CONTENTS

HANDBOOK
FOR A MODULAR COURSE IN
HEALTH PROMOTION AND
HEALTH EDUCATION

MODULE 1

DEFINITION OF THE PROBLEM
AND
CHOICE OF SOLUTIONS

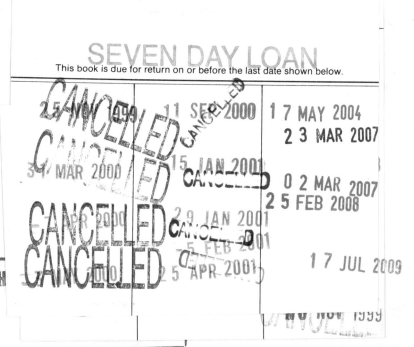

Copyright © Leo Barić
First Edition 1990
Second Edition 1991

ISBN 0 9516973 0 7

Published by Barns Publications, 14 High Elm Road,
Hale Barns,
Altrincham, Cheshire, WA15 0HS, England.
FAX: 061 980 7446

UNIT 3 Available methods and approaches 147

Introduction   147

UNIT 4 : Planning an intervention   251

Introduction   251

Examples   273

PREFACE TO THE SECOND EDITION

The main reason for printing the second edition of this handbook so rapidly has been the high demand, which quickly put the first edition out of print and has left a lengthy waiting list.

Another, equally important reason has been the feed-back received from purchasers of the handbook. It appears to have met an existing need for a down-to-earth, practical handbook, which can be used both by teachers as well as students engaged in educational programmes on different levels and for different purposes.

Some of the comments that came from the feed-back raised the question of the appropriateness of a "modular" format to the course. Evidently, various educational institutions such as universities, polytechnics and colleges, have different interpretations of the requirements for a "modular" course. Since, however, most share the view that the attractiveness of a modular structure lies in the choice of how to use the modules and in what combination for meeting different qualification requirements, it was decided to keep the name "modular course" with the understanding that, where necessary, the label "module" can be translated into "unit" and the course used as appropriate.

The feed-back from some other users of the handbook confirmed the need for the further handbooks, which will accompany Modules 2 and 3, and stressed the urgency for their publication. This allowed for some readjustment and focussing of the contents of all handbooks, which will ensure that the practical needs will be met.

These practical needs have been clearly defined by recent events in Europe. As a member of the WHO team engaged in helping a number of countries in Central Europe in their endeavours to adjust their health promotion and health education services to meet established European standards, I have been able to share knowledge with them in assessing their immediate and long term needs. The development of educational programmes in health promotion and health education on different levels clearly emerges as one of their needs and this course will represent a contribution towards meeting this requirement.

Consequently, I was very pleased when Dr Ilona Kickbusch agreed to write the Foreword for this second edition. In the light of her high status and acknowledged expertise in the field of health promotion and health education, as well as her outstanding contributions to the developments in this field following the Alma Ata Declaration, it is most encouraging to have her strong support for the appropriateness of the approach represented in the structure of the course and in the contents of the handbook.

Leo Baric,

Salford, 1991

FOREWORD

Ilona Kickbusch PhD, Director Lifestyles and Health, World Health Organisation, European Office, Copenhagen.

Over the last ten years we have witnessed a major change of emphasis in the health debate. The shift has been from infectious to behavioural diseases and risk factors, followed by an increasing emphasis on the "environmental" factors that create and maintain health. The aim now is to influence the context of health actions and make the social and physical environment supportive to health and to provide individuals with strategies of health improvement and maintenance that can be integrated with meaning into a person's overall life pattern. This has led to a renewed interest in health promotion and health education as central strategies with which these new problems can be faced and solved, as expressed forcefully by the Ottawa Charter on Health Promotion. This is further supported by the growth of the "green" movement and a renewed interest in population issues as two factors affecting survival on a planet with limited resources.

Consequently we are witnessing a shift in responsibility from the medical profession to a multisectoral sharing of responsibilities for health. The multisectoral approach has consequences for training programmes in health promotion and helath education, which now need to be flexible and easily accessible to a wide range of actors involved in creating health. This has led to a growth of "modular" courses on a wide range of levels (undergraduate, graduate and postgraduate) which has enabled the integration of health promotion and health education teaching into training programmes of different professions, either as part of their regular training programmes or as a specialisation accoridng to their specific roles. The WHO Health for All strategy based on target setting has been used to help focus on priority issues.

The modular course developed by the author reflects the new trend in training on three levels: non-graduate (certificate), graduate (diploma) and postgraduate (master's degree). It is flexible to allow the use of one, two or all three modules according to the needs and the educational background of the students. Each module is accompanied by a handbook which can be used by students as well as teachers and which provides the content of each module. Module 1 deals with general aspects of health promotion and health education such as the definition of the problem and the choice of solutions. Module 2 deals with the problems of applying health promotion and health education in practice and gives information about planning health promotion and health education interventions in different situations such as family, community, school, hospital etc. Module 3 deals with problems of research and provides a very good summary of principles and methods of research, evaluation and auditing. The approach chosen by the author attempts to strike a balance between the need for a scientifically respectable way of defining the problem and the importance of choosing the appropriate practical solution. It gives a concrete guidance for planning programmes and provides a number of useful examples from existing practice.

This handbook is the first of a set of three. Its emphasis on environmental factors and flexibility in its use according to different needs of the student population represents an important contribution to the new developments in health promotion and health education training programmes.

INTRODUCTION TO THE MODULAR COURSE

The role of health promotion and education in the improvement of health of a population within the general movement towards "Health for All by the Year 2000" is in the process of rapid development and change. The existing tendency to create a "profession" active in this field is changing, owing to the acceptance of a multisectoral approach as the most promising way of achieving the set goal of health for all.

The participation of many different professions and occupations in health promotion and education has required a revision of the existing training programmes. The new modular training programme presented here takes into account the different kind and amount of involvement of all these professions as well as their specific educational needs and background.

This modular course has been designed with these needs in mind. It is organised in a way which should enable the course modules to be organised on different levels and with the emphasis on different aspects of knowledge and skills. It is divided into three modules:

Module 1: Definition of problems and choice of solutions;

Module 2: Health promotion and education in practice;

Module 3: Research, evaluation and aduiting.

The modules are intended to provide participants with knowledge and skills as well as qualifications on three different levels:

LEVEL	CONTENTS	QUALIFICATION
1. Basic training	Module 1	Certificate
2. Intermediate	Module 1	
	Module 2	Diploma
3. Higher	Module 1	
	Module 2	
	Module 3	
	Thesis	Masters Degree

The participants are selected for each level according to the regulations of the educational institution concerned, based on their educational background and their involvement in health promotion and education activities.

Module 1: Definition of problems and choice of solutions

It is envisaged that people working in other professions and occupations and having a lilmited or marginal role in health promotion and education as part of their existing roles will need some general knowledge about the possibilities and requirements necessary for the integration of certain health promotion and health education aspects into their everyday work. For them the Module 1 should provide the necessary background and enable them to acquire the necessary skills which are required for a **Certificate** qualification.

Aims and objectives

The **aims** of Module 1 are to enable the participants to achieve a general understanding of the practice of health promotion and health education and to become acquainted with the processes involved in the definition of problems and the choice of appropriate solution which are the basis for planning a health promotion and health education intervention.

To achieve these aims, the **objectives** of this Module are to provide the participants with knowledge and skills in the following areas which are also reflected in the contents of the handbook accompanying this Module:

1) Definition of the problem
   i. medical aspects
   ii. health promotional aspects
   iii. health educational aspects
   iv. methodology

2) Choice of solutions
   i. medical solutions
   ii. health promotional solutions
   iii. health educational solutions

3) Available methods and approaches
   i. personal approach
   ii. group approach
   iii. community approach
   iv. mass media approach

4) Planning an intervention
   i. health promotion
   ii. health education

5) Examples

Module 2: Health promotion and health education in practice

There are, however, professions and occupations which have taken or are now taking over health promotion and education as part of their professional role. For them, the **Diploma** level of training, which includes Modules 1 and 2, will provide, in addition to knowledge and skills, the necessary theoretical understanding of the various aspects of health promotion and education in different situations and for different groups, so that they know not only what to do but also why they are doing it in a certain way.

Aims and Objectives:

The **aims** of Module 2 are to give the participants an insight into the
most recent advances in health promotion and education, provide them
with a theoretical justification for the choice of available methods for
a health promotion and education intervention and provide them with
an opportunity of learning about the needs and possibilities of health
promotion and education in specific situations. The aims are supported
by relevant theories and accompanied by the steps involved in the planning of interventions for each situation and population group, making
a differentiation between the processes of defining the problem and
choosing the appropriate solution. To achieve the aims, the objectives
of Module 2 are presented in the accompanying second handbook
under the following topics:

Introduction: World Health Organisation

1) conditions of radical change
   - i. radical changes in various situations
   - ii. theoretical aspects of radical changes
   - iii. intervention for coping with change

2) the family
   - i. agent for procreation and socialisation
   - ii. theoretical aspects
   - iii. intervention affecting family competence

3) education
   - i. levels and institutions
   - ii. theoretical aspects
   - iii .interventions on different levels

4) work
   - i. employers and the work force
   - ii. theoretical aspects
   - iii. problem-specific interventions

5) retirement, unemployment, leisure
    i. situation specific needs and problems
    ii. theoretical aspects
    iii. group-specific interventions

6) special institutions
    i. hospitals, homes, prisons, army, etc.
    ii. theoretical aspects
    iii. situation specific interventions

7) special groups
    i. patient groups, community groups, self-help
       groups etc.
    ii. theoretical aspects
    iii. specific interventions

Module 3: Research, evaluation and auditing

The third level, which is envisaged as providing a **Master's degree** in the subject matter, is becoming increasingly the expected standard of education for specialists in health promotion and education as well as for researchers in this field. For this reason the candidates for a MSc will have to take, in addition to Modules 1 and 2, Module 3, which will give them an insight into research, evaluation and auditing skills, and should enable them to carry out a research project which they will present in the form of a thesis. This should also help them to assess other people's work as well as their own in terms of professional responsibility and accountability.

Aim and Objectives:

The aim of Module 3 is to provide the participants with knowledge and skills necessary for planning and carrying out research, integrating evaluation into the planning process and for auditing an intervention. To achieve this aim, the objectives of Module 3 are presented in the third handbook under the following topics:

1) principles and methods of research
    i. planning requirements
    ii. indicators and criteria
    iii. instruments, data collection, analysis

2) principles and methods of evaluation
    i. definition of aims and objectives
    ii. choice of indicators and criteria
    iii. methods and inferences

3) principles and methods of auditing
    i. setting the standards
    ii. indicators and criteria
    iii. data collection and analysis

ASSESSMENT

The assessment will be carried out differently for each level of the training programme:

- for the basic level the assessment will take the form of "continuous assessment", which includes the observation of participants' work on the course, their contributions and diligence as well as their feeling of competence to carry out this kind of work in the future. At the end of the course they will receive a **Certificate** of Attendance;

- for the intermediate level the assessment will include, in addition to continuous assessment, also a set examination, and after successful completion, the participants will be awarded a **Diploma** in Health Promotion and Education;

- the assessment for the higher level training leading to a **Master's degree** is defined by the regulations of the Institution which will award the degree but usually includes a written and/or oral examination and the submission of a written thesis.

MODULE 1: PROBLEMS AND SOLUTIONS

Introduction to the Teaching Units

This Module deals with the topics related to the definition of the problem(s) and the choice of solutions which are the basis for health promotion and education interventions. They are intended to provide participants with the skills necessary for their endeavours in improving health in a population as well as on an individual level.

To be able to achieve this, the Module has been divided into 4 teaching units with the following aims and objectives (Diagram 1):

Unit 1: The aim of this unit is to enable the participants to appreciate the relevant factors of importance in defining an intervention strategy for prevention of disease and improvement of health; to achieve this aim the Module will have the following objectives:

1.1 to examine the relevant aspects of a medical definition of the problem, looking at the aetiology or causation of a problem and the epidemiology or distribution of the problem in a population, thus enabling the participants to carry out a medical diagnosis of the problem;

1.2 to examine the health promotional aspects of a problem, looking at the societal factors influencing a person's health, and the personal adjustment to these societal conditions which can affect a person's chances of avoiding a health threat or regaining his/her health, thus enabling participants to make a health promotional diagnosis of a problem;

1.3 to examine the health educational aspect of a problem, looking at a person's knowledge, attitudes and skills relevant for self care and protection as well as for more general prevention of risk factors and management of illness, thus enabling participants to make a health educational diagnosis of a problem.

1.4 to provide the participants with knowledge and skills in carrying out the necessary investigations and measurements concerning the definition of a problem in medical, health promotional and educational terms.

Unit 2: the aim of this unit is to enable the participants to translate the results of the diagnosis of the problem into the appropriate solutions in the form of health promotional and educational interventions; to achieve this aim, the Module will have the following objectives:

2.1 to acquaint the participants with available medical solutions in terms of prevention, treatment and management of risk factors and disease;

2.2 to enable the participants to understand the available options for planning a health promotion intervention on an environmental as well as individual level;

2.3 to give the participants an insight into the mechanisms operating on a personal level which can affect the health of an individual and which include knowledge, attitudes and skills, representing the level of competence of that individual.

Unit 3: the aim of this unit is to acquaint the participants with the methods which they could use in planning and executing a health promotional and educational intervention and enable them to acquire appropriate skills necessary for their practical work; to achieve this aim, the Module will have the following objectives:

3.1 to provide the participants with knowledge and skills related to a personal approach when carrying out health promotional and educational work;

3.2 to provide the participants with knowledge and skills related to group work;

3.3 to provide the participants with knowledge and skills in planning and carrying out a community programme based on community participation.

Unit 4: the aim of this unit is to provide the participants with knowledge and skills necessary for planning and carrying out a health promotion and/or health education intervention; to achieve this aim, the Module will have the following objectives:

4.1 to provide the participants with an insight into the requirements for planning a health promotion intervention;

4.2 to provide the participants with an insight into the requirements for planning a health education intervention.

The **method** of work intended to achieve the aims of the four units will include the distribution of written materials, a knowledge input, a discussion session and work on tasks resulting in the presentation of a written programmes which should be relevant to the needs of the participants and their future roles.

The participants taking Module 1 will undergo a process of continuous **assessment** using the following indicators:

- ability to select, from the variety of causes of a health problem, those which are amenable to a health education and promotion intervention;

- competence in planning a health promotion and/or health education intervention;

- performance in task work situations, associated with various intervention skills.

It is expected that the participants will be able to produce, under professional supervision, an action programme for their own needs which is appropriate to their future roles.

UNIT 1	**DEFINITION OF THE PROBLEM**
	• Medical aspects
	• Promotional aspects
	• Educational aspects
UNIT 2	**CHOICE OF SOLUTIONS**
	• Medical solutions
	• Promotional solutions
	• Educational solutions
UNIT 3	**METHODS AND APPROACHES**
	• Personal approach
	• Group approach
	• Community approach
	• Mass media approach
UNIT 4	**PLANNING AN INTERVENTION**
	• Health promotion
	• Health education

Diagram 1   Contents of Units

UNIT 1 : Definition of the problem

Introduction

This unit deals with the advances in medical knowledge and medical technology that have resulted in extending the definition of health to include in addition to medical factors, and also with a number of environmental and personal factors that not only contribute to the spread of disease and can directly cause certain diseases but can also be affected by diseases. At the same time, advances in the understanding of social processes and the psychology of individuals are reflected in the new definition of problems facing health promotion and education. It is because of this that health promotion and education have to consider all these factors when defining the problem which they are aiming to solve. (Diagram 2)

The unit is composed of three parts, each examining one aspect of the definition of the problems facing health promotion and education.

The *medical* aspect of the definition of the problem includes two approaches: the aetiological and the epidemiological. The aetiological approach looks at the medical, social/environmental and personal factors; the epidemiological approach looks at risk factors and human behaviour.

The health *promotional* aspect includes the environmental approach and the individual adjustment to it. The environmental approach looks at physical, social and organisational factors; the individual adjustment looks at physical and social factors as well as services.

The health *educational* aspect of the definition of the problem includes the knowledge, attitudes and skills approaches. The knowledge is concerned with health threats, services and supportive systems; the attitudes to problems and to solutions are examined; the skills include coping, communication and behaviour modification skills.

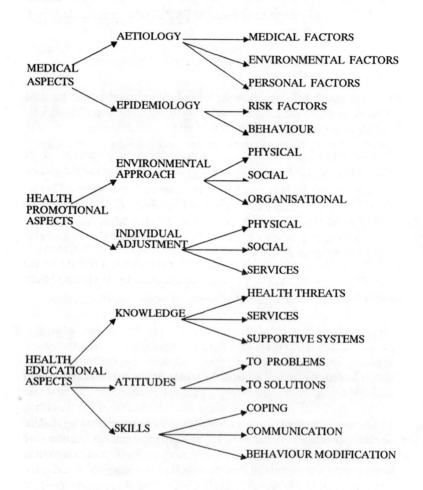

Diagram 2 Aspects of the problem

The method of using this unit includes:

- the study of the written text and recommended readings;

- lectures giving a summary of the topics;

- work on tasks and producing a report;

- group discussions with experts.

The task includes the selection of a problem by each member of the class and applying the principles of all the three aspects of the definition to the problem of their choice. In exceptional cases it will be possible for a number of members to form a team and work jointly on the same problem. (See examples 1 to 7).

Group discussions with experts should enable the members of the class to find out more about some of the prevalent health problems in our society, and allow them to check the definition of the problem of their choice against that of the experts.

Medical aspects

There are two ways the medical definition of the problem and health promotion and education interventions are interlinked. The first one is concerned with the findings of medical research into the causation of a disease, and possible ways of preventing and/or treating it. This approach includes laboratory tests and experiments, designed to find the cause of a certain disease, as well as population studies aimed at mapping out the distribution of the problem in a population and gaining some insight into possible causes by looking at the characteristics of the population most affected.

The second way the medical definition is relevant concerns the situation with which the medical practitioner is faced in diagnosing a disease on the strength of the symptoms or descriptions presented by the patient. Since the outcome depends on the interaction between the two actors, studies have been concerned with the ways the patient presents the case and the ways the medical practitioner interprets them in terms of necessary procedures and treatment.

Health promotion and education will benefit from medical research concerned with the definition of the problem, and will be able to contribute to the effectiveness of diagnosis by sensitizing the patient to the important signals or signs the body provides as an indication of a disease.

Aetiology

The history of medicine is characterised by changes in the assumptions concerning the causation, character and the means of abolishing disease. The beliefs of yesterday are obsolete today, and today's beliefs will almost certainly be obsolete tomorrow. The progression of our understanding of disease and its prevention and management follows the general pattern of scientific development with all its potentials, doubts, uncertainties and mistakes. It is important to bear this in mind when one talks about the way a health threat or a disease can be prevented and/or treated.

The methodology of medical research is highly specialised and attempts to follow the requirements of strict scientific norms supported by a code of ethics which governs research on human beings. Here only certain aspects of this methodology and its consequences will be mentioned, which could have a bearing on their application in health promotion and education.

To understand the way people "perceive" a health threat or a disease one has to examine the developments in the psychology of perception (Dember,1969) which has established that "people perceive what they expect to perceive, and they expect to perceive what they have learned to expect to perceive". In other words, people start off by perceiving within a familiar framework of existing expectations, disregarding details and using abstracted pictures, which have been called "gestalt". Instead of observing every detail in a picture, people see "gestalts" or "whole" images which are based on existing experiences. To accept a

new image it is necessary to look in greater detail for specific characteristics which are different from the expected ones and to devote more
time to such observations.

The next question to be considered is the way knowledge is accumulated and new knowledge established. This has been the concern of
philosophers, one of whom (Kuhn,1970) developed a four-step progression in the development of knowledge: the first is the "pre-normal"
stage where individual scientists study problems without sharing their
ideas, methodology or findings. Each has to solve all the problems
from the start, uses different terminology and theories, and progression is slow. The second stage is "normal science", where the scientists
share information, methodology and findings and there is a possibility
of building the body of new knowledge on the existing one. The third
stage is the "crisis" stage when the findings challenge the existing beliefs and question the accepted practices; the outcome is the fourth or
the "revolution" stage when the new practices and ideas are being accepted and become the new "paradigm" on which the understanding
of some scientific idea is based.

While a paradigm must always start from and be based on some theory, there is an important difference between these two concepts: theory usually is concerned with the explanation of a phenomenon, and
need not necessarily have been tested or widely accepted; a theory can
be raised to the level of a paradigm if it is tested by means of scientifically sound research and if it is as such accepted by the majority of
scientists.

As the paradigm becomes more generally accepted it becomes applied
in increasingly new situations, some of which may produce some anomalies or unexpected outcomes. It will require some time and effort before these new anomalies will be successful in changing the existing
gestalt of the perceived reality associated with the observation explained by a certain theory. The existence of such paradigm shifts
characterise the process of maturation of a science.

The study of the history of development of scientific thought has made
important contributions to our understanding of the character and
limitations of existing research methods. This has been achieved by a
better insight into the meaning of cause-effect relationships as the main

preoccupation of scientific research. The statement that one cannot prove something empirically but only disprove it (Popper,1959) has become widely known, as has the following analogy: an observer standing on the bend of a river and observing the passing of swans records that they are all white; he will, however, not be in a position to say that "all swans are white" since he does not know whether the next one coming round the bend might not be black. If one translates this general view of the development of knowledge to medicine, it becomes obvious that the existing knowledge about some health threat or disease is exposed to a high degree of uncertainty and possible changes and redefinitions following the new experiences and new research findings. It is important to bear this in mind when one deals with clients who want to "know the truth" and are not satisfied with different degrees of probability.

In addition to philosophical issues associated with proof and the difficulties in coping with paradigm shifts in medicine, a number of recent research findings have added to the existing uncertainty by exposing the enormous complexity of the causation of a number of medical problems. Gone are the days of simple cause-effect discoveries associated with infectious diseases. More refined research methods and a more holistic approach to research have produced insights into the complex processes associated with certain diseases. A well known example is often quoted to illustrate this point (Dubos, 1960), referring to research on cancer of the breast in mice.

It seems that the occurrence of this disease in mice is very rare. When it does occur it is usually in special strains in which a proportion of offspring develop spontaneously this form of cancer, which indicates a genetic factor at play. A virus has also been detected in the milk of lactating mothers of this strain of mice. The occurrence of the disease among the young of this strain can be avoided by removing them from their mothers and allowing them to be suckled by mice who do not have the virus in their milk. If the offspring of mothers who do not carry the virus are removed and suckled by mice who do have the virus they will not develop cancer. It seems, therefore, that although both the genetic factors and the virus are associated with the occurrence of the disease, one without the other cannot bring about the disease in young mice.

Young mice with both the genetic factor and the virus present will only develop cancer if they are females. Males will not develop breast cancer even if both factors are present. Only when the female sex hormone oestrogen is injected into these male mice will they become susceptible to breast cancer in the same way as the females. One could, therefore, conclude that the susceptibility to breast cancer in mice will depend on genetic factors, presence of a virus and of the female sex hormone.

Even if all the three factors (genetic, virus, hormone) are present, by placing the young mice on a low calorie diet, one can significantly reduce the incidence of mice breast cancer.

The history of medical discoveries is full of breakthroughs in understanding causation and the way a disease is acquired or spread. It is also interspersed with occasional discoveries of new diseases which have in the past been unnoticed or wrongly labelled. The methods used are mainly limited to laboratory experimentation and trials with the aim of confirming experiences and turning them into paradigms recognised by medical scientists. Some medical discoveries, however, are based on the study of the association of different factors which can be interpreted as the probable causation of a disease even if the actual causative mechanism is not as yet known or understood.

This progression is best illustrated by the changes in the interpretation of major health threats in terms of causation. One is aware of the important breakthrough which signalled the emphasis on "infectious diseases". Since then we have moved to "behavioral" diseases (lung cancer, etc.), to "environmental" diseases (leukemia, etc.) and to present recognition of "genetic" diseases (breast cancer, etc.).

The existing body of medical knowledge and skills is transmitted to new generations of medical and paramedical professionals by means of the process of education. Since education is socialisation into new roles, the new generations, in addition to knowledge and skills, also acquire sets of values which enable them to deal with the problems as well as the uncertainties associated with some solutions. The professional practice of medicine has a strict code of ethics, a defined process of legitimation of the practitioners and mechanisms which audit the practice.

All this has been devised with the sole purpose of protecting the clients and their rights.

The topic of "human rights" has been a minefield of conflicting interpretations in general, and even more so in the field of health and disease. The fact that the WHO Constitution (1948) declared health as one of the basic human rights, does not mean that such rights are automatically respected throughout the world. For human rights to be implemented and protected it will be necessary to match them with corresponding "civil rights" which are expressed in the country's legislation. In general, civil rights recognise the basic human rights within certain boundaries which are defined by laws. Some human rights (i.e. freedom from slavery) are generally accepted, whereas some others are accepted with limitations and restrictions in order to define their boundaries. In the latter case, the basic human right represents the "core" of the civil right which also includes additional prescriptions when this right can be disregarded. These can include as justification such concepts as "national security", "public interest" etc. In the last few decades we have seen a whole range of new laws aiming at redressing the inequities which are a part of any human society. We have seen laws concerning "equality of opportunity" which included the famous "GI Bill" in the US which was intended to give equal opportunities of education to GIs returning from war; this was followed by laws against discrimination, firstly against blacks, followed by discrimination against women, followed by homosexuals and most recently laws against discrimination against disabled persons. All these laws are directed at redressing the disadvantages of certain population groups and the most recent ones concerning equity in health and the access to health services raises the question of a socialised medicine, which is difficult to sustain in a free market economy.

In general, however, one takes the issue of human (and civil) rights for granted as far as the established ways of treatment of common diseases is concerned. Only when a new disease occurs or is discovered does the issue of rights and duties come to the fore and becomes a topic of discussion and consequently of new legislation. An illustration of this has been the occurrence of AIDS or "acquired immune deficiency syndrome", a cluster of symptoms manifested by patients whose immunological defences have been severely compromised and who have, therefore, fallen prey to a variety of infectious or other diseases. At present there is no cure for AIDS, although there may be ways of preventing it by means of immunisation and there are treatments that can delay its progression. The literature on AIDS is considerable and rapidly increasing in volume. Here only the aspects of human rights relevant to patients and their environment will be considered.

In the first place, there are measures which do not directly affect human rights and include (a) research into causation and the development of vaccines and means of treatment; (b) ensuring the safety of blood transfusion, sterility of needles for injections and provision of protective devices used during sexual intercourse (condoms); (c) promotion and education of the general population and high risk groups in particular.

Secondly, there are measures that, according to present laws, require explicit consent, such as (a) voluntary testing of individuals for HIV infection; (b) counselling of individuals both before and after they are tested; (c) voluntary treatment and modification of individual behaviour.

The third area includes measures entailing compulsion which can invoke the use of force and are supported by sanctions and could be concerned with (a) compulsory testing, (b) outlawing practices which increase the probability of the spread of the disease, (c) exclusion from jobs, (d) entering a country, (e) participating in education, (f) exclusion from marriage, (g) housing, (h) social services, (i) having children, (j) introduction of quarantine, (k) isolation or detention etc.

Some of these measures are already adopted for some other disease, (for instance, infectious diseases, mental disease, some behavioral problems such as addictions etc). These need to be legalised for AIDS, whereas some others which are not applied to other disease may become legalised for AIDS because of its specific nature of contraction, incubation, spread and lack of any effective prevention and treatment. At present there are serious discussions concerning these issues within the framework of human rights and the lack of any definitive decisions has allowed for the spread of prejudice, stigmatisation and prosecution of people at risk or infected by the virus.

The development of medical practice has been continuously concerned with the issue of human (and civil) rights in the light of the doctor-patient relationship. The medical professional body has been concerned with the development of medical code of practice which formalises this relationship in the light of rights and duties of both the doctor and the patient. This has been one of the most fertile fields of study and research and has attracted the interest of many different branches of science. Some studies have been concerned with the processes taking place between the two actors, others with the ways these interactions can be improved, whereas some others (e.g. Illich, 1974) have been critical of the ways such interactions are conducted at the expense of the rights of the patients.

It is important to understand this complex picture when one talks about the medical definition of health problems (McKeown,1977). One tends to assume that such a definition is clear cut and can be derived from examining the medical literature. When one makes such an effort, however, one soon discovers the uncertainty and controversies even within the medical profession about such definitions. The reason for defining a problem in medical terms for health promotion and education purpose is vital and can still be useful if one understands the processes by which the medical profession arrived at their definitions.

It is important also to bear in mind the way medical students are trained to carry out a diagnosis of a medical problem. They are mostly confronted with a patient who presents certain symptoms. The students are taught to combine certain symptoms into a disease entity. If the patient mentions only some of the symptoms that are associated with a disease, the doctor will probe by questioning the patient or by carrying out certain tests to establish what kind of indicators are present and in what combination. This stepwise approach can be described as a differential diagnosis in which symptoms are combined into patterns which are associated with specific diseases.

If, however, the doctor is faced with an "educated" patient he or she may be misled by the symptoms presented. The patient may suspect that he suffers from a certain disease (e.g. a heart attack) and will either invent or imagine the symptoms which he knows are associated with a specific disease (e.g. pain in the chest, tingling in the left arm, indigestion, etc.) and will mention them to the doctor who, being conditioned to react to certain combination of symptoms in a specific way, will have little hesitation in diagnosing a disease (e.g. a heart attack), will act appropriately and the patient will end up in the intensive care unit of the nearest hospital.

Since the doctor cannot be absolutely certain in most cases about the accuracy of the diagnosis as well as the effectiveness of the treatment, he or she must learn to cope with uncertainty. The problem of uncertainty can be reduced by a continuous contact of the doctor with the patient which will enable the doctor to react to the feedback and adjust the treatment accordingly.

Taking these reservations into account, one can examine the aetiology or causation of a health problem according to present day knowledge, which includes the causal agent, the means of acquisition and/or transmission, the incubation period, the symptoms, the process and the expected outcome. These aspects can be considered as parts of a life-style system and can be differentiated according to the main characteristics of the following relevant factors:

Medical factors

Out of a whole range of medical factors which are relevant to the diagnosis, management and treatment of a disease, one should be able to highlight those that are of direct relevance for a health education or promotion intervention:

- *causal factors* are in general considered to be those which deal with the mode of acquisition and/or transmission of the disease in terms of specific agents or processes which have at present been found to be associated with that particular disease;

- *risk factors* are in general considered to be those which have been found to contribute to the increased probability of acquiring or transmitting a disease.

Social/environmental factors

There are external factors which have been found to be associated with the acquisition or transmission of certain diseases. They can originate in the:

- *physical environment* and be related to air, water, food, climate, pests, transport, communication etc. and in the

- *social environment* and can determine the social position of the target population, their income and occupation, culture and religion, their belief and value system, norms and role performance, available services, access to professional help, etc.

Personal factors

Within a given physical and social environment, various individuals may act differently and in different ways react to health threats or utilise the existing resources. These individuals and groups will have specific characteristics which are associated with their genetic makeup as well as their exposure to certain risk factors, their competence in dealing with a health problem and their preference of the choices available. The personality and the competence of individuals will be reflected in:

- *life style*, which has been found to be associated with the probability of acquiring and transmitting certain diseases;

- *habits and routines*, which represent learned reactions to certain stimuli and can be associated with the incidence of certain diseases;

- *actions*, which may or may not take place and which can be associated with certain diseases.

Epidemiology

Epidemiology, or the study of the distribution of a disease in a population, has made some major contributions to the understanding of the causation of a diseases and has raised a number of other important issues associated with planning the provision of health care, the protection of human rights associated with inequalities in health and the treatment of disease, as well as about the influence of the environment (physical and social) on the health of a population.

For example, by looking at the shared common characteristics of patients with lung cancer, an association between cigarette smoking and lung cancer was established long before the discovery of the specific agents in cigarette smoke which cause cancer of the lung. Similarly, by tracing the distribution of certain infectious diseases, associations have been established between some environmental factors and the disease which could then be pursued and confirmed by laboratory research procedures. Another outcome of population studies has been the realisation that certain diseases are related to certain life styles and the association of some diseases with poverty has been the basis for the attempts to remove the inequalities in health which exist between the developed and developing nations, between the north and the south, between rural and industrialised societies, etc. These associations between certain agents, conditions or behaviour with a disease are based on the interpretation of probability of whether this association could occur by chance or is significant enough to cause concern. By convention a 5% cut off point is chosen for assessing whether an association is considered to be statistically significant or not.

It is also necessary to make the distinction between the concepts of "possibility" and "probability". For something to be probable (at whatever level) it should be possible. At present we are witnessing a "food scare epidemic" where any possibility of an association is accepted as significant enough to merit some behavioral changes. Some of the better known are the scares about eating eggs, milk and milk products, chicken, beef, shellfish, sugar, fat, margarine, artificial sweetners, etc. All these foods have been identified as associated with some disease or health threat. An interesting case is the association between beef and BSE or "mad cow disease", where although the possibility of transmitting infection to humans has not as yet been demonstrated, and therefore, one cannot calculate the probability of this occurring, the panic is sufficient enough for countries to ban the import of British beef and for people to stop eating it. To use Popper's analogy, one never knows when the possibility of human infection will be established.

Since epidemiology is based on population studies, specific methods have been developed to accommodate the requirements of scientific rigour for the inferences made, as well as their reliability and validity.

The development of social medicine has resulted in a matched development of the epidemiological method appropriate for the study of health and disease in society. The importance of disease in society will depend on its duration and the degree of disability it may produce, as well as on its frequency and its fatal effect on the population.

The distribution of a disease in a population will be associated with the distribution of medical, social/environmental and personal factors in a population. It helps to define as a system the community/group at risk or the target population. For health education and promotion of special interest is the distribution of risk factors.

Risk factors

The distribution of different risk factors associated with a health threat or a disease is of importance for the definition of a segment of a population at risk in health education and health promotion terms. The different levels of risk are associated with the distribution of the following types of risk factors in a population, which are usually interrelated and need not be mutually exclusive:

- *environmental* risk factors such as air or water pollution can contribute to the spread of a disease;

- *socioeconomic* risk factors include housing, income, employment, social class, education and number of others which have been found to be associated with the prevalence of a health threat or a disease in a population;

- *behavioral* risk factors include smoking, diet, leisure, stressful life style, alcohol and drug abuse, certain patterns of sexual activities and others which are associated with individual attitudes and behaviour related to health and disease.

Behaviour

One of the main determinants of risk from a certain health threat or disease is people's behaviour. The distribution of different kinds of behaviour in a population will help in defining the target population for health education and health promotion interventions. The types of behaviour related to the definition of a medical problem are:

- *orientation to health care*, which can differ according to the "parochial" or "cosmopolitan" characteristics of the population (Suchman 1965) ;

- *utilisation of health services*, which depends on people's relationship with the health professions and the amount of self confidence and competence they have in dealing with health problems;

- *perception of health threats*, which is associated with the socioeconomic and educational characteristics of a population.

Health promotional aspects

In the summary report of the Working Group on Concepts and Principles of Health Promotion (WHO EURO, Copenhagen, 9-13.7.84) the following interpretation of health promotion is given:

> "...At a general level, health promotion has come to represent a unifying concept for those who recognise the need for change in the ways and conditions of living, in order to promote health. Health promotion represents a mediating strategy between people and their environments, synthesising personal choice and social responsibility in health to create a healthier future....Health promotion is the process of enabling people to increase control over, and improve, their health....Health is, therefore, seen as a resource for everyday life, not the objective of living; it is a positive concept emphasising social and personal resources, as well as physical capacities".

The **characteristics** of health promotion can be described as follows:

1. Health promotion **involves the population as a whole** in the context of their everyday life, rather than focusing on people at risk for specific diseases. It enables people to take control over, and responsibility for, their health as an important component of everyday life - both as spontaneous and organised action for health. This requires full and continuing access to information about health and how it might be sought for by all the population, using all dissemination methods available:

2. Health promotion **is directed towards action** on the determinants or causes of health. Health promotion, therefore, requires a close cooperation of sectors beyond health services, reflecting the diversity of conditions which influence health. Government, at both local and national levels, has a unique responsibility to act appropriately and in a timely way to ensure that the "total" environment, which is beyond the control of individuals and groups, is conducive to health;

3. Health promotion **combines diverse, but complementary, methods or approaches,** including communication, education, legislation, fiscal measures, organisation change, community development and spontaneous local activities against health hazards;

4. Health promotion **aims particularly at effective and concrete public participation.** This focus requires the further development of problem-defining and decision-making lifeskills both individually and collectively;

5. While health promotion is **basically an activity in the health and social fields,** and not a medical service, health professionals - particularly in primary health care - have an important role in nurturing and enabling health promotion. Health professionals should work towards developing their special contributions in education and health advocacy.

Health promotion best enhances health through integrated action at different levels on factors influencing health, economic environmental, social and personal. Given these basic principles an almost unlimited list of issues for health promotion could be generated: food policy, housing, smoking, coping skills, social networks. The working group sought to frame the **general subjects for health promotion** in the following areas:

1. The focus of health promotion is *access to health* to reduce inequalities in health and to increase opportunities to improve health. This involves changing public and corporate policies to make them conducive to health, and involves reorienting health services to the maintenance and development of health in the population, regardless of current health status;

2. The improvement of health depends upon the *development of an environment conducive to health* especially in conditions at work and in the home. Since this environment is dynamic, health promotion involves monitoring and assessment of the technological, cultural and economic status and trends;

3. Health promotion involves the *strengthening of social networks and social support.* This is based on the recognition of the im-

portance of social forces and social relationships as determinants of values and behaviour relevant to health, and as significant resources for coping with stress and maintaining health;

4. The predominant way of life in society is central to health promotion, since it fosters personal behaviour patterns that are either beneficial or detrimental to health. The promotion of life-styles conducive to health involves consideration of personal coping strategies and dispositions as well as beliefs and values relevant to health, all shaped by lifelong experiences and living conditions. *Promoting positive health behaviour and appropriate coping strategies* is a key aim in health promotion;

5. Information and education provide the informed base for making choices. They are necessary and core components of health promotion, which aims at *increasing knowledge and disseminating information* related to health. This should include: the public's perceptions and experiences of health and how it might be sought; knowledge from epidemiology, social and other sciences on the patterns of health and disease and factors affecting them; and descriptions of the "total" environment in which health and health choices are shaped. The mass media and new information technologies are particularly important.

At present health promotion activities are based on what is known as the "OTTAWA CHARTER" signed by the participants of the First International Conference on Health Promotion held in Ottawa in 1986.

The prerequisites for health, according to the Charter are peace, shelter, education, food, income, a stable ecosystem, sustainable resources, social justice and equity.

There are three main activities related to the fulfilment of these prerequisites. These activities are:

- *Advocacy:* good health is a major resource for social, economic and personal development and an important dimension of quality of life. Political, economic, social, cultural, environmental, behavioral and biological factors can all favour health or be harmful to it. Health promotion action aims at making these conditions favourable through advocacy for health;

- *Enabling*: health promotion focuses on achieving equity in health. Health promotion action aims at reducing differences in current health status and ensuring equal opportunities and resources to enable all people to achieve their fullest health potential. This includes a secure foundation in a supportive environment, access to information, life skills and opportunities for making healthy choices. People cannot achieve their fullest health potential unless they are able to take control of those things which determine their health. This must apply equally to women and men.

- *Mediating*: the prerequisites and prospects for health cannot be ensured by the health sector alone. More importantly, health promotion demands coordinated action by all concerned: by governments, by health and other social and economic sectors, by non-governmental and voluntary organisations, by local authorities, by industry and by the media. People in all walks of life are involved as individuals, families and communities. Professional and social groups and health personnel have a major responsibility to mediate between differing interests in society for the pursuit of health.

Health promotion action means building healthy public policy, creating supportive environments, strengthening community action, developing personal skills and reorienting health services.

This Charter was signed by all the participants at the Conference, has been adopted by WHO and represents the basis for the new "healthy city movement".

The health promotional aspect of preventing and managing a disease in a population is mainly concerned with population or community interventions. It includes a multisectoral approach expressed in multisectoral cooperation. Because of this, the definition of a problem in health promotional terms will include various factors.

Environmental factors

The definition of an existing problem for a health promotion intervention will have to include an examination of certain environmental factors which will affect the level of people's self-reliance and competence in dealing with a health threat or a disease. These factors are:

Physical environment

There are many characteristics of the physical environment in which people live that can be a cause of a disease or a contributing factors to its spread and persistence.

Some of the more obvious characteristics, such as climatic conditions, communication and transportation systems etc., will require different health promotion interventions: some will be aimed at raising people's competence in adjusting to the living conditions and some will be concerned with changing these conditions and reducing the adverse effects on people's health.

Social environment

Norms or social expectations reflect the predominant value system in a community associated with dealing with a health threat or disease. These norms can be related to:

- *life style*, which reflects the individual's position in a society, his values and beliefs, his behaviour and actions and the ranking order of preferences or issues of importance, which together can be subsumed under the general concept of our life style;

- *risky behaviour*, which represents specific forms of behaviour or action associated with an increased risk from a health threat or a disease. Generally speaking this risky behaviour will be associated with the type of social norms and specific norm characteristics (historicity, social support, sanctions etc.);

- *support systems*, which are complementary to the health care system and originate in the community to provide knowledge, skills and support in the form of self-help groups. An examination of the existing supportive services as well as those which could be helpful if they existed, will contribute to the definition of the problem in health promotional terms.

Organisational structures

The existing organisational and administrative bodies which will be relevant for a health threat or a disease will include medical services associated with management and treatment, as well as other supportive systems. These will be relevant for the following:

- *diagnosis* of the problem, which will include the presence of risk factors which can be medical or behavioral. It will include screening services as well as studies carried out by the public health services;

- *treatment* in health promotional terms will include the manipulation of social policies and norms and creation of new or reinforcement of existing services, which will be influenced by the distribution of a risk factor or a disease in a population;

- *utilisation of services* will reflect the type of norms that exist in relation to dealing with a specific health threat or disease.

Individual adjustment

Individuals and groups will be exposed to different kinds of health threats and diseases within the same social environment. This will be of great importance for the definition of a problem in health promotional terms and will form a part of the aims and objectives of a health promotional intervention. The following will be important areas in which individual adjustment must be made:

The physical environment

The way individuals cope with the environment will depend on their awareness of its dangers as well as their confidence in being able to affect it and improve it. Health promotion has an important role in raising people's competence in dealing with environmental issues either individually or through some other social mechanisms. One way of influencing the environment is by joining some existing environmental movement or creating one for the specific and local purposes. Another way is to create political pressure on the governmental bodies to recognise such issues and include them into their policies.

The social environment

Even where there are social expectations aimed at reducing risk and preventing a disease, individual perception of those expectations or norms may be decisive for the type of behaviour or action within a certain life style that is in operation. This perception may be related to the following aspects of norms:

- *to the accurate interpretation* of existing expectations relevant to the situation in which an individual finds himself;

- *to existing legitimation,* which includes the professional as well as lay support for conformist behaviour related to that norm;

- *to existing sanctions,* which are associated with the deviant behaviour related to a norm.

Services

Even where certain services exist they may not be known or attractive enough to individuals or groups, which could reduce the utilisation of the same. In health promotional terms it will be necessary to define any problems related to the utilisation of the following services:

- *preventive*: which may include screening services, antenatal clinics etc. aimed at preventing certain health threats or diseases;

- *management services:* which can include certain types of hospitals as well as self-help groups;

- *treatment services*: which may include general practitioners, hospitals, as well as certain outlets for alternative medicine.

Health educational aspects

For years the attempts to improve people's health by means of education has been the main responsibility of health education. With the introduction of the concept of health promotion it became necessary to redefine health education within this new framework. To understand the new role of health education it will be necessary to compare the two activities according to present day role definition of each (Baric,1985).

1. What is health education?

It is the process of transmission and/or acquisition of knowledge and skills necessary for survival and the improvement of quality of life. There are many definitions emphasizing different aspects of this process. The main objection is that the definition is too general and cannot be operationalised.

2. What is health promotion?

It is a wider concept which includes the health education aspect as well as a number of other activities aimed at manipulating the physical and social environment of the target population.

There are many definitions and interpretations of this concept and at present there is a general confusion in this area.

3. What is the difference (if any)?

The difference is in the interpretation of the scope of the activity and in the type of agents involved.

- *ACTIVITY: Formal - Informal*

- *AGENTS: Direct - Indirect (access to clients)*

There are those who believe that health promotion is part of health education, whereas others believe the opposite. i.e. that health promotion is something wider which includes health education as one aspect of its activities.

4. Interpretation depends on the organisational model:

The prevalent interpretation depends on the existing organisational model of health related and health directed activities. In general terms, there are several organisational models in existence:

- Dispersed

- Specialist

- Coexisting

- Cooperative

5. The dispersed model

The organisation of health education activities is distributed amongst many professions and institutions. There is no specific health education service and no specialists. There is a strong tendency to adopt team approach and role differentiation. Health education and promotion are considered to be two interchangeable concepts, including all the activities necessary for promotion of health, prevention and treatment of illness.

6. The specialist and coexisting models

The activities are divided between health education specialists and other agents (professionals or non-professionals). There is a strict differentiation between health education and health promotion. Health education is what health education specialists do, and health promotion is what others do. Whereas in the past one could say that other agents are involved in health education as part of their professional and/or occupational role, this is now changing. Other professions (doctors, etc.) prefer the term health promotion to underline the difference between their activities and those of health education specialists.

7. The aims

The need to differentiate between health education and promotion came up only recently, due to the developments initiated by WHO.

a) Health education aims:

The main aim of health education is health behaviour of individuals and groups. This includes routines as well as decisions about certain behaviour, and actions in terms of prevention and treatment of illnesses. A certain health behaviour can have several different consequences, depending on specific characteristics.

b) Health promotion aims:

Health promotion uses a wider concept of health as the result of interaction of internal and external factors. Taking an ecological approach, it looks at behaviour-action continuum in terms of the existing norms and decisions, concentrating on the social aspects which influence behaviour and actions.

8. Methods

According to the different aims, there will be a difference also in the methods used to achieve these aims.

a) Health education:

The methods used in achieving health education aims will depend on the conceptualisation of the health education problems, i.e. problems due to health behaviour. There are a number of models of health education interventions in existence. They deal with knowledge and skills, decision making, perception of norms etc.

b) Health promotion:

The methods will also depend on the aims which in the case of health promotion include also the manipulation of the social environment. The methods will, therefore, include legislation and lobbying of members of parliament, changing social norms, provision and distribution of resources (finances and services), influencing values, etc.

9. From the clients' point of view

So far we have been talking about what we can and should do for our clients or target populations. How does the client experience a health threat or the onset of an illness? What are the alternatives available to him/her? To find an answer one can examine the problem in terms of a process which includes a set of steps

       a. Awareness of the risk/symptom

       b. Self-diagnosis

       c. Assessment of the finding

       d. Choice of actions available:

           i) primary health care (no action, self-help,

             self-care, community help)

           ii) primary medical care (clinic, hospital,

             general practitioner).

10. Primary health care

In countries with a limited access to medical services the primary health care is of greatest importance. The main objective of health education/promotion is to create a certain level of competence in diagnosing and treating a certain health problem.

11. Primary medical care

In countries with a well developed and easily accessible health care system, one notices the tendency for treating primary health and medical care as interchangeable concepts. This is because the first four steps are, for the client, compressed into a simple decision to see a doctor. Primary medical care is provided for everybody and the medical profession takes over the responsibility for the diagnosis and treatment of health problems. The main objective of health education/promotion will be to to motivate clients to seek medical help early, to follow the advice and treatment, utilise preventive services, etc.

The health educational intervention is now limited to dealing with individuals and groups, as compared to the health promotional intervention which deals with societal factors. Drawing these demarcation lines between health education and health promotion requires a new approach to the definition of a problem in health educational terms. Taking this view, the definition of the health educational aspects of a health problem should consider a number of factors, set out below.

Knowledge

The awareness or knowledge about the existence of a health threat or a disease is considered to be an important, although not absolutely necessary precondition for prevention, management and treatment on an individual or group basis. In the period before the Second World War the main emphasis of health education was on transmitting knowledge to the "ignorant" populations. This approach was supported by the studies carried out in developing countries where ignorance and poverty were thought to be the main cause of low life expectancy, high infant mortality and widely spread morbidity. Most health education interventions were concentrated on improving the ways and means of transmitting information and knowledge about the causes and the means of preventing certain diseases.

With the expansion of health education in industrial societies, it soon became apparent that even with considerable knowledge, the prevalence of certain diseases has not been reduced. Further studies have found that health related and health directed behaviour is a function of a number of factors, of which knowledge is only one. The reaction of health educators was to disregard the role of knowledge and place the emphasis on other psychological factors such as attitudes and motivation.

With the present revolution in the field of information technology, the transmission of knowledge/information has obtained a new importance. In the past, knowledge and information was aimed at individuals and the individuals were used for the evaluation of effectiveness in transmitting health education messages. New technology has enabled the simultaneous spread or access to knowledge/information by a whole community, nation or even the world. The fact that a whole population hears a "bit" of information simultaneously means that this can be instrumental in changing the value system or norms of that society or community. In this way the importance of knowledge/information has come full circle back into the forefront of importance as a health promotion/education method.

At present we are faced with a contradiction: the transmission of information by means of modern technology is important - not so much because it increases individual knowledge about the diseases and the means of prevention and management - but because it affects the value system and norms related to health behaviour and actions in a population.

On an individual level, however, it will be important to examine the existing knowledge or awareness about the following:

Health threats and diseases

Although everybody is exposed to all the health threats and diseases that are prevalent in a society, some people are exposed more than others. In this sense the knowledge about relative probability associated with a health threat or a disease should provide a positive motivation for adjustment and changes.

Services

The knowledge about the existence and the availability of certain services can be an important precondition for their utilisation. This includes not only knowledge about the existence of a service and its character, but also such details as address and telephone number, transport, hours of work, available personnel etc. It will also include the type of services provided and the expectations which a certain service can meet.

Supportive systems

The awareness of existing supportive systems which can be organised by the health care system (anti-smoking clinic) or as self-help groups (mothers with handicapped children), is an important precondition for their utilisation. Awareness about their existence as well as details about their character and provision of support will help people to decide about their utilisation.

Attitudes

One of the consequences of the disappointment with the attempts to improve health by means of increasing individual levels of knowledge has been to place emphasis on the way people felt about the health threat and the measures necessary for preventing it. The emphasis was given to people's feelings expressed in their attitudes which became the main target of health educational interventions.

Today we are aware of the importance of attitudes in the decision making process, but not solely because they represent people's feelings about health actions. They are also important because they represent people's internalisation of social expectations (norms) as a part of the more general value system concerning a health issue. This means that in a society where there are norms (social expectations) which support a positive preventive action, people with positive attitudes to that action will be labelled as conformists and will be more likely to undertake such an action. Those with negative attitudes will be labelled deviants and health education will have the task to change the deviants into conformists, or to change social expectations (norms). This involves a different set of measures, compared with the attempts in the past to change people's attitudes on an individual level. Many of such attempts failed, because the attitudes were not accompanied with supportive norms, and those who changed became deviants.

Bearing in mind this new interpretation of the importance of attitudes for health behaviour and actions, people's attitudes or orientation towards certain risk factors or diseases will be an important indicator for planning a health education intervention. Attitudes relate to::

The problem

Some problems have acquired a certain image which is reflected in the attitudes that people have towards them. Some health problems have the image of a killer disease (cancer) or carry a social stigma (STD) or are associated with particular life styles (CHD). Attitudes towards different problems may enhance or inhibit people's decisions about changes in life styles or behaviours which are associated with their prevention and management;

The solutions

There is a difference between motivational power of attitudes towards a problem and attitudes towards a solution. Even if the attitude towards the problem is positive in terms of its severity and a person's susceptibility to it, a negative attitude towards the solution may act as an inhibiting factor. The cost benefit assessment of the proposed solution supported by a positive attitude may act as a motivational cue to trigger off a change in people's life style or behaviour.

Skills

Reducing a health threat or preventing an illness may often depend on people's competence, which can also include a certain set of skills required to do something about the problem. The definition of the required skills and the information about their distribution in a population will be important when planning a health education intervention. Among a number of skills as a part of people's competence the following are considered to be important.

Coping skills

The awareness of any health threat or risk from a disease, whether imposed from outside or due to internal factors, represents an upheaval which demands certain skills to be able to cope with it. These coping skills can be associated with avoiding a certain threat, with reducing it, or with integrating it positively into one's life style.

Communication skills

To learn about a health threat or a disease, to be able to mobilise support and to acquire help demands that individuals and groups communicate with each other and with the professionals. There are a number of aspects of skills that are involved in a process of communication, which may include linguistic abilities and coping with social barriers. Defining the problem in this area is of importance for planning any health education intervention.

Behaviour modification skills

Even in the case of appropriate knowledge and positive attitudes to the problem and its solution there is a need for a certain set of skills, which will enable individuals to modify their life style or behaviour. Those skills can be learned and practised, and the information about lack of those skills should be taken into account when planning a health education intervention.

Methodology

The definition of the problem needs to relate to the three aspects: the medical, the health promotional and the health educational. Each of these aspects of the problem has a specific methodology appropriate for its definition and requires a special set of approaches backed up by appropriate indicators, criteria and instruments.

The general approach adopted in the medical definition is that of a "differential diagnosis" as contrasted with the simple cause-effect approach usually applied in health promotion and education. This means that the exploration of the events leading to a health problem or risk is carried out in greater depth than before, using a systems model of exploration.

The main objection to such an approach in health promotion and education has been the difficulty in exploring a problem in depth due to the difficulties associated with the access to necessary data relevant for such a diagnosis. It is, therefore, necessary to develop and refine the diagnostic tools for health promotion and education to match the quality of tools used in a medical "differential diagnosis". It is accepted that this may be a time consuming exercise which is, however, necessary if health promotion and education are to match the professional standards of the medical profession, be accountable and submit to auditing as well as evaluation of its activities.

Definition of medical problems

Health promotion and education deal with threats to health and prevention and management of diseases. For this reason it is necessary for people engaged in health promotion and education to understand the methods of medical diagnosis of such problems. The medical definition is based on two main approaches, i.e. the study of causation (aetiology) and the study of the distribution (epidemiology), each of which has specific methods of approach.

The study of causation

Our fight against disease and for the improvement of health is based on the ever-changing body of medical knowledge; in addition, practitioners have to learn how to perform their activities within the constraints of medical ethics, which is based on human and civil rights of the patients including the existing value system, so practitioners must learn how to deal with uncertainties associated with the complexity of the interpretation of today's health problems.

Health promotion and education use medical knowledge as the basis for defining the aims of their interventions. It is, therefore, very important to bear in mind this "relativistic" character of existing medical knowledge when one plans an intervention involving some fundamental changes which may be irreversible. This is of special importance for health promotion which deals with changes in the social environment. Such changes are difficult to achieve and if and when they are achieved it is practically impossible to revert to the original state.

The uncertainty in medical knowledge, which is either due to the awareness of possible new discoveries, or to the levels of probability associated with the established associations, has to be encompassed by a doctor-patient interaction or a health promotion and education intervention.

Another problem in translating causality into health promotion and education aims arises from the tendency to use simple cause-effect models. Medical science has long since abandoned such models and has fully recognised the complexity of the origins of health threats and diseases. In health promotion and education one is still limited to simple models expressed in statements of what is good or bad for a person's health.

The methodology used in the definition of medical problem includes the assessment of medical, social and personal factors:

1. Medical factors

Medical factors influencing health and disease are based on the medical discoveries and can be discovered from the medical literature or from interviews with the representatives of the medical profession. These factors include:

   a. *causal factors*, which are usually complex and change with the new medical discoveries;

   b. *risk factors*, which have been found to contribute to the risk from a certain disease and which are also changing with the discovery of new associations between certain factors and the incidence of health threats.

It is important to make a critical selection of relevant information from the available medical knowledge concerning the causal and risk factors and choose only these factors that are amenable to health promotion and education. The factors chosen should be classified according to their relationship with the health threat or disease in terms of the level of probability or certainty of such an association.

2. Social/environmental factors

The social/environment factors influencing health and disease can have a causative or a contributory character. The association between the environment and the health threat or disease is usually the outcome of a study of some disease which has been published in a learned journal. The information about these factors can be obtained from literature or from a survey of the experts dealing with that health threat or disease. A differentiation will have to be made between the origins of these contributory or causative factors in terms of:

   a. the *physical environment*, which has more recently been under intensive scrutiny by many professionals. This kind of information includes housing, sanitation, transport, etc., and will be available not only from medical but from a number of other professional journals;

   b. the *social environment*, which can be a causative as well as a contributory factor in terms of the living conditions, poverty, habits, etc. The information about social factors is usually available from the results of studies concerned with the social position of the individual and can be found in a wide range of professional publications including journals devoted to curative and preventive medicine. It should, however, be mentioned that these factors are not often referred to in medical literature or used by the medical profession in the prevention and treatment of disease.

3. Personal factors

Personal factors are associated with a number of diseases and risk factors in the following areas:

a. lifestyle, which is used as a general description of different behavioral patterns and has been found to be associated with increased risk or incidence of certain diseases. The information is usually derived from special studies which use indicators appropriate for the study of lifestyles. It should be mentioned that this is a most recent development and that one can only find a limited number of studies of this kind;

b. *habits and routines* relating to different forms of behaviour such as smoking, overeating etc..are associated with risk factors and diseases. Information on these problems in a population is gained from the secondary analysis of existing records and from the outcomes of population surveys. The kind of information used for an epidemiological analysis includes mortality and morbidity data as well as information about social characteristics and behavioral patterns of specific population groups.

c. *actions*, can either cause, increase or affect the reduction of risk from a disease. These actions are associated with certain occupations, utilisation of services, compliance with the treatment, etc. The source of information about such actions comes from surveys, or from existing records from hospitals, police, clinics, general practices, social services, etc.

Distribution

The information used by epidemiology for the study of the distribution of medical problems in a population is gained from the secondary analysis of existing records and from the outcomes of population surveys. The kind of information used for an epidemiological analysis includes mortality and morbidity data as well as information about social characteristics and behavioral patterns of specific population groups.

1. Existing records

The types of national and regional data collected on a regular basis include information about authenticated causes of death. The information is based on the *International Certificate of Death*, which is in use in most countries with a developed health service. The reliability of the information on such certificates depends on who completes them. In some countries a non-medical person is authorised to sign a certificate of death, in which case there is some doubt about the accuracy of the cause of death. Epidemiological analysis of mortality data examines death by cause, age, sex, location, occupation, season, etc.

The information concerning non-fatal diseases or *morbidity data* is more difficult to come by since it is not collected on a regular basis for the whole country. There are records about notifiable diseases such as certain infectious diseases, cancers, HIV, etc. The most important source of morbidity data consists of hospital records. These can be supplemented by records from General Practitioners, although neither of them are published on a regular basis. The introduction of age-sex register and computerised data banks have made the access to General Practitioners' data much easier. To a large extent, however, the acquisition of morbidity data depends on population surveys.

Another source of national data is the *birth register* which in some cases (if the birth was attended by a medical person) could include information about possible congenital malformations.

The development of the epidemiological method has, therefore, been mainly concerned with survey techniques and data analysis. The survey method depends on the choice of the population which is in most cases represented by a sample if the total population cannot be included for various reasons. There are specific techniques of insuring that the sample represents the population from which it is drawn: the most common is the random sample, although, a stratified random sample is also often used. There are other types of samples such as quota sample etc.

The more specific a sample is the more difficult it is to ensure its representativeness of the whole population.

In addition to the choice of a sample, the survey method depends on the construction of the instrument (usually a questionnaire) which is used to collect the data. The design of a questionnaire must conform to certain standards which will enable the expected analysis of the findings. It can include questions which deal with factual data (i.e. age), questions that are related to a composite characteristic of the respondent (such as social class, which is composed from the occupation and the status of the respondent), or some theoretical construct, for example, attitude which is derived from a battery of specially selected and pretested questions).

In whatever way the data are collected, epidemiological methods have paid special attention to the analysis of the information that should justify the inferences made. The methods are usually based on the comparison of disease occurrence between identifiable groups of people. The main assumption is that the disease is due to certain characteristics of a group of people, their behaviour or the place they live in and work, or to some other external influences. These variations in time and space are expected to highlight the decisive factors which differentiate people who suffer from a disease as compared to those who are healthy, and are intended to help in the understanding of the causation of a specific disease.

Based on this insight, the next step is to define the *population at risk* from that disease. Since everybody is at risk from something, the population at risk is defined as such only if their risk is greater than what could be expected under 'normal' conditions. To be more precise, the notion of relative risk needs to be introduced, which denotes the level of risk in two populations, where all the other factors have been taken into account.

To be able to calculate the relative risk in a population it is necessary to know the number of new cases in that population during a defined period of time. This proportion is called the *incidence rate*. It is calculated by dividing the number of cases by the size of the population and is usually expressed by a number per thousand, ten thousand or hundred thousand population (i.e for positive cervical cancer smear tests it was 7 per 1000). The incidence rate is useful in the study of causation of a disease and for short term acute diseases. To study chronic disease, it is better to look at the number of cases in a population, which is described by the *prevalence rate*. The prevalence rate is calculated by taking the number of cases in a population at a certain point in time and dividing it by the size of the relevant population at the same time. It is expressed as a percentage or any other more suitable rate. Both the incidence and prevalence rates can be translated into a statement of the risk from a particular disease for a certain population.

There are numerous rates that are commonly used when analysing mortality statistics. *Mortality rates* are derived from dividing the number of deaths during a year by the size of a population in the same year. *Crude death rate* is calculated at the mid year for a whole population. The main reason for differences in death rates between different countries is usually the different age distributions of the countries' population. It is known that the death rate is highest in first few weeks of life, then falls towards middle age to rise again in the older population.

This difference can be avoided by calculating *age specific death rates*. This is appropriate for small populations, but for large populations the usual measure is the *standard mortality ratio (SMR)* which is calculated by taking each population and calculating the number of deaths that would occur in it, if at each age it experienced the age specific death rates of a certain standard population. It serves for comparisons between populations with different age distributions of their populations. The standard population is usually the whole population in a country with corresponding characteristics of the study population.

Since the number of deaths in early childhood contributes most to the measurement of mortality rates in a population, there are various measures that are used to study mortality for that age group. The simplest is the *infant mortality rate*, which is calculated by dividing the number of deaths among children under one year of age with the number of live births in that population. It is expressed as rate per 1000 live births.

The number of deaths in the first month of life is expressed by *neonatal mortality rate* which is calculated by dividing the number of deaths of infants under 28 days old with the number of living births in that year.

Mortality among infants between one and 12 months old is expressed by *post-neonatal mortality rate*, which is calculated by dividing the number of infants dying between 1-12 months old by the number of live births during the year. To measure prenatal mortality one can use the *stillbirth rate* which is calculated by dividing the number of stillbirths by the number of all births in a year and expressing it as a rate per 1000 total births. It is, however, difficult to define precisely what is a stillbirth (before, during or immediately after birth) and it is, therefore, more common to study *perinatal mortality*, which is calculated by taking the number of stillbirths and deaths within the first week of life and dividing them by the total number of births (stillbirths and live births) in that year.

There are situations when it is useful to know the *life expectancy at birth* for a certain population. This measure is commonly used by life insurance companies and is simplified by being presented in *life tables*. These are calculated by taking a imaginary population of new born individuals and applying standardised mortality ratios for each age group of that invented population and see how the population diminishes through time. In this way one can easily see the life expectancy of any individual of any age, although for the purpose of life insurance a number of other factors are being taken into consideration.

One of the problems for comparative studies based on mortality and morbidity data is the way the diseases have been classified. To avoid unnecessary confusion an International Statistical Classification of Diseases has been sponsored by the World Health Organisation and is in general use.

2. Survey data

The usual way of finding out what is happening in a population is to either observe that population or question them. A structured means of asking people about certain topics of interest is to carry out a survey. The main elements of a survey are the population under study, the topic of inquiry, the instruments used to collect the information and the inferences made from the findings:

a. *The population.* This can include all the people or a sample according to the number of people relevant to the study. In case of a survey of the whole population, the inferences made from the data collected will reflect what is going on in the population; in case of a sample, special methods of sampling and interpreting the sample data will have to be used if one wishes to generalise from the sample to the whole population. One can sample members of a community, group, profession, etc., or some institutions such as schools in an area, some districts or any other part of a classificatory system which can be identified as representative of some larger entity.

There are different kinds of samples, such as a random sample, stratified random sample, quota sample etc. Each has specific advantages and limitations which will affect the possibility of generalising from the sample to the whole population.

Most common is the random sample: it includes the decision about the size of the sample selected from the whole population and the choice of individuals to be included by using a "random numbers table". The idea is that every individual in the total population should have an equal chance of being selected, thus reducing any possible bias in the representation of that population;

b. *The topic.* This will reflect the aims and objectives of the study. It can be concentrated on one aim or can have several aims, in which case, each aim will have to be accompanied by a separate set of objectives. It is generally accepted that the aim reflects what one wants to achieve, and the objectives define how it is intended to be achieved. This differentiation between aims and objectives is important as is the link between the two. If there is no logical or theoretical justification for the expectation that certain objectives will achieve, or could achieve, a certain aim, then the interpretations of findings from a survey will be meaningless as far as the aims are concerned. This, however, need not be obvious if one does not start by critically examining the relationship between the aims and objectives of a study. In addition to the logical link between the aims and objectives, it will be necessary to specify them in concrete and measurable terms;

c. *The instruments:.* These can be in the form of an "aide memoire" which is used in an in-depth interview, or a questionnaire. The latter can be administered by an interviewer or can be handed/sent to the subject to complete it and return it to the sender.

The questions in the questionnaire will be the product of the process which is a part of research design, which includes the selection of indicators and criteria that can then be translated into a questionnaire. Indicators are factors which the study assumes will produce relevant information concerning the aims and the contribution of objectives to the achievement of these aims. The criteria represent the qualitative/quantitative aspects of the indicators which should be reflected in the questionnaire.

The usual procedure is to carry out a pilot study which is concerned with finding out about the relevant questions, their reliability and validity, as well as their acceptance by the respondents. Once the questionnaire has been pretested in this way, the final questionnaire will be produced and administered to the population under study.

There are various forms of questions that can be included in a questionnaire: one can use open-ended questions, multiple choice questions, factual questions (age etc.) or batteries of questions in the case of a composite construct (i.e. attitudes, etc.).

d. *Inferences.* These will be made on the basis of the analysis of the collected data. They can take a descriptive form or can be the result of a statistical analysis. In other words, one can use either descriptive or inferential statistics, or both.

Descriptive statistics are based on aggregation of data and produce a "frequency distribution", which can be further analysed in terms of patterns which such a distribution manifests. One can look at central values (mode, median, average etc.) trends, percentages, etc. These can be presented in the form of tables or diagrams.

Inferential statistics are meant to examine the relationships between two or more variables in a study. This examination is usually carried out by cross tabulation of variables in two- or more- dimensional tables and will include tests of significance concerning the patterns presented in such a table. It can also include other measures of association such as correlations, or other more complex statistical methods of analysis.

It is important to bear in mind the precision of the elements of measurement represented by the indicators and criteria, and adjust the statistical methods accordingly. Lack of precision in measurement cannot be improved by a sophisticated statistical analysis.

One should also bear in mind that the relationship between certain variables is usually expressed in terms of probability and one should interpret the meaning of probability accordingly and not assume that a high level of probability can be equated with "near" certainty, since there is no such thing as near certainty. This is important for the application of inferences to certain health promotion and education activities; all should take into account the difference between possibility, probability and certainty.

Definition of health promotional problems

The health of a population has been defined as a function of the interaction between external conditions (environmental factors) and personal characteristics (psychosocial factors). It is consequently desirable in defining a problem to examine under what conditions people live and fight for their survival. This is done by visiting the place where people live, talking to the people themselves and observing the situation, talking with those in positions of authority, members of the health services and examining the existing records. The systematisation of the information is achieved by the use of an "aide memoire", which covers the following areas of inquiry, some of which will be more appropriate for rural than urban populations or agricultural rather than industrial societies, but are included to provide a complete picture of the definition of the environmental factors influencing health (Baric,1982):

Location

The background information should include a description of the location of the study population, including:

1. the *name* of the place in which the study population lives;

2. *type of settlement*, its approximate size and general character on an urban/rural level;

3. *climatic conditions* of the area including the average temperatures, rainfall and seasonal changes. These conditions will influence the priority given to certain needs such as heating, clothing, time spent outdoors, adequacy of shelter and possible restrictions in movement during certain seasons;

4. *water supply* available to the families, which will influence the possibility of carrying out personal hygiene, the access to clean, good quality water, cooking patterns, need for boiling water, available hot water supply for personal hygiene, washing clothes and dishes or heating; the description of water supply to include its type such as wells, springs, river or lake, rain water, piped water, as well as the distance of the living quarters from the source which can imply transportation as compared to immediate access;

5. *sewage disposal*, which can be an important source of infection and infestation; the description to include the ways people in that area dispose of waste either in fields or forests, by using various types of latrines, or by means of centralised collection in sewers including outside or inside toilets;

6. *energy sources* available in that area, which influence the ways people heat their living quarters, the way they cook their food and move around; for heating purposes the energy source can be rubbish, wood, dung, coal, oil, gas, electricity, and the need for it can range from not being required for heating at all, to being self-collected or purchased; for cooking and washing purposes, the same categories and consideration; the energy sources for transportation to include reference to manpower, animal power or mechanical power;

7. *housing*, to be described in terms of the type of dwellings common in that area, average size in terms of number of rooms per person, available amenities such as heating, lighting, cooking, water supply, waste disposal; protection from the elements; pests and insects depending on the ventilation system, window and door screens. An important aspect

of the dwelling circumstances will be the density of the population and the proximity between the different households in that area.

Economy

The information on the economic conditions of the area of study in general should provide us with an insight into a number of factors relevant to the state of health as well as the accessibility of the health services for the sample population:

1. *prosperity* of the population under study in terms of annual income per capita and a description of possible deprivation;

2. level of technological *development* of the area, relating either to industry or to agriculture, investment policies and outlook for future developments;

3. the main source of family *income* in that area, described in terms of predominant occupations of family members;

4. level of *employment* among the members of families in the area with specific reference to the problems of unemployment and provisions made to deal with it;

5. level of *migration* among the families in general and the working population in particular with special reference to commuting to work, emigrating permanently or of new work force immigrating into the area;

6. availability of local, national or international *help* to the economy of the area or its specific parts and the effects it has on the area under study;

7. presence of local, national or international *organisations* running specific health, social or other programmes.

Social organisation

The type of society in which the family/household lives and earns its livelihood will to a large extent influence its state of health and the demands on the family's own capability to take care of itself. Aspects of society include:

1. *political system*, which defines the amount of participation expected and allowed to certain family members in influencing their own destiny and the priorities in terms of budgetary expenditure; if there is more than one political party, different party orientation to health care; emphasis on professional or indigenous health system, coverage of the population in terms of freely available health care, orientation towards work, social security and social help;

2. *social stratification*, which relates to the criteria along which the population is differentiated; this involves examination of different social classes, castes, religious groups, age groups or income and occupations;

3. *position of women*, which directly affects their role in taking care and educating their children; employment of women in industry, home craft, agriculture or in housework, which decides on the time available to be spent with children and the need for substitute child minders either within the family or the social environment;

4. *social mobility*, which depends on the socio-political system, as well as the position of women in that society, and is achieved either through marriage or through education and employment, this indicates to a certain degree the future-orientation of family members and perceptions of possibilities for economic advancement;

5. *type of organisations* existing on the local level, including political, social trade union, voluntary and other, which can provide support, direct help or services to the local population.

Communications

The information available to a population in a certain area will to a large extent depend on the existing communication system by means of which news can travel and be exchanged. It will also depend on the existing transportation system and subsequently geographical mobility, since either information can be disseminated among the population or the members of that population can travel to places where information is more readily available:

1. *type of communication* system available locally, such as radio, TV, telephone, press, mass meetings, social gatherings, patterns of visiting and the availability of professional and nonprofessional informants;

2. *type of local organisations* and bodies such as assemblies, councils, committees, voluntary organisations, self-help groups and gatherings, where the population meets and which can serve as an opportunity for exchange of news, information and ideas;

3. the *transportation infrastructure* within the area, as well as that linking the area with the outside world, including roads, railways, bus routes, water transport;

4. *available links* in the area by means of the existing transportation system with important locations such as workplace, school, health services, shopping centre;

5. *available means of transport* in the area such as pedestrian travel, bicycles, animal-drawn carts, boats or motor transport;

6. *costs of transport* relative to the income and priorities in expenditure of the population in the area.

Value system

The way a population thinks, the priorities they cherish and the taboos they observe will be supported by the general value system of that population, which also defines the social expectations of norms prevalent in that society, people's attitudes to certain goals and the use made of information and resources in achieving aims:

1. *prevalent religion*, which still has a great influence on the value system in many societies, whether or not the population strictly observes the codes and participates in the rituals; it may have its most significant influence on health-related behaviour and practices connected with nutrition, personal hygiene, sexual habits and the rules concerning the bringing up of children;

2. *status of religious leaders* in a society, which can have important consequences on the health of a population, on their participation in health campaigns, their support for certain health measures and reinforcement of certain health practices;

3. *existing legal norms*, which are in direct relationship with the health practices related to family health and the care of young children; their historicity, coercive power and sanctions will influence people's conformity and utilisation of such norms to achieve the best health for its members;

4. *existing social norms* will directly influence people's health-related behaviour, whether it is covered by legal norms or not; their historicity, coercive power and sanctions will influence the level of conformity and social support available to the population.

Education

There is an association between the level of education and the mortality and morbidity of a population. In developing countries this will be not so much the level of education as the difference between any education or none, between illiteracy and literacy of the population. Where education is available, the state of health of the population may be directly influenced by the inclusion of certain health-educational topics in the curriculum. It is also possible that in certain areas there will be a generational difference in literacy and education which can be remedied by extra-curricular activities of the local teaching staff:

1. *level of education* of the population as a whole in the area, including generational differences, level of illiteracy and trends for the improvement of the educational level;

2. *type of education* available locally and within commuting distance of the settlement, which may be of different types such as compulsory, at various levels, professional and skilled education;

3. *type of extramural educational activity,* including special courses (domestic science, first aid etc.) and special classes as a part of health care (e.g. mothercraft);

4. *location of schools* in relation to the habitat of the study population, with special reference to locally-based schools as compared with those within commuting distance, given type of transport and distance covered;

5. *quality of education* offered, depending on the size of classes and the number and training of teachers;

6. *content of the curricula* with special reference to subjects which indirectly (biology) or directly (health education) contribute to the increase in the health knowledge of the pupils;

7. *provision for teaching of health topics* by the local or visiting health personnel, on a regular or ad hoc basis;

8. *special programmes on health educational topics* initiated by the school or by others and carried out through the school and by the school personnel.

State of health

It will be important to know something about the general state of health in a country since this could reflect on the state of health of the population in the study area. A crude but useful way of measuring the state of health is by looking at mortality and morbidity data. In summary, the following information will be required:

1. *mortality rates,* general and especially infant mortality, with possible indication of the causes of death for the study area;

2. *morbidity rates,* general and infant morbidity with special reference to most common diseases in the study area;

3. *utilisation* of services;

4. *general assessment* of physical, mental and social wellbeing of the study population;

5. *endemic and epidemic diseases,* especially prevalent in the study area and their consequences (such as malnutrition and infestations).

Health care

The level and kind of family competence will to a large extent depend on whether or not health care is available locally and within easy reach or whether the families are dependent on their own resources, either totally or for everything except major illnesses. This will also be related to the kind of treatment available, and the expected consequences. Even where health care is available, its effectiveness depends on the relationship between type of services offered, and the potential user's financial involvement, social expectations and the ability to recognise the need for help in the first place. It is thus important to know what kind of curative, preventive and supportive services are within reach of the population:

1. *kinds of health care system* that exists in the country in terms of payment and coverage by insurance;

2. *special provisions* for mother and child health (MCH) and other special diseases such as sexually transmitted diseases (STD), tuberculosis, trachoma and others;

3. *organisation of health care,* in terms of numbers of professionals per capita, number of hospital beds, type of primary health care and the existence of complementary nonprofessional or indigenous health care systems;

4. *location of primary health care* and its accessibility to the indigenous population of the area under study;

5. *special provisions for preventive health services* in terms of screening programmes, vaccination and control of the environment;

6. *organisation and execution of health education activities,* in terms of regular services or special programmes and campaigns;

7. *special provisions* for socially endangered, chronically ill, handicapped and elderly population groups on a national and local level.

Definition of health educational problems

Since health education is now being treated as a complementary aspect of health promotion, its activities have been limited to interventions on a personal and group level. For this reason the definition of health educational problems will be based on information about the personal health-related characteristics of individuals and the groups they live in and depend on (e.g. their families/households), as well as on the assessment of their competence in dealing with health problems.

Individual characteristics

1. Personal information

Each respondent is asked a number of personal questions which will be grouped into more general categories, such as:

a. age and sex of the respondent

b. position in the family

c. marital status

d. education

This information is collected by the inclusion of relevant questions into the questionnaire to be administered by the interviewer. Other questions collect information about specific characteristics or situations in which each respondent lives and works. The questions presented could apply to people living in rural as well as urban areas and cover the following topics:

2. Residence

a. *type of residence* in which an individual or family lives, which is influenced by the socio-cultural, economic and geographical environments; its type may reflect the social position and may define their access to resources and services; the kind of friends and neighbours they have and will be able to mobilise in case of a need of emergency; because of the differences within an area or a settlement it will be necessary to find out which of the existing resources and services are accessible to each individual or family in the sample;

b. *water supply*   available to an individual or family in terms of piped water, wells, springs, rivers, lakes, rain water or the need to transport water from a distance such as a central distribution centre outside the settlement;

c. *sewage disposal*   directly available to a particular individual or family will considerably influence the risk from infections, infestations, personal hygiene and cooking practices, whether it is a system with a central collecting point and links to each house, a separate facility for each house or no system at all, where the inhabitants use fields, bushes or forest for waste disposal;

d. *energy source*   available to each individual or family must be assessed according to family needs; whether they are adequate or not; whether there are possible restrictions and limitations owing to the lack of adequate energy resources. It is necessary to bear in mind that these limitations could affect such aspects as the lighting and heating of premises, cooking facilities, washing clothes and cooking utensils, personal hygiene, etc. Mobility of the individual or family can depend on available resources in terms of limitations in transport and communication.

3. Spatial mobility

The length of time spent living in a community will affect a person's position in that community as well as his/her interaction with the social environment. One can look at this in terms of mobility and say that an individual's movement from one community to another will be closely related to a number of factors such as social position and degree of social interaction with others. It is generally accepted that place of residence and length of stay are influenced by a person's occupation and marital status. Therefore, spatial mobility is a very important social characteristic in the assessment of types of social interaction, particularly because of its association with the social class of the individual.

The influence of spatial mobility is expressed in two ways: one is closely related to social mobility and therefore is decisive for social status and for achieved social class; and the other is its influence on the kind of social interaction, including type of household, type of kin relationship and, to a certain extent, type of conjugal role distribution, which takes place within a social network.

a. *Type of spatial mobility*. The definition of an individual or family as spatially static or mobile will depend on the origins of the spouses in relation to their place of residence. Mobility may be expressed in terms of the type of marriage which includes:

- *circumscribed marriage*, where both husband and wife are native born;

- *extraneous marriage*, where one of the spouses is native born, and the other comes from some other place;

- *immigrant marriage*, where both spouses were born somewhere else, and moved to the place of residence;

b. *Method of measurement*. To establish the spatial mobility of an individual or family group, the questions include the place of birth of each spouse. The answers can be presented in the following matrix:

	Wife	Husband
Native		
Stranger		

The answers can be coded in two categories: static (circumscribed) marriage or mobile (extraneous, immigrant) marriage.

4. Housing

The place of residence and the available amenities will directly influence the appropriateness of the housing circumstances in which an individual or family lives and brings up its children. It is, therefore, important to find out the housing conditions for each individual or family in the study and assess them in absolute terms according to their adequacy for a healthy family life, and in relative terms, according to a comparison with other houses in the settlement. The factors to look for are:

a. *Type of dwelling* in terms of a detached, semidetached or terraced house, farmhouse with additional outbuildings (stables, barns etc.), a cottage, hut, house in a compound, shack, tent, flat etc.;

b. *Living space* according to the room/person ratio, sleeping space, cooking space, proximity to domestic animals etc.;

c. *Protection* in terms of insulation from elements, pests, insects, vermin, dampness, cold or heat, fresh air etc.;

d. *Amenities* according to the type and location of water supply, waste and sewage disposal, heating, lighting, food storage, cooking facilities, eating facilities etc.;

5. Subsistence

It will also depend on the spending priorities and the availability of additional sources of income or existing savings.

a. *Income*, or the acquisition of the necessary means of subsistance, will depend on the type of occupation of the individual or family members. It will also depend on the spending priorities and the availability of additional sources of income or existing savings.

b. *Employment*, in terms of being self-employed, working for wages, living from land or capital or from outside help. In the case of working for a living, the availability of employment, unemployment benefits, or possibilities for emigration will be of importance. The type of employment according to the required expertise and skills will be reflected in the security of income in long terms and possibilities for occupational mobility, retraining a job or changing it. Additional security can be obtained by the earning capacity of more than one member of a family and pooling of resources.

c. The *wealth* of an individual or family will largely define its standing in that society in relation to other individuals or families; in absolute terms it will define the spending capacity including the basic needs as well as luxuries.

6. Familial environment : Domestic group

The immediate environment into which a child is born and which can in general terms be described as the "family" can take many different forms and include a number of people with different relationships. It is because of this that this environment should be more accurately defined as the "domestic group" into which a child is born and within which most adults operate. The description of the domestic group can be made in terms of its structure or the kind of people that live in it, and in terms of their relationship and activities usually performed by the members of a domestic group of a certain kind.

a. *Type of domestic groups.* In terms of the structure of a domestic group a typology can be developed:

i. *matricentered group* : the minimal two-generation domestic group which consists of mother and child/ren. In most societies it is considered aberrant, but it has been argued that in some societies (e.g. parts of West Indies) it is so common as to be the norm. In our society it is becoming increasingly more prevalent and accepted under the name "one parent family";

ii. *elementary family* : sometimes referred to as the nuclear family, simple family or restricted family, which usually consists of husband (H), wife (W) and child(ren) (C); as a domestic group the set of H W C forms a unit of consumption and very often also of production;

iii. *compound family* : occurs in societies in which polygamy is permitted; in polyandrous societies, a wife may have more than one husband, usually brothers (fraternal polyandry); but the more common form is polygyny, in which a husband has more than one wife (wives are sometimes but not usually related); domestic arrangements in general take the form of a group of houses or huts, typically enclosed by a wall or fence;

iv. *extended family (or extended household)*, of which there are different types, all presuming the presence of three or more generations of kin in one household; kin may all be living under one roof, or may be living in nearby dwellings, but the crucial characteristic is commensality, which implies common budget, common food preparation and sharing of meals; types of extended household include:

- patrilocal, the commonest type, in which a couple, upon marriage, come to live with the husband's parents, while their sons and son's wives are expected in turn to come to live with them;

- matrilocal type, of the same form or pattern, except that the married couple live with the wife's parents, and in turn, their daughters and daughter's husbands come to join them;

- rarer types of extended family in which other patterns of kin affiliation occur, such as residence with the husband's mother's brother, which sets up an avunculocal extended family.

v. *domestic cycle*, arising from regular cycles in family formation, as one generation replaces another; from the point of view of an individual in the system, he/she forms part of a family in which he/she is a child, and later, a family in which he/she is a parent; in view of the effect of the family in moulding the child to fit society, the first type is often called the family of orientation, while the second type is the family of procreation. In terms of the structure of sequences of families, it is possible to identify what has been called the developmental cycle of the domestic group; if this cycle is not taken into account, the different phases in the cycle of one normal form appear misleadingly to be different types of family system.

b. *Relationships and activities*. Whereas the structural typology presented is valuable in providing a framework, the real potential of a domestic group as a place of bringing up children will be better understood if one learns something about the real-life activities and relationships among its members. These differ according to culture, social norms, and the type of the domestic group and can be generalised according to their distinctive features as follows:

i. *matricentered group* : the tie between mother and child is most decisive in the earliest years of a child's life, including prenatal and perinatal influences; the health of the mother up until the time of weaning is of great importance; in the course of urbanisation the incidence of one-parent families of a matricentered variety appears to be increasing; there may also be one-parent patricentered families, but these tend to contain older children and are rare; where there is a weak kinship system, there is the least support for the matricentered family and mothers must cope on their own often in the most difficult circumstances;

ii. *the elementary family* emphasises conjugal roles and the accepted domestic division of labour has a great influence in establishing patterns of food preparation, nutrition, and child rearing, as well as being influential in establishing gender patterns very early in a child's life; the relationship between father and child, mother and child, and father and mother form an important triad; where there are siblings in the household, their influence may be great in establishing appropriate patterns for second and subsequent children; in some societies male children are more highly regarded than female, and may get differential treatment in terms of food, care, education etc.;

iii. *the compound family* in its most common polygynous form, rests on the relationship among wives, which may be structured so that there is a senior wife with authority over others; in general it is regarded as an important duty of the husband to share appropriately among wives, and the taking of subsequent wives may be welcomed by a senior wife, since it increases the available domestic labour and shares burdens; allowing for problems of mutual adjustment, a compound family need not necessarily be riven with conflict, while children in a compound family usually grow up in larger groups of similar age consisting of siblings and half siblings and learn to adjust to more adults and cooperative groups; since polygyny is often a sign of high status and wealth, such families may be well provided for;

iv. *the extended family* offers an opportunity for a child to be greatly influenced by grandparents, setting up in many societies, a particular closeness between grandparents and grandchildren; this allows for greater stability, although it may be a source of conflict in a rapidly changing society; since grandparents usually provide a great deal of advice and quasi-medical care; older women and grandmothers particularly figure in childbirth and the early stages of child rearing;

v. *domestic cycle stages* influence the perceived appropriateness of the time of establishing a new family; late marriage or late beginning of procreation is associated with limiting the size of family; it may be adopted as a conscious policy and even be enforced by law rather than custom; in the case of some forms of kinship and inheritance, for example those in which access to land passes from father to son but only when the son has married and the parents are more or less retired, marriage may be much delayed; the domestic cycle is concerned with the patterns of continuity of the domestic group as family replaces family.

c. *Method of measurement.* To explore the structure of the domestic group under study it will be necessary to collect the following information:

- the number of generations living together;

- which members constitute a domestic group;

- presence of kin in the domestic group;

- stage in the cycle of family development.

d. *The investigation* of the real life activities and relationships related to the members of a domestic group will require the following information:

- parental roles related to the children;

- child's relationship to the parents and siblings;

- relationship between the parents;

- relationship between the siblings;

- child's relationship with kin.

These are the general areas where the information will be required to describe the characteristics of the domestic group. Some of the areas of investigation have been worked out in greater detail as to the methods of collecting data and the ways of summarising the findings.

7. Cycle of family development.

The aim of this section of the study is to add still another dimension to the measurement of the exposure of the individual to social influence. This new dimension is concerned with the attempt to isolate and conceptualise the time factor in relation to the continuity in social structure. It examines a social system in terms of a life cycle, including the elements of maintenance and replacement constituting the process of social reproduction.

a. *The development phases.* A family can be considered in terms of a living organism as undergoing a certain set of established phases of change in a certain order. According to the membership of the group and the relationship between them at certain points in time one can differentiate the following phases in the cycle of family development:

- phase of expansion, which begins with marriage, and continues until the youngest child achieves adult status;

- phase of dispersion, which begins when the first child achieves adulthood and can leave home, if that is the custom;

- phase of independence, which begins when all the children have left home, and the parents again live alone;

- phase of replacement, which begins when the parents retire and ends when they die.

b. *Method of measurement.* To collect the necessary data for allocation of each family (only of married subjects) into the appropriate phase of family development, the questions should include: who lives in thehousehold, the relations between the members, number and age of children, occupation and status of parents, children, and other members of the household, how long have the parents been married. When these answers are combined in a matrix, it is possible to allocate each family into one of the categories according to the phase in the cycle of family development.

8. Conjugal roles

From the description of the composite concept of a familial environment it is easy to see that the interaction of spouses is of greatest importance. This interaction can be measured by looking at the different types of conjugal roles in families. It seems that there is a circular interrelationship between the type of family, the role distribution between the spouses and their expected relationships and activities; the health educational activity of the spouses concerning the newly born baby and the infant will reflect this interrelationship. This is highly relevant in case of two-parent families, where one of the parents can be the active agent and the other can serve as support and either may serve as a model for the child. In other cases, both parents can share the responsibility, or in some cases one of the parents can be excluded from this activity altogether. It is important not only to examine role relationships in terms of activities, but also in terms of decision-making. One spouse may carry out an activity, whereas both parents may make a joint decision, or both carry out an activity, while one alone makes a decision.

a. *Types of roles*: there are a number of ways one can differentiate conjugal roles and each study has to describe the way and the rationale of the classificatory system used. In one appropriate conceptual model, a continuum of different degrees of segregation of roles is measured by aggregating the degree of segregation of all activities and decisions. Thus, the following classificatory system containing three major types of conjugal roles can be used:

- merged roles, where the percentage of joint activities and decisions, or joint decisions alone, outweighs the percentage of husband's and/or wife's independent activities and decisions;

- co-operative roles, where husband's participation in family activities is great (over 40%) but the wife makes the majority of decisions (over 40%), and the percentage of joint activities and decisions is small;

- divergent roles, where either wife's or husband's independent activities and decisions are both over 40%.

There are, thus, two decisive aspects to allocating types of roles to different families: one is the proportion of activities and decisions which the respondents will classify as joint ones, and the other, the proportion of independent activities and decisions the respondents say that are being carried out by each spouse.

b. *Measurement of conjugal roles.* The measurement of roles will depend on the purpose it will be used which can include different areas of family activities. For the purpose of finding out the family potential in health education of their children, the measurement of conjugal roles will be carried out by a set of questions which deal with different relevant family characteristics. The questions are designed to cover the following areas of child care:

- Looking after the child

- Child's illness

- Child's health

- Nutrition

- Personal hygiene

- Discipline

The questions are designed to deal with parent's actions (A) and decisions (D) and the answers are expected to be: usually (U), sometimes (S) and never (N). The questions are asked about the activities and decisions of father (F), mother (M), both jointly (J), as well as those carried out or made by others (O). The question may also be not applicable (N/A). The instrument is designed to be used as a battery of questions and the answer to each is scored, thus obtaining a numerical value which can be aggregated to give a cumulative score. This cumulative score expressed in percentages enables the choice of the appropriate role. Although only the scores for father's, mother's or joint activities and decisions are used for the allocation of a role type, the possibility of employing with greater precision the category "others" should enable the research to throw some light on the support that the parents receive in bringing up their child, since answers in this category can denote the participation of grandparents, uncles, aunts and cousins.

The scoring of answers is carried out by allocating a weighted numerical value to each kind of answer: usually = 2, sometimes = 1, never = 0. The answers are scored, after which the appropriate role is allocated.

c. *Interpretation of roles.* The general description and classification of domestic groups includes a description of patterns of actions and relationships associated with each family type. The study of conjugal roles is aimed at finding out whether this general pattern applies to the families under study. It is possible that individual families deviate from the general expectations due to certain factors such as illness of one spouse, employment of both spouses, housing shortage forcing people to live in three generational households, and so on.

The exploration of conjugal roles can cover many areas of family life, such as providing the necessary income, household chores, social activities, as well as looking after children. In terms of establishing family competence in bringing up a healthy new generation, the conjugal roles related to bringing up children are most relevant. In the various types of roles according to different patterns of interaction among the spouses, the most important factor for health education concerns who makes the decisions about health matters and in what way are the decisions made. The dominant question is whether one parent carries the responsibility or whether it is shared by them both. This kind of information should be obtainable from an analysis of conjugal roles and will be crucial in defining the aims of a health education intervention..

9. Kin networks

In addition to the child's immediate domestic group composed of father (F) and mother (M) in an elementary family, or grandparents (FF, FM), uncle (FB), aunt (FBW), and cousins (FBS, FBD) in, for example, a patrilocal extended household, there are other kin important to the child. These are represented by the extended kin network, which is usually structured according to a number of fairly limited principles embodied in law and custom.

a. *Types of kin networks.* The kin network can be according to structure of the domestic group classified in the following terms:

i.*patrilineal descent groups*, in which descent is traced through males, which does not imply that a child has no relationship with the female side of the family, but that certain rights and duties, such as for instance the right to inherit or the duty of legal responsibility, descends in a particular line; a son belongs to the same descent group as his father and so do his children, whereas a daughter belongs to the same descent group as her father, but her children belong to the descent group of her husband; the effect of a patrilineal descent group system consistently carried through, is to provide clearly demarcated, non-overlapping groups of kin within a society, which may take on corporate functions, important in, for example, landholding or in occupying political office;

ii. *matrilineal descent groups* trace descent through the female line, are not mirror images of the patrilineal system, since political power and responsibility still remain, in most known societies, with the senior male members of the group, and in matrilineal societies the mother's brother takes a dominant role in managing family affairs; the same principle of demarcated groupings forming potential corporate entities with economic and political functions remains;

iii. *double unilineal kinship systems* operate in rare cases, in which both patrilineal kin groups and matrilineal kin groups coexist, but with different functions; for example, a patrilineal group may be concerned with land holding, while a matrilineal group may have largely ritual functions to perform;

iv. *bilateral kin systems* (also called 'non-unilineal') reflect the large amount of prior research on unilineal kinship systems are those systems in which no unilineal descent groups appear to be present and kin relationships are traced indifferently through both male and female parents; the effect of a bilateral kinship system is to establish wide ranges of kin, focussed on a particular individual identified as the reference person in the system (called *ego*) ; ego's bilateral kin's set may be shared by *siblings* (brothers and sisters) but not by any other person in the society; the overall effect of such a system is to provide a society with overlapping groups of kin ramifying throughout a community, with more distant kin in this system consisting of second, third and fourth cousins; when a unilineal system breaks down, it is frequently the case that a sort of bilateral system emerges, although this may not be fully established and with more distant kin not recognised; according to circumstances, it may be flexible or unreliable as a form of support;

v. *affines* exist in every kinship system, as the relatives who are acquired by marriage; as a contract, marriage is always important not only in setting up a relationship between the married couple, but also in establishing links between formerly unrelated people.

b. *Types (activity).* According to the kind of activities and relationships of its members the kin networks can be characterised in the following way:

i. *patrilineal lineages,* in which the loyalties of a child may extend beyond his/her elementary family or household to a large number of kin, named and identified clearly as descendants of an originating ancestor, which provides a ready-made community for the child and locates him or her firmly within it, with concomitant rights and duties, operating as a resource in the economic sense, and one of the main means of support for the impoverished in developing countries; it is possible to rely on kin in a way that it is not possible to rely so much on friends and neighbours, since outside the kin group the laws of morality may not apply so strongly; the patrilineal kin group has proved to be extremely resilient and is still of great importance in many parts of the world; members of such a group may club together to support and educate children and may plan a total family strategy built round their resources of income and members;

ii. *matrilineal lineages* should theoretically allow for the same considerations to apply, although in effect this is not so, and matrilineal kinship systems have tended to disappear in economic change and have turned into some form of bilateral system, as a result of the complexity of a system which relied on transmission of wealth, authority and influence from mother's brother to sister's son; one legacy of such systems when they do tend to alter, is that the status of women remains high; although a matrilineal kinship system is not a matriarchy, nevertheless it does provide a particular role for women within it;

iii. *double unilineal and complex systems* have tended to turn into patrilineal systems with residual functions on the mother's side, or into a bilateral type;

iv. *bilateral kinship*, recognising kin without customary bias on the mother's or father's side, can provide a network of influence, aid and support which is potentially very flexible and may be activated in times of crisis; if need be a mother's sister or father's sister may be called upon to help look after a child; more distant cousins on both mother's and father's side may be used as a means of support in migration to towns an cities; and a network of latent kin may be known to older members of society and only called upon in need; this kinship system has long been characteristic of northwestern Europe and may have been associated with the speed of economic development in that area as cause rather than consequence; it also emerges as a consequence of the disruption of traditional ties in societies which formerly had corporate unilineal kin groups.

Despite flexibility, it has the disadvantage that it is amorphous and kin ties within it are easily lost, so that a bilateral kinship system may readily turn into a practically non-existent and haphazard selection of kin who hardly recognise formal rights and duties to one another, and do not provide the support for children of an established traditional system;

v. *affines* are established through marriage, which sets up formal relationships between two groups of kin; cohabitation without marriage may serve the elementary family household well, but it does not establish links of mutual responsibility with outside kin; in many societies these affinal relationships are taken most seriously and, under those circumstances, marriage is not an individual choice based on personal affection of the couple concerned, so much as an alliance between two groups of people suitably solemnized by the marriage; hence bride-wealth or dowry payments and their equivalents, such as extremely expensive wedding ceremonies and the like, are still extremely important, being an investment in the future children of the marriage; even in very poor countries these considerations still apply and savings are sometimes made for years in order to properly solemnize a marriage and establish appropriate affinal relationships;

vi. *informal kin relationships* should be stressed in the health context, since, even though there may be a formal kinship system of unilineal variety or one in which clearly delimited kin rights and duties persist, the other kin are extremely important as well; they may not have the same recognised responsibilities, but they nevertheless form part of the network of information, influence and support on which a child may rely.

c. *Method of measurement.* In terms of the structure of kin networks, for the understanding of the development of a classificatory system, it is necessary to trace the descent of the members of a domestic group, and discover those they recognise as kin. To find out about the relationships and activities it is necessary to ask about the proportions of different types of contact since it is difficult to investigate such relationships in depth by means of a survey-type questionnaire.

It is hoped that from the indicated proportions of different types of contact at least some idea about the kind of interrelationship will be gained. To explore this the following questions should be asked:

(Interviewer's Questions)

We would be interested in the amount of contact you have with your kin:

(a) Could you tell me with how many of your relatives you have a close relationship (visit them and/or write letters frequently, expect mutual aid, and in general consider close or intimate)?

(b) With how many of them is your relationship more distant or does not exist except for what you hear from others about them, and for an eting at a family gathering or Christmas card?

(c) How many do you know of only by name and have no contact with at all?

The answers can be coded in such a way that the subjects are divided into the following categories according to the kind of relations they have with their kin:

- Answer (a)   relationship with intimate kin;

- Answer (b)   relationship with effective kin;

- Answer (c)   relationship with non-effective kin;

- Answer (a + b) relationship with intimate and effective kin;

- Answer (a + b + c) no predominant pattern

For the purpose of a statistical analysis, these categories can be grouped into two: relationship with intimate kin and relationship with effective and/or non-effective kin.

10. Social networks

When faced with a health problem in the family, it may not be sufficient to rely on one's own resources or help from one's own kin. It will sometimes be necessary to seek help and advice from friends and neighbours who are part of the family's wider social environment. The amount of help that a family can expect will depend on the kind of relationship it has with its friends and neighbours. This can be measured by examining the kind of social interaction that exists and classifying it into different types of networks.

a. *Types of networks.* The relationships which link the family with its social environment are expressed in terms of social networks. According to the intensity of these links one can distinguish four main types:

- close-knit

- medium-knit

- loose-knit

- transitional.

The fourth category is defined as transitional and defines the links of a family in transition, either coming into or going out of the community.

In classifying social interaction in terms of a network, one has to take into account the difference between the more limited aspects of the concept as well as its wider implications. In its narrower sense, one can think of social sets which denote the social interactions between a person (ego) and recognises others. These others may have their own sets of relationships so that ego may also be linked to them. It is in this wider sense that the concept of a network describes the structure of relationships in a certain field such as a city, neighbourhood or a community. This means that there are now two possibilities of analysing social interaction: one is the "set" or the amount of interaction recognised by and associated with ego, and the other is the "network" or a wider pattern of interaction, including not only the part recognised by ego, but also by other people who in part form ego's set. Although there is a need for a more precise distinction between "bounded" and "unbounded" fields of social interaction i.e. between "sets" and "networks", it seems that the already familiar term "network" is still used in a more general way in most of the studies dealing with this problem.

b. *Measurement of networks.* In a survey, an attempt is being made to find out something about the existing social interaction described by a family, both in terms of their "set" as well as the "network" of which they are a part. Whereas the establishment of a set can be achieved by asking the family to name its social contacts, the definition of a network should include a survey of these contacts to establish their sets. In this way one could obtain a picture of the whole network in that area, by using the appropriate approach if one wanted to study the network of an area. In this study, however, the interest in sets and networks is of a practical nature. It is aimed at finding out the perception of the family members about the people in the area whom they could contact in case of a need for help or advice. This perceived network may be different from the existing one but is real and important in terms of the help as an available resource for the family under study.

The perceived latent social network which could be mobilised in the case of a crisis includes extra-household kin and non-kin, relatives, neighbours, friends and colleagues at work. The potential support is measured by the closeness of the relationship.

As an illustration, the information about the network of a family under study will include the following questions:

Question 1:   How long have you been living in the area? The answer should be recorded in terms of 'long', not very long' and 'only a short time';

Question 2:   Who are your friends and companions? The answer should be recorded in terms of three categories i.e. 'mainly', 'partly', 'not at all'; the choice should be given as 'members of the family (husband's or wife's), neighbours, colleagues at work (husband's or wife's), others.

Question 3: What would you say is the relationship between the friends and relatives you mentioned? The answers should be recorded in terms of: 'Do they mostly have contact among themselves?', 'Or do they rarely have contact and do not even know each other in most cases?', 'Do a few have contact among themselves while others do not?'

Question 4: Which of your own or your husband's relatives live close by? The answer should be recorded in terms of 'Living in your neighbourhood (within walking distance)?' or 'Living in the same town/village/settlement?'

The answers to the questions should allow for the classification of the family into one of the four types of networks: close-knit, medium-knit, loose-knit, or transitional.

11. Educational level and parity

The level of education is a very significant indicator of the general position of a domestic group in a society, of its economic power and its ability to process and utilise information relevant to preservation of health and treatment of diseases.

Another important factor in assessing the general level of education is the predominant language in the domestic group under study. In case of immigrant marriages, some members may not speak the official language, or may be bilingual, using both their native and the official language.

The lack of appropriate education of some members of the domestic group can be compensated for by marriage to a spouse with a higher education level. In this way the highest achieved level of education by any one member of the domestic group can influence the capability of that group to utilise existing knowledge and information in dealing with matters of health and illness. It can also influence the way the received information is interpreted as a part of the decision making process.

a. *Levels of education.* There are many differences between the educational systems in different countries, and it will be necessary for reasons of comparison to use some general categories which can be understood everywhere and, it is hoped, interpreted in a similar way once their definitions are agreed. These are:

- illiteracy

- literacy without education

- primary education

- secondary education (and professional educatio)

- higher education.

b. *Methods of measurement.*

      i. *level of education*, will include the questions about the ability to read and write in the official language of the country, the amount of schooling, and the acquisition of any skills or professional knowledge;

      ii. *language*, questions will be asked about the native language spoken in the domestic group and whether or not it is the same as the official language in that country;

      iii. *parity*, which relates to the level of literacy and education between the spouses, which will be compared to find the highest level achieved by any member of the group.

12. Social position

There is enough evidence that the health of the members of a family is closely related to their position or status in that society. There are many reasons for this, one being that the social position of a person represents and is associated with such characteristics as wealth, type of occupation, educational level and place of residence. Each of these characteristics, in one way or another, contributes to the chances for a person to live a longer and healthier life.

a. *Types of social stratification.* Social stratification is the term used to describe the location of persons in a hierarchy of statuses or positions in a society. There are a number of coexisting systems of social strati-fication such as social class system, social status system, caste system etc. All of them have specific ideological bases and use different sets of indicators in identifying a person's place on a social scale. It would, therefore, be practically impossible to use social stratification as a characteristic in comparative studies, if it were not for one common factor: all the systems of stratification employ a high-low continuum of some sort. Furthermore, in each society, no matter what the system of stratification is, the people placed in high positions have better chances of survival and better health than those lower down on the scale. It is because of this that for the purpose of this study the following stratification is used:

- high

- middle

- low

- transitional

The last category denotes people who cannot be allocated a definite category.

b. *Method of measurement.* The social position of a person has a relative character since it depends whether one applies an objective indicator or looks at the subjective perception of an individual about his/her placement on a social scale. To assess an objective position, the stratification scale 'high-middle-low' will use the information about education, occupation, income and type of housing as criteria and a way of defining a person's social position profile. This can be done by using a matrix of information, as shown in the following sample table:

Method of Allocating Social Position for a Person

	High	Middle	Low
Education of head of household			
Illiterate/literate, no schooling			L
Primary/secondary education		M	
Higher education	H		
Occupation of head of household			
Unskilled labour (agriculture/others), land or business owner-small			L
Skilled workers, clerical, teachers, nurses, land or business owner-medium		M	
Physicians, lawyers, manager, banker, land or business owner-large	H		
*Income**			
Low			L
Moderate		M	
High	H		
Housing			
More than 4 persons per room			L
2-4 persons per room		M	
Less than 2 persons per room	H		

* See note.

(*Note. The level of income will be relative and can only be assessed in these three general categories according to the subjective assessment of the respondent.)

For simple coding purpose, a family with three or more High (H) or Low (L) scores will be allocated into the appropriate social status, whereas any other distribution will place the family into middle social status.

13. Values : Religion

There are many dimensions along which one can differentiate the objective social and cultural realities of the outside world in which parents live and bring up their children. An important one is the value system that is predominant in a country, area or community, which moulds the way that people should feel, think and act. Within many value systems, religion is the dominant force, defining the beliefs and practices shaping the ethic manifested in the behaviour of its adherents. There are, however, countries in which religion is replaced by a set of secular values, decreed by the dominant political ideology.

The existing value system, whether based on religion or ideology, exerts a powerful influence on people's beliefs and practices, many of which are directly or indirectly relevant to the maintenance of health and prevention and treatment of diseases.

a. *Areas of values.* If one takes as a starting point the many areas of activity in which religious or ideological beliefs can play an important role, one can produce a list which can serve as a check list for the purpose of studying the influence of these values on health behaviour. These areas can be listed as follows:

  i. *courtship, mating and marriage:* the prevalent patterns, the age at which it takes place, the choice of partners, the place of residence and the sexual practices as affected by the system of beliefs prevalent in that area;

  ii. *conception, delivery and child care,* which will all be to some extent governed by the existing beliefs;

iii. *health practices*, as affected by existing rituals concerning personal hygiene, waste disposal, the care of the newly born, available help in case of crisis, as well as the interpretation of symptoms in terms of their origin, meaning and treatment;

iv. *nutrition*, which is an area regulated by most of existing religions in terms of kind of food, preparation, time and place of eating or fasting, with special meals related to certain feasts or rituals; even in secular states, this influence persists.

b. *Methods of measurement*. The effects of individual religious practices and ideologies on family health in general and that of the infant in particular, can only be measured within the general value system of a specific religion dominant in that area. It is, therefore, assumed that the description of the prevalent religion, in terms of its effects on health, will already be available from the first part of the inquiry dealing with external conditions. The measurement of family characteristics should concentrate on the aspects of adherence and coping with consequences.

To find out about adherence, a set of questions should be asked, including a direct and an indirect approach. The respondents are directly asked whether they consider themselves to be strict, moderate or non-adherers to the prevalent religious norms in general, and the health-related or health-directed norms in particular. The questions cover all the areas of influence mentioned.

The consequences of strict adherence as well as of non-adherence may cause certain problems in families. Questions will be asked whether any such difficulties are perceived by the respondents and in what way they are able to cope with such problems.

14. Values : Norms

A value system in a society denotes the broader standards which, when related to the actualities of social life, can give rise to complexes of institutionalised norms. Norms can be defined as shared expectations in a population relating to a certain behaviour or action. Most of the activities concerning the preservation of health and prevention and treatment of diseases are regulated by a whole range of institutionalised norms, which define the role expectations and role perceptions of the healing professions as well as of their clients.

a. *Types of norms.* Norms can be in general terms differentiated, according to their prevalence in a society, into two main groups:

- *statistical norms*, which denote the average or modal action, i.e. the most typical behaviour, attitude, opinion or perception in a group;

- *social norms*, which denote, in addition to a clustering in terms of modes or averages, the attitudes, opinions or acts of the members of a social group, which they perceive to be constrained by social sanctions.

It is also very important to distinguish between the existing social norms and the perception of social norms relating to different social positions and roles.

For the exploration of social norms, it will, therefore, be important to examine the element of constraint which is expressed in the *coercive power* of the norm. There are three elements which will influence the coercive power of a norm:

- *historicity*, which implies that although the actors are not aware of the origins or even the functions of habitualised behaviour, they accept it as part of their objective reality and conform to its expectations;

- *legitimation*, which can either be implicit or explicit, and denotes the approval and support for some attitude, opinion or behaviour, by significant others, accepted in that area;

- *sanctions*, which express most directly the element of constraint and the coercive power of a norm; there are four main characteristics of sanctions, depending on whether they are positive or negative and whether they are diffused or organised.

b. *Method of measurement.* The existence of a social norm can be established by examining the laws and regulations concerning the relevant expectation, or if there is no written evidence, by carrying out a survey of a random sample of the population with the aim of investigating what their expectations in that area are and what kind of sanctions they would envisage for nonconformists. Whereas legislation as a topic is outside the scope of the present study, the examination of records and laws seems feasible to throw light on the nature of sanctions.

Whether written laws and regulations exist or not, the perception of a social norm by the segment of the population at which the norm is directed, can be measured by carrying out a survey of the affected population group.

The measurement of people's perception of a social norm can be carried out by asking such questions as: "How do you think that most of the people you know feel about corporal punishment for the small child?" The answers can range from the belief that people strongly approve to the belief that most of the people strongly disapprove. According to the answer, one can make deductions about a norm, as in the following illustration:

Question: How do you think that most people you know feel about corporal punishment?

Possible sets of answers:

Strongly approve/approve	65%	10%	40%	30%
Be indifferent	5%	5%	10%	30%
Disapprove/strongly disapprove	10%	65%	40%	30%
You do not know	20%	20%	10%	10%

- if the majority of respondents think that most of the people they know approve of corporal punishment this can be taken as an indication of the existence of a norm approving corporal punishment;

- if the majority think that most of the people they know would disapprove of corporal punishment, then a norm of non-punishment can be assumed to exist;

- if the number of people thinking that most of the people approve is similar to the number of people who disapprove, then one can conclude that two opposite norms coexist;

- if the numbers are equally distributed among the answers, then one can conclude that there is no definite norm concerning corporal punishment according to the perception of the respondents.

The other characteristics of a social norm reflecting the constraint element can be measured in relation to the following:

a. *historicity*, where the respondents are asked whether they know how the expectation originated or not, the possible answers include such statements as "I do not know, it was always like this" or "It's normal" or "It's natural" and so on.

b.*legitimation*, where the respondents are asked if, in for example, the case of a medical norm, any member of the medical profession confirmed that expectation, or it was confirmed in any other form (medical literature);

c. *sanctions*, where the respondents are asked whether they would expect certain sanctions in case of nonconformity, what form the sanction/s would take, and who could implement them. From the answers the following combination of characteristics can be derived:

SANCTIONS:	Positive	Negative
Organised		
Diffuse		

d. *social support*, where the respondents are asked whether the friends and relatives share the respondents opinion about an expectation or not; from the answer one can deduce whether the respondent thinks that there is social support for her opinions or not. One can find out whether the support is implicit or explicit by asking the respondent to mention what kind of support she would expect from her friends and relatives;

e. *ethnocentrism*, where the respondents are asked whether the norm that they perceive to exist is shared by other ethnic, religious or political groups. One can deduce its ethnocentrism according to the group to which the norm is linked;

f. *conformity*, where the respondents are asked whether their behaviour or actions correspond to the perceived norm in that area, the answers being classified into conformity, variance and deviance, with the latitude of variance - the grey area of expectations taken to be the middle position between conformity and deviance, representing opposite extremes.

15. State of health

The actual experience of illnesses will be directly related to the need for competence in dealing with them. For this reason it will be necessary to establish the state of health of an individual or the family and its members.

a. *Classification of experience.* To find out what the health related experience of an individual or a family are, it will be necessary to distinguish the state of health at the time of the study as well as any past experiences the individual or family members did have in relation to health and disease:

i. *the present state* can be described in terms of hard data, i.e. by listing any illnesses present in the family at the time of interview; it can also be described in terms of the general opinions of the respondent about the state of health of the members of that family;

ii. *the past history* is of importance in examining the continuity in experiences dealing with illness; it can be subdivided into: hard data including information on past mortality and morbidity in the family; and recall of past experiences in special situations such as pregnancy, delivery and child care.

b. *Methods of measurement.* The information about the state of health will be collected by asking a set of questions, which for the hard data will be of a direct nature; opinions and recall will be investigated by asking the respondent to mark the answer on a scale containing different options:

i. *present state,* where questions will include information about any illness at the time of the interview, its nature and means of dealing with it; to assess the present general state of health of the family, the respondent will be asked to place the family on a scale, the range of which will offer choices from excellent health to very bad health; the questions will ask about the family as whole, and about each member separately; the health of the small child will be investigated in greater detail;

ii. *past history,* where the respondent will be asked about the deaths in the family in recent past, and death of any children born to the respondent; the respondent will be asked to recall any illness among the members in recent past, with special emphasis on the health of the small child; further questions will deal with specific experiences the respondent had during pregnancy, delivery and caring for the newly born baby; methods of coping with these situations will also be investigated.

16. Utilisation of services

The utilisation of services will be the function of needs as experienced and the available services at the disposal of an individual or family. The needs as experienced by the individual or family can also be assessed objectively and the services can be defined in terms of the minimal adequate care available.

a. *Types of utilisation.* One can objectively differentiate three types of needs:

- mass and emergency problems

- problems of risk groups

- random distribution of illness in a community.

A subjective assessment of needs as experienced by the individual or family can be assessed by asking the respondent to list the recent occasions when a need was experienced and the kind of help required.

To satisfy these needs different types of services will be required:

i. for mass and emergency problems organised mass campaigns are the most appropriate intervention and the formation of mobile units it an efficient operational programme;

ii. for the problems of risk groups in a population both an organised community approach and a family approach will be necessary, with continuous care for the individual;

iii. when the diseases are randomly distributed in a population group, an individual approach will be necessary for the treatment of episodes of illness.

Utilisation of medical care services can be assessed according to the availability and the needs in terms of under- or over-utilisation as two extremes, and optimal utilisation as the mid-point on the scale.

The grouping of the type of services available will include the following categories:

    i.   no services;

    ii. intermittent services (mobile units)

    iii. regular services   -   access: in the area, or in the settlement/village

    iv. regular services - type: primary care; minimal adequate care; full medical care

    v.   regular care - payment: free medical care; payment for services (partly); payment for all services.

b. *Methods of measurement.* The assessment of utilisation for an individual or family can be carried out only on a subjective level, by asking the respondent to indicate the needs within the last month/year, the perceived availability of services appropriate to deal with that need and the actual utilisation.

Measurement of competence

For the purpose of health education the concept of competence defines the ability of individuals alone or in groups (such as a family) to look after their own health and/or the health of their social environment (which includes the members of the family). This definition of the concept of competence is very general, and although one could imagine the possibility of assessing someone's "general competence" for staying healthy, this would be of little practical use for the purpose of improving it by means of health education. People need different aspects of "competence" at different stages in their life career, which is characterised by age specific and status specific roles and requirements. It is, therefore, more practical to ask the question "competence for what?" and gear the educational programmes to meet these specific needs. For example, a mother bringing up a child will put emphasis on different aspects of competence compared to a worker in a factory, a lorry driver or an old age pensioner. Another type of competence could be the ability to render 'first aid' to someone in an accident or other type of distress. (See examples).

Since the concept of "competence" is a theoretical construct it will be necessary to take into account the specific needs of different populations and define the indicators which will be measured as important part of a specific "competence".

The approach presented here postulates that a person to be competent in health matters, needs to have a certain level of knowledge about prevention and management of health threats and disease, as well as about improvement of health. In addition to knowledge, a person needs a positive attitude to health and skills concerning the necessary actions such as self-care, mobilisation of support and help, etc.

The measurement of competence will, therefore, require the measurements of the main domains of which the concept is composed. Each of these domains, however, is a theoretical construct in its own right and will require special methods of measurement appropriate for theoretical constructs. It will also require the choice of emphasis within each domain according to the specific needs of the subjects. One can assume that the accumulation of findings from measurements for each domain will produce an insight into the level of competence for each subject, which can be used as a guideline for health education interventions. If it is deemed that the level is too low and, therefore, could inhibit expected behaviour or action on the part of that individual, the aim of health education intervention will be to raise it to an optimal level.

Before going into detailed examination of the possibilities of measuring each domain, it will be useful to summarise the methods of measurement appropriate for theoretical constructs. This will depend on the way a construct has been defined:

1. *Tests.* Personality traits can be useful in understanding and predicting people's chances of staying healthy or becoming ill, since a number of 'personality traits' have been associated with certain diseases in a positive or negative way.

To measure such personality traits one uses tests which are composed of a battery of questions, statements or images. A person is exposed to such a test and has to react in a given time. His reactions are scored in a way that is specific for that test. On the basis of such a score one can establish the presence or absence of a trait, the direction and the strength, or any other characteristic that has been built into the test. To be valid a test must meet certain standards. There are four main types of validity:

a. *Content validity.* A test has content validity to the extent that the items in the test are judged to constitute a representative sample of some clearly specified universe of knowledge or skills. This judgment is usually based on a consensus of experts in the field of knowledge or skills that the test items are expected to sample. This type of validity is most relevant to achievement tests, job-knowledge tests and work-sample tests. There are other tests, such as aptitude tests, for which content validity is important but not a crucial feature.

For example, a test of general musical knowledge will include items that musical experts think are relevant for such testing, and will include a broad and varied selection of factual information about music. Any musician seeing the test should agree that it is a test of musical knowledge.

A work-sample test is a performance test consisting of a representative sample of the kinds of skills that analysis of a job reveals a person must actually posses to perform adequately on the job (typist, computer programmer,etc.).

Specific aptitude tests (clerical, mechanical, musical,etc.) often aim for content validity, although the test must depend on other types of validation. One could have aptitude for music without having the necessary musical knowledge.

b. *Criterion validity.* This is the ability of test scores to predict performance in some endeavour that is external to the test itself, called the criterion. A test's validity coefficient is simply the correlation between the test scores and measurement of the criterion performance.

For example a college aptitude test would be said to have a good criterion validity (also called predictive validity) to the extent that the test scores are correlated with grades in college (the criterion).

The criterion performance can be measured by other tests such as scholastic-achievement test and job-knowledge tests, using as the criterion grades in courses, supervisor's ratings of performance on the job, or by direct indices of work proficiency and productivity.

Criterion validity is probably the most important, defensible and convincing type of validation in the practical use of psychological tests. Its objectivity is derived from the fact that the results depend on the correlation of a performance with clearly defined and measurable criteria.

Sensitive decisions such as employment should, however, be made by using as the validity coefficient scores from multiple correlations with a number of tests called the predictor variables and the criterion.

c. *Concurrent validity.* This is used in two ways. It can mean that the correlation between a test and a criterion are measured at practically the same point in time (scholastic aptitude test and scholastic achievement test administered on the same day); the other meaning concerns correlation between a new invalidated test and another test of already established value.

There are instances when a new shorter or simpler test has been developed in a specific area where a more cumbersome test has been validated. The correlation between the new and the old test may serve instead of the long process of validating the new test. This can be done but it could be dangerous.

d. *Construct validity.* This is most important from a scientific standpoint. It is more difficult to explain. It attempts to define in scientific terms what is it that the test measures. The validity of the test will depend on the accuracy of the definition of the 'construct' that it tests. Constructs are for example intelligence, happiness etc., as well as a number of other personality traits.

Construct validity will depend on the soundness of theories explaining the construct. In that sense the questions associated with the test should sound reasonable and relevant to the construct that they are supposed to measure. This will affect the attitude of the person taking the test as well as his or her motivation and performance.

2. *Index.* This measure is appropriate for the measurement of complex constructs in behavioral and social sciences which cannot be measured by one item in a questionnaire (political orientation, religiosity,etc.). It is useful if one adds a "quantitative" aspect to the concept under study. One can take the case of knowledge, as for example with the subject of malaria, where the knowledge will include (1) the cause, (2) the transmission and (3) the prevention of the disease. There will be a number of respondents who will answer one out of three questions, some will answer two, and some will answer all three questions. One should notice that in this case it does not matter which two have been answered (1 and 3, 1 and 2, or 2 and 3) and it will still be possible to say that the person answering 2 questions knows more than the person answering one question. If one carries out such a study among a population of men and women, one could, depending on the findings, say that "women know more than men" about malaria if the answer more questions.

3.*Scales*. When one measures a concept that includes a qualitative as well as a quantitative dimension, then the answers will have to be ordered in terms of a qualitative assessment such as "more or less relevant", or "more or less appropriate", or "positive or negative", etc., which are all expressions of an intensity structure. This type of measurement will require "scales" along which one can order the answers given by a respondent who will then be placed on a certain position on that scale. The ordering of answers will, obviously, require that the questions should be also ordered along a certain dimension of intensity. The questions should also allow the respondent to express the intensity of his/her feelings, as for example when having to chose one of the following answers "strongly agree, agree, indifferent, disagree, strongly disagree" when faced with a statement about a subject matter. A scale would include a number of statements considered relevant to the subject under study, and the respondents would be said to have "scored high (or low)" on such a scale. If one takes again the example of malaria, and the questions are ordered in terms of importance from 1 to 3, this will imply that a person answering the question 3 will also have known the answers to questions 1 and 2, and the person answering the question 2 will have known the answer to question 1. It will also imply that along a certain dimension (e.g. the competence in preventing malaria), the person answering the question 3 will score the highest. The questions can be presented in the form of statements, and the answers can be ordered in terms of intensity, in which case the person "strongly agreeing" with the right statements will score the highest on this "competence scale".

Whether one will need a simple test, an index or a scale depends on the level of sensitivity that is required from an instrument, which will in turn depend on the definition of the construct under study. The examples given are in fact too simple to explain all the refined differences between indexes and scales, but serve merely to give an insight into the fact that such differences do exist and that they can be measured with appropriate instruments. They should also prevent the health educator from acting "naively" out of ignorance about the availability of complex and scientifically tested methods of the measurement of highly complex constructs.

In terms of measuring "competence", which includes the dimensions of knowledge, attitudes and skills, it will be necessary to use indexes and scales which have been specifically designed for each topic.

One should mention that the construction of such instruments is a highly professional job, and the health educators who do not possess such expertise, should buy it in by engaging some relevant professional, or use pre-prepared instruments which are on sale. Sometimes even the commercially available instruments are restricted for the use of professionals only, which should be taken into account when defining a problem in terms of the required financial resources.

a. *Knowledge/information*

There is a semantic difference between knowledge and information, although in general use the two terms can be interchangeable. One usually thinks about a "body of knowledge" which includes all that is known about a topic, subject or a problem, and which, when analysed, can be broken down into "bits of information".

One can, therefore, say that knowledge is mostly transmitted in formal setting (schools) whereas information can also be obtained from informal sources (e.g. newspapers).

Since the transmission of knowledge is mostly carried out in formal institutions it is based on a curriculum, which includes aims (what one wants to achieve), objectives (how one expects to achieve it) and the methods of assessment (how far was the recipient successful in achieving the aims). The detailed development of a curriculum is necessary for the formal approval of the training programme within a formal institution, as well as for the evaluation of the training programme which will include the programme performance and the student achievements.

There are many different ways of measuring or assessing knowledge and information, most of which have been developed and applied within the field of formal education and deal with student achievements. The most popular way of measurement is by using tests. At present there is a discussion going on about the advantages and disadvantages of tests and examinations as means of assessing student achievements. Those in favour of examinations (and tests) argue that they provide an overall aim and purpose for the teacher, as well as a goal and motivation for the students; they can provide "objective" data; they test student's ability to discriminate, reason and work under pressure and at speed; and they provide a feed-back for the teachers and their superiors.

The arguments for abolishing examinations and tests are based on the assumption that examinations include the danger of forcing a teacher to adhere strictly to a syllabus; limit exploration and put stress on recall and memory; and depend on a special ability for "passing tests" as compared to the more general improvement in the level of knowledge. This is an ongoing discussion and one can find institutions with formal examinations as well as those with a continuous assessment and no formal end examinations. One should, however, bear in mind that if the outcome of a formal education programme is the achievement of a professionally recognised status, then the teaching institutions must follow the prescriptions concerning the assessment procedure set by the relevant professional body.

The tests developed for the measurement of achievements of students attending formal education, can also be used for the assessment of knowledge in a population derived from other informal sources. Such tests are composed of a set of questions which can be presented to the respondent in a number of forms: (a) questions demanding an answer which can be right or wrong; (b) multiple choice questions, where the respondent has to mark the right answers from a number of possibilities provided; (c) a question which demands that the respondent writes an answer in the form of an essay, which is then assessed according to the number of "right" arguments included and the completeness of the topic covered in the essay; (d) a question in the form of a task which the respondent must perform in the "right" way as, for example, in mathematical tests.

The assessment of achievement based on a test will be predefined by the examiner by establishing the success or failure depending on the aggregated number of "right" answers.

For the purpose of health education, however, the assessment of knowledge/information can be carried out either in a formal institution as a part of a formal curriculum, or in informal settings such as a part of an interview or a survey. In either case it will be necessary to take into account the following aspects:

i. *Content.*   One can differentiate between the relevant and irrelevant knowledge (or information) concerning a health threat or disease in terms of its prevention, treatment and management. There is, however, a general assumption that "the more knowledge the better" which has been dominant in health education in the past. The assessment of knowledge has taken the form of a set of questions concerning the information about the problem in hand, which explored the subjects ability to recall the facts transmitted in a written or spoken form. In this sense, the recall was the indicator. The criteria were based on the available body of knowledge developed by the professionals and transmitted to the subjects.

ii. *Amount.*   More recently, the emphasis has changed, and health education programmes have been selective in the kind of knowledge they transferred to the client-population. In practice this meant that out of the existing body of knowledge about a problem, a selection has been made of the relevant knowledge which was deemed to be necessary for a health action to take place. Although the indicator has still been the recall of the transmitted knowledge, the criteria were concerned with the motivational force of this knowledge for a desired action to follow.

iii. *Motivational power.* Health educators were soon to realise that the content and the amount of information are not enough to produce a desirable action and that the transmitted information must have a specific message which will tell the recipient how the information should be used. It should also include an "appeal" element which should act as a motivation for the recipient to want to follow the advice included in the message. For this purpose the transmission of knowledge was designed to include the reason why an action is necessary (cost and benefit) and the information about the ways and means an action should be carried out, presented in an attractive and appealing form.

The assessment of the success of transmitting certain knowledge/information can include a number of indicators such as the recall of the transmitted message, understanding of the message in terms of its linguistic characteristics, and the motivational power of the message in terms of the action that should follow.

b. *Measurement of attitudes*

Attitudes do not exist as natural phenomena but are theoretical constructs of a complex nature. Because of this, the measurement of attitudes will be only possible if we define what we understand by the theoretical constructs and if we describe how we intend to measure them (Henerson et.al, 1987; Himmelfarb et .al, 1974). There have been many attempts to define attitude, and the definitions depend on the preferential orientation of the person who defines it. Since a theoretical construct is directly associated with the way it is measured, one could say that attitudes are what attitude scales measure. Most of the definitions, however, have affect as a central common core and this allows a general description of attitudes as *"affects, feelings, values or beliefs towards an object"*. Some authors emphasise the evaluative aspect of an attitude in terms of a predisposition of an individual to evaluate some symbol or object, or aspect of his/her world in a favourable or unfavourable manner.

This evaluative aspect has been a subject of many studies which have tried to establish a functional relationship between attitudes and behaviour. If one accepts that attitudes can be decisive in terms of whether an action will take place or not, and if it does take place, what form will it take, then the concept of attitude has direct bearing on the way health promotional and educational interventions need to be planned. This belief has, however, been questioned and it is at present accepted that attitudes could influence behaviour but need not. One can have a positive attitude towards a political party, but need not vote for it.

Since it is impossible to measure attitudes directly, it will be necessary to rely on inferences based on the instruments which are being used to measure "attitude". Before discussing instruments, it will be necessary to examine the ways attitudes can be measured. One can envisage a number of situations, each of which will require a different approach:

i. if the respondent is aware of his/her attitude (or feelings) about an object or a situation and does not feel embarrassed or endangered by disclosing it, then it will be simply necessary to ask a direct question. The choices will be from "strongly agree" to "strongly disagree", which will enable the investigator to establish the direction and the strength of the respondents attitude towards the subject raised in the question;

ii. if the respondent is aware of his/her attitude towards an object or a situation, but feels that disclosing it could embarrass or endanger him/her, then it will be necessary to establish the attitude by a battery of questions about the subject matter in general instead of asking directly. There are a number of ways such questions have been organised and validated, producing "attitude scales", associated with different authors, some of them commercially available. One could envisage the situation where, for the purpose of secondary prevention of AIDS, the attitudes of people towards AIDS infected persons would be highly relevant for any health promotion and education intervention. Since any negative feeling or attitude could be labelled as prejudice, one can assume that people would not want to be labelled as such. The use of attitude scales could provide an insight into the feelings of people without asking them directly;

iii. if the respondent is not aware of his/her attitude towards an object or a situation, or if he/she simply does not have an established attitude towards that object, then whatever method of measurement will be employed, the outcome will be doubtful. Even the highest level of sophistication in measuring something that does not exist, cannot produce a valid result. One could imagine the situation where one would like to measure someone's attitude towards " the black hole at the centre of our galaxy", and the respondent not being clear about the meaning of a galaxy, let alone the meaning of a black hole. This has lead some investigators to differentiate the following aspects of an attitude: the cognitive or the knowledge aspect, the affective or the feeling's aspect and the action or the behavioral aspect. This differentiation is only useful for research purpose since in a real life situation they are only aspects of a whole which cannot be divided into separate parts. This differentiation does, however, help in measuring attitudes towards a health issue and has been used in the "Health Belief Model" which postulates that for a health action to take place, people should know about the threat, should perceive its seriousness, should perceive that they are susceptible to it (that it could happen to them) and that the way out is acceptable in terms of cost-benefit comparison.

It is not possible to decide in advance which of the above mentioned situations one will face, and it has, therefore, been the usual practice to use a variety of approaches for collecting information about people's attitudes. Some of the methods used are:

i. self-report which can take the form of oral report included in an interview, survey or poll, and written report based on answering questions from a questionnaire, attitude rating scale, log, journal or a diary;

ii. reports of others which include interviews, questionnaires, logs, journals, reports and observational methods;

iii. secondary analysis of records which include attendance records, counsellor's files or any other record that includes information relevant for attitude measurement.

The field of attitude measurement is very prolific in terms of commercially available ready-made attitude tests. In general terms, according to the area of interest, there are available test for the following types of attitudes:

i. attitudes towards self: these include measurement of self-esteem, self-concept, self-perception, self-confidence, locus of control, etc.; (Some of available tests are: Piers-Harris Children's Self Concept Scale; Tennessee Self Concept Scale; Self-esteem Inventory by Coopersmith; Intellectual Achievement Responsibility Questionnaire by Crandall; Locus of Control Scale by Nowicki & Strickland, etc.)

ii. attitudes towards school and school related concerns: these include measurements of attitudes towards specific school subjects, schoolmates, teachers, school environment, learning process, etc.; (Some of commercially available tests are: Childhood Attitude Inventory for Problem Solving; The Minnesota School Affect Assessment; Self-concept as a Learner Scale; Student Attitude Survey; Interest Inventory for Elementary Grades;etc.)

iii. attitudes towards others: include faith and trust in others, acceptance and concern for others, strategies for dealing with others, attitudes towards others of different sex, race, religion, culture, age, etc.; (Some available tests are: Cross-national Scales for Measuring Attitudes in Civic Education; Katz-Zalk Opinion Questionnaire; Russell Sage Social Relations Test; etc.)

iv. attitudes towards vocation and general interests: these include preferences for future roles and jobs, future aspirations, job satisfaction, working conditions, relations with superiors and management, status and recognition, pay and benefits, other rewards, etc. (Some available tests are: Minnesota Vocational Interest Inventory; Kuder Occupational Interest Survey; Career Maturity Inventory; Work Values Inventory; Minnesota Satisfaction Questionnaire; Management Burnout Scale; Stress Evaluation Inventory; etc.)

Since there is a wide variety of commercially available tests from which to choose, it will be, therefore, necessary to ask oneself certain relevant questions which could help in making the right choice. These are:

i. how does the test relate to the attitude objective in the programme? In other words does the programme depend on the findings
from a specific measurement, and how can the programme utilise the
findings?

ii. does the test do what it implies it will do, and if yes, will the
findings be reliable and valid? This includes the critical assessment of
the questions and situations used to establish an attitude in terms of
one's own objectives and will also depend on the reputation the test
has gained by being used in the past;

iii. does the test seem appropriate for the population in the
study, in terms of age, culture, language, etc.;

If after critical examination, one comes to the conclusion that the available tests are not appropriate, one can undertake to develop one's own
test or buy in external expertise to do this job. The main requirements
for developing one's own test are:

i. it will be necessary to define in a precise form the aims and
objectives which the test should achieve and which will define the contents of the test;

ii. it will be necessary to carefully select the items or questions
which will be included in a test, pretest them for validity and reliability
and appropriateness concerning the topic, the population and the expected outcome;

iii. each test needs to be standardised and that is the advantage of commercially available tests as compared to one's own tests.
Standardisation means that a test has a standard form of administration and interpretation which has been derived from the application of
that test during its development on a series of population groups, has
been validated and is accompanied by a manual which sets down the
way the test should be used and interpreted.

One should bear in mind that this kind of attitude measurement is a
recognised professional activity, and that many of the tests can be
bought and used only by people with a recognised professional status
(i.e. psychologists, etc.)

Even when one overcomes all the hurdles mentioned, the most important question to be answered is "why do I need to measure attitudes, and how will I use the findings"? In health promotion and education the aims are related to the improvement of health, and according to the "Knowledge, Attitude, Practice" (or KAP) model, the assumption is that one needs to modify attitudes to achieve desired behavioral changes or actions. This assumption has been questioned and better ways of influencing behaviour and actions have been developed. If, however, the existing attitudes are the problem, then the aim will be to modify them for their own sake. This is a justified use of the outcomes of attitude measurement if they are a part of the aims of the intervention.

An example of a test which could be used to find out whether the existing attitudes are the main problem and should be the goal of an intervention, is the Bogardus Social Distance Scale which examines the attitude as well as the strength of that attitude towards a specific population group or a minority. One can take, for example, the problem resulting from some people having a strong negative attitude towards associating, working together, living nearby or going to school with someone who is infected by HIV and is potential AIDS patient. One would design a set of questions with an increased personal aspect: "Are you willing to allow HIV positive people to live in UK?", "Are you willing to allow HIV positive people to live in your neighbourhood?", "Are you willing to allow HIV positive people to sit in the same school class with you?", "Would you encourage your daughter to marry a HIV positive man?", etc. According to the rules of building scales, the issue becomes increasingly personal, and one can assume that a person accepting the last statement would also accept all the previous ones. The Bogardus social distance scale illustrates the advantages of scaling as a data-reduction device. By knowing which of the statements a person has accepted, one can assume that this person would also accept all the preceding ones. By finding out the predominant attitudes in a community towards an issue, it will be possible to anticipate the problems or a lack of them, if one tries to mobilise that community for support and acceptance of a certain population with shared characteristics.

c. Measurement of skills

There are many situations where the competence in looking after one's own health or the health of others will involve a mastery of certain skills. Since these skills can be of different nature, the measurements will also be different. Here are some of the skills and the ways they can be measured:

i. *manual skills* can include the ability to take the temperature of a child, administer a medicine to an old person, bandage a wound due to an accident, give an injection to oneself as in the case of diabetes, etc. All these skills can be learned and the performance can be assessed by a test which will include verbal explanations and practical performances. Most widely spread test of this kind are used in assessing the performance of participants on a First Aid Course before being given a certificate of proficiency. Another way to assess manual skills is by observation. It will be necessary to structure such assessment observations and in some cases the observations will have to be made by experts. A structured observation allows for administration to a number of subjects, producing a comparable result. Finally, the assessment of skills can be made on the basis of a task that the subject has to perform. This kind of assessment has been used for generations by apprentices who had to produce a "masterpiece" as the proof of mastering the necessary skills for the practice of that occupation or profession. This kind of assessment is well known to students in subjects which depend on manual dexterity for practising the profession (teachers, engeneers, doctors, nurses, etc.)

ii. *social skills* include interaction with others, coping with stressful situations, getting on with ones friends, colleagues, etc. The simplest way of measuring social skills is by observation of the subjects behaviour in artificial and/or real life situations. One can also use records, if they are available, which note the conflicts in particular situations, etc. Another way of exploring social skills is by means of a sociometric test. This is a test administered to a population or a group, where the participants are asked to note persons with whom they would like to be close friends, would like to work closely together, would like to go on holidays, etc. The negative statements (i.e. whom do you dislike most?) are avoided because they could lead to stigmatisation and isolation of certain people who would score high on such negative choices. Each subject writes down a name for each question, and this is the basis for the development of a sociogram, where all the links (or choices) are recorded and the persons are ranked according to the number of times they have been chosen by others. In this way one can make inferences according to the context of the questions about certain people who are most popular or who are social isolates. If one repeats this test after a certain time, one can also monitor the trends of social development of certain persons in terms of their movement within the sociogram.

iii. *group skills*: make up a specialised variety of skills, which can include the skills of leadership or the skills of participation. The measurement of these skills can take the form of observation, diary, log keeping, interviews and questionnaires. Each of these methods can be successful if it follows certain rules and is carried out by skilled researchers.

4. *Observational method.* This can take one of several forms. The main difference will be according to the interaction between the observer and the group members.The observer can be a member of the group in which case he/she will carry out participant observation; he/she can be placed outside the group with the group being aware of the observers presence, or it can be carried out with the observer being placed behind a one-way mirror and the group not being aware of the observer. With the development of video technology, observation can be carried out by analysing video tapes of group meetings, after the event.

One can also differentiate between structured, semi-structured and unstructured observation. Structured observation is based on a pre-prepared schedule or instrument which requires the observer to make observations covering a prescribed set of activities or contents and to record them in a certain order. With semi-structured observation, the observer is asked to prepare anecdotal accounts of the events and behaviours within the group, which can serve as a basis for developing an instrument and analysing the anecdotal observations within the structural framework of that instrument. Unstructured observation requires the assistance of a skilled professional who will be able to observe and analyse group behaviour within a scientific framework which is a part of the professional's expertise.

5. Sociometric method. This is a specific method for recording group interactions and the relative position of group members in terms of modelling, power structure, affective relationships, etc. It requires a structured instrument which will include all the questions deemed relevant to the programme. The questions can take the following form: "Who in your group produces best new ideas?", "Who in your group is most productive?", "With whom in your group you would like to spend most of your time?", "Who in your group is the person you would wish to be most like?" etc.The analysis of the instrument will produce a ranking order of members along certain dimensions which have been included in the instrument such as popularity, authority, attractiveness, intellect, etc. This method can be useful in trying to find the natural leaders in a group, which can be a very important factor in implementing a health promotion/education intervention.

6.Leadership assessment. To assess the performance of a group leader it will be necessary to design an instrument which will include the break-down of the leadership role into its constituent parts. A leadership role aimed at meeting the needs of the group on the task level will include leadership functions as a facilitator and coordinator of group efforts in defining the common aims or tasks of the group and will include initiating the relevant ideas, opinion-seeking and opinion-giving, clarifying, elaborating, interpreting and summarising the group activities. The role of the leader on the group maintenance level is aimed at ensuring the smooth running of the group processes and continuation of group activities until the group task is fulfilled. This maintenance function includes encouraging members' participation, expressing group feelings, harmonising members' interactions, resolving conflicts, protecting weaker members from dominance of the stronger members, compromising the opposed views, gate-keeping or keeping the channels of communication in a group open, and setting standards for group interactions and achievements. It is assumed that each of these functions contributes to the effectiveness of the leadership role and should be included in the assessment of leadership performance.

7. Group processes and members' performance. Since group processes can only be observed through members' interactions, it will be necessary to produce an instrument with a number of items which are considered to be relevant for this kind of study. The first group of observations will be concerned with group problems. These can be due to conflict, apathy and non-participation, and/or inadequate decision-making. There are a number of indicators of the existence of each of these contributory factors to a group that has problems, which can be established by observation and analysed for the reasons of occurring in that particular group. Another group of observations will be concerned with factors which can contribute to group efficiency, such as the group atmosphere, quantity and quality of work accomplished, members' contributions and the leadership behaviour.

Since a group is a dynamic mechanism, one way of assessing its performance will be to monitor group's growth which includes the group's ability to transit through the various stages of group development without any problems. A scale for measuring group growth can include members' opinions on such topics as goal setting, trust among the members, group's sensitivity and perceptiveness, attention, leadership support, use of resources, decision-making process and loyalty together with the sense of belonging within the group. The members should be able to express the strength of their opinions by a choice of qualitatively different answers (for instance, strongly agree / strongly disagree; none contributed / all contributed; no loyalty / full sense of belonging).

UNIT 2:Choice of solutions

Introduction

Based on an appropriate definition of a problem, including the medical, health promotional and health educational aspects, an insight should be gained into the best available solutions which could be applied in a specific situation. One should, however, bear in mind that health behaviour and actions are a part of a life-style which is the function of an interaction between external and personal factors, as represented by medical, health promotional and health educational aspects, and that any solution will have to take into consideration all the three aspects within a holistic intervention. It should be noted that this tripartite differentiation is only a means of learning more about different aspects of a problem, and cannot be segregated in an intervention.

This has been recognised by WHO, when they introduced health promotion as a means of influencing the environment (physical and social) in addition to the well established health education, which has been more concerned with the personal factors. In this way the potential of an intervention has been extended to cover both aspects of the same thing. It has also been reflected in the change of emphasis from various risk factors and diseases to a life-style approach, since health is a product of a life-style and affects the whole life-style.

The **aim** of this unit is to enable the participant to translate the results of the diagnosis of the problem into the appropriate solutions in the form health promotional and educational interventions; to achieve this aim, the unit will have the following **objectives**:

1. to acquaint the participants with available medical solutions in terms of prevention, treatment and management of risk factors and disease;

2. to enable the participants to understand the available options for planning a health promotion intervention on an environmental as well as individual level;

3. to give the participants an insight into the mechanisms operating on a personal level which can affect the health of an individual and which include knowledge, attitudes and skills, representing the level of competence of that individual.

The **method** applied in Unit 2 consists of written material, lectures, individual learning, group work and work on tasks.

The **assessment** of the achievements concerning this Unit will be based on continuous assessment and written material.

Medical solutions

It is important to remind oneself that most medical problems have medical solutions. They may take the form of prevention, treatment and/or management of health threats and disease. This implies that health education and health promotion can only be considered as complementary and supportive to medical solutions. There are, however, sadly still a number of medical problems for which there is no medical solution. In this case the role of health promotion and education is to enable the afflicted individuals to cope with all the aspects of such a problem, and to help them in mobilising all the support necessary from the medical and social services as well as from their immediate and wider social environment.

Prevention

When we talk about prevention we mean, in most cases, primary prevention. One should realise that there are different levels of prevention which must be taken into consideration since they will require specific solutions. In general terms, one can differentiate between primary, secondary and tertiary prevention, although there are some other more complex classificatory systems.

Primary prevention

Primary prevention is concerned with preventing the onset of a disease. This means that it is limited to a "healthy" population which could be or is exposed to an unacceptable level of risk from a health threat. Medicine has been the branch of science that has mostly contributed to our present day body of knowledge about the causation and the spread of a disease. Based on this knowledge it is possible to define that segment of a population which runs a higher than average risk from a health threat and which should be included in a preventive intervention. Since disease is caused by external and personal factors, or a combination of both, the preventive interventions will take into account both in the attempt to reduce the risk and protect individuals.

The methods used can include a number of activities: one can attempt to eliminate the cause from the environment, as in the case of malaria eradication, prevention of salmonella poisoning, ensuring safe drinking water and reducing air pollution, implementing safety measures at work, prohibiting, driving after drinking, isolating the carriers of a disease, etc.; one can attempt to raise the natural resistance in a person by boosting the immune system through vaccination and immunisation, preventing contact with carriers, promoting the use of protective practices, etc.; one can also use the combination of approaches which will affect both the environment and the individual.

Some of these measures will be generally applied to the whole population, whereas, others will be appropriate only for a population that is at an unacceptable level of risk from a health threat. In the latter case it will be necessary to define this part of the population at high risk by means of screening programmes, examination of behavioral patterns and general life-styles.

The medical solution, in many cases will be concerned with the provision of appropriate knowledge about prevention, adequate supplies of preventive materials, provision of adequate services for their implementation, and in general terms the accessibility of prevention to the population at risk.

When planning a medical preventive intervention, it will also be necessary to differentiate between the prevention of disease and prevention of risk factors. The former is concerned with specific medical causes, whereas the latter is more concerned with prevention of the acquisition of certain types of behaviour which could increase the risk from a health threat. Here one immediately thinks of preventing children from experimenting with smoking, young people using precautions in their sexual relationships within the existing social, moral, religious and legal norms, preventing drug abuse, preventing parents' incompetence in raising their children, etc.

The importance of primary prevention is recognised by the medical profession and is reflected in a number of specialties which have been developed, such as social and preventive medicine, public health, epidemiology, immunology, etc.

There are a number of existing measures and services provided by the health care system which are aimed at prevention. Since most of them depend on health promotion and education for success, some of them will be described in greater detail:

1. *Prevention in early childhood*

Prevention of health threats starts during pregnancy, concentrates on delivery and continues during the early childhood:

a. *pregnancy*: This is the time when a number of later problems can be prevented and the health care system is adjusted to this by providing pregnant women with a whole range of services, i.e. the initial examination, the follow-up monitoring, and preparation for childbirth. During pregnancy a woman is expected to keep a diary where she will record the important events relevant to pregnancy, such as the duration of pregnancy, appointments with the GP or visits to the Clinic, weight/height, movements of the baby, general feelings, etc. Keeping records is a useful preventive measure since it helps with providing accurate information to the medical staff during the visits to the antenatal clinic. Some of the troublesome problems during pregnancy concern sickness, diet and weight, constipation, passing water frequently, tiredness, apathy, and feelings of anxiety about the welfare of the expected baby. Prevention is mainly concerned with establishing and maintaining of close contact of the pregnant woman with the health care system and her understanding of the purpose and the mechanics of various tests and examinations. The most common preventive topics include diet, smoking during pregnancy, regular utilisation of services, medication and drug taking, and coping with possible anxieties;

b. *delivery*: Even before the baby is due, the parents will have to decide where the delivery will take place and whether the mother has any objections to drug assisted delivery and possible induction. Taking care of these issues can reduce the anxiety and avoid problems related to delivery. In any case the delivery will be carried out under medical control, which does not exclude the presence of a supportive person such as the husband;

c. *the first years*: There are a number of preventive medical services available to a family with a young baby. Immediately after the birth, the baby will be examined to establish whether it is "normal", although it is impossible to define a "normal" baby, since there are so many variations and one prefers to define a baby as healthy. This is usually done by administering the 'apgar' test to the baby which examines heart rate, respiratory function, muscle tone, reflexes and colour. It will also include visual examination of the general appearance and the detailed examination of all the parts of the body such as limbs, genitals, eyes, etc. Once at home, the parents will be expected to use the existing postnatal clinics or well-baby clinics, as well as keep in close contact with their general practitioner. At this stage the mother is visited by the health visitor, and the prevention is concerned with the problems that a new mother may face as well as the probof a small baby. Medical prevention will be only possible if the mother is aware of the significance of certain symptoms and is willing to seek medical advice.

2. *Immunisation and vaccination*

One of the most common ways of preventing illnesses in childhood as well as in later life is by immunising the child. Local authorities and/or general practitioners carry out a set of immunisations at different age of the baby and for different diseases.

Local authorities have produced a "schedule for immunisation" according to the age of the child. It includes immunisation for a number of most common childhood diseases, as follows:

- at birth the children from immigrant parents and those in contact with TB patients receive a BCG vaccination;

- at 3 months all children are immunised against diphtheria, tetanus, pertussis in a triple vaccine (DTP), and receive an oral polio vaccine;

- between 4 1/2 and 5 months they receive the second triple vaccine (DTP) and oral polio vaccine;

- between 8 and 11 months they receive the third triple vaccine (DTP) and oral polio vaccine;

- between 12 and 18 months they receive measles, mumps and rubella triple vaccine (MMR);

- between 4 and 5 years of age or at school entry they receive diphtheria and tetanus vaccine, oral polio, and MMR if they did not receive already;

- between 10 and 14 years they receive the BCG vaccine, and girls receive rubella vaccine;

- between 15 and 18 years of age they receive tetanus and oral polio vaccine.

This complicated schedule extending through time requires a highly organised approach which consists of parents being expected to know what their child had and what it is still due to have and when, and the general practitioners and local authorities keeping records of all the children on their list which is used to sent letters of invitation to parents as a reminder that their child is due for immunisation.

In addition to technical problems of keeping track of what a child had and is due to have, there are some problems related to the possible side-effects of some vaccines such as the pertussis vaccine. There is a considerable fear amongst the parents who can opt out of allowing their children to have the triple vaccine (DTP), by leaving out the pertussis vaccine and letting their child have only the diphtheria and tetanus vaccine. It is important to note that this immunisation programme is not compulsory and that it needs parent's approval. This is an important aspect which influences the chances of litigation and compensation in case of side-effects due to the programme. It will, therefore, depend on the way the services phrase their invitation addressed to the parents, the promises they make and the motivational appeals they use.

There are a number of other immunisation programmes, most of which are offered to or demanded from people who travel into parts of the world where certain infectious diseases are endemic. The World Health Organisation has produced a programme and issues travellers with a certificate in which the various vaccinations are recorded. Some of the countries do not allow people to enter the country without such a proof of vaccination. The most common diseases against which vaccination is required are smallpox, yellow fever, cholera, typhoid and some others depending on the area and the country. For some countries it is recommended that a preventive medication for malaria be undertaken a week before travelling into the area and continue with it two weeks after returning home. With the advent of AIDS, travellers are advised to carry with them sterilised syringes and possibly also blood for transfusion, if they travel to countries where blood and plasma are not checked for AIDS infection.

People in certain important public occupations (doctors, nurses, teachers, bus drivers, etc) or of certain age (old people) are offered immunisation against common cold, since an epidemic of this kind could disrupt the normal life in a community.

3. Prevention of AIDS

At present there is no medical way of primary prevention of AIDS. There is a hope that a vaccine will be developed in time, but this is still in distant future. The only possibility for a healthy person to protect himself/herself from getting infected is by controlling their sexual habits and choosing their sexual partners. Another way of preventing infection is by checking the blood used for transfusion and preventing cross-infection in the medical and dental services. In the past primary prevention has been concentrating on high risk groups (homosexuals and drug users). This has now been abandoned with the increased spread of the infection in the heterosexual population, and targeting "high risk" groups is considered to be wrong and counterproductive. The most common advice, approved by the medical profession, for primary prevention of AIDS is to avoid any sex without proper protection (condom), and the reduction of promiscuity in the population.

4. Prevention of cardiovascular disease

Since cardiovascular disease is the most common cause of death in the developed world, medicine has concentrated on methods of primary prevention by investing considerable resources in research (Robb-Smith,1967). For health promotion and education purpose it is important to differentiate between the diseases of the heart and of the blood vessels. The function of the heart can be affected either by inadequate blood supply or by complete blockage of a blood vessel supplying the heart muscle. Inadequate blood supply, such as in arteriosclerosis occurs when the blood vessels become narrow in places and slow down the supply of blood to the heart. Complete blockage of a blood vessel can occur due to embolism or blockage of smaller vessels or thrombosis which refers to a blood clot within the vessel of the heart. Arteriosclerotic changes in coronary artery disease are very often accompanied by high blood pressure or hypertension, and/or the raised level of serum cholesterol in blood (serum being a part of blood which includes fatty substances such as lipids, a component of which is cholesterol).

Most of the evidence for causation of cardiovascular diseases has been produced by epidemiological studies, and is based on higher than expected (or statistically significant) associations between certain factors and the diseases. These include environmental factors (atmospheric pollution, cold weather, hardness of drinking water, high elevation of the locality), occupational factors (stress, toxic factors), behavioral factors (diet, cigarette smoking, alcohol). There are, however, certain medical factors which also contribute to the risk and which include hyperlipidaemic states, arterial hypertension, diabetes mellitus and hyperuricaemia, and certain genetic factors. (See example.)

One can also examine the natural history of ischaemic heart disease in stages and divide it into 'causes', 'precursor pathology' and 'early incidence'. In this way one can examine which of the factors are most likely to contribute to the increased risk from the disease. These are age, family history, stature, blood pressure, occupation, exercise, diet and cigarette smoking. Primary prevention of coronary heart diseases is well developed and includes the avoidance and control of most of contributory factors mentioned.

Primary prevention in this area is concentrating on early discovery of the presence of certain risk factors which may increase the probability of a person suffering a heart attack. This usually takes the form of the 'Health Checkup' for the healthy population and is carried out in general practices, local authority clinics and by the occupational health service at the work place. In the past it was concentrated on the managerial staff, whereas, now it is offered to everyone. Once the population at risk has been defined, primary prevention depends on preventive medication and health education with the aim of reducing risk factors and changing the behaviour.

5. Cancers

Most people still think of cancer as one deadly disease. The differentiation of cancers of different sites has produced sufficient evidence that there is a strong case for primary prevention of at least some cancers. This is especially the case of lung cancer which can be prevented in a great number of instances by preventing people from smoking. There is evidence that cervical cancer can be prevented by avoiding early sex (teenage) and by discovering early changes in the cervix which if left untreated could develop into cancer. Similarly one can avoid breast cancer by early detection and removal of lumps in the breast, although some think that with cervical and breast cancer one deals with secondary and not primary prevention. There is some disagreement as to whether every abnormality in cervical cells and every lump in the breasts is the first stage of cancer or not. More recently, there has been some evidence about the increased risk from cancer of the scrotum due to nude sunbathing, which is also associated with skin cancer. Skin cancer in general has been related to increased sunbathing. There are also occupations which increase risk from cancer due to toxic substances or irradiation. Health promotion and education is mainly concerned with eliminating smoking, early detection of any abnormality which could be associated with cervical or breast cancer, reducing exposure to sunlight and protection at work.

6. Accidents

There are a number of medical factors which can increase the risk from accident. These include reduced perception and reflexes due to alcohol and drugs, exposure to dangerous environment (at work, home or leisure) and certain high risk practices. Primary prevention has been mainly concentrated on drinking and driving, physical fitness, and other safety measures.

Secondary prevention

It is mainly concerned with the prevention of the further development of existing diseases or precursors leading to a diseases, controlling the situation and attempting to reverse the processes.

In the case of childhood, secondary prevention will emphasise the early diagnosis and treatment of any disease and the isolation of the patient to avoid contact and spread of that disease into the healthy population. Health promotion and education will use the medical knowledge to improve people's competence in recognising the most common diseases and in seeking timely medical help as well as to enable them to cope with the management of the disease and the patient.

Secondary prevention of AIDS will include the control of the spread of the infection and the treatment of people who are already infected. Health promotion and education is mainly concerned with avoiding spread through sharing of needles among drug-abusers, use of condoms and control of blood-donors. An important and so far neglected area is reducing prejudice in dealing with infected persons. This is of importance due to the long incubation period (several years) from infection to the development of the disease. The medical evidence clearly states the ways the infection can spread and the ways of interacting with infected persons without danger of infection. This is, however, not widely accepted, and causes a number of problems for infected people who wish to live in a normal social environment. The questions have been raised about accepting infected children into normal schools, the possibility for infected people to continue working in a normal working environment, their position in the community, conditions for insurance, mortgages, etc.

Secondary prevention of coronary heart disease is mainly concerned with people who have had a previous incident or have some condition (hypertension, etc.) which can increase the risk from the disease. Health promotion and education will concentrate mainly on the life-style to exclude behavioral patterns such as smoking, stress, obesity, etc. It will emphasise the importance of regular check-ups and self monitoring of blood pressure and the level blood cholesterol.

In the case of secondary prevention of cancers, people concerned will be women who had a positive cervical smear test, a lump in the breast, solar keratosis, or any similar condition which makes them at higher than average risk from cancer, and makes them aware of that risk. The health promotion and education intervention will be concentrated on developing coping mechanisms which will enable these people to lead a relatively normal life.

Secondary prevention of accidents is in the first instance concerned with rendering first aid at the place where the accident occurred. It is also concerned with the control of after-effects and will depend on speedy and competent dealing with the victim on the spot as well as treatment in medical institutions. In the case of an accident (in the home, at work, in the street etc.) the first help will usually be provided by lay people who happen to be on the spot at the time of the accident.. Secondary prevention is, therefore, concerned with improving the competence of the general public in dealing with accidents until the ar-rival of professional help. This is for the most part achieved by provid-ing the general public, as well as specific groups, with the opportunity to learn about first aid by attending special courses. A number of or-ganisations provide such courses, the promotion of which has so far been a neglected part of general health promotion and education.

Tertiary prevention

Tertiary prevention is concerned with people who have recovered from a disease and may have some consequences which will restrict their normal life. This may include children who are born with certain han-dicaps, suffered some consequences from a childhood disease, people with infectious diseases which turned into chronic states or for which there is no known cure, suffers from AIDS, cancer patients including terminal cases, and people suffering some disability due to a disease or an accident. An example is the case of diabetes. People need to learn how to monitor their state, how to control it and how to deal with emergencies . The role of health promotion and education will be to raise their competence and enable them to utilise the support systems.

Treatment

Treatment as a medical solution usually includes medication, surgical intervention or radiation therapy. It can be concerned with:

Acute episodes

In case of acute episodes of disease the medical profession goes through the process of legitimising the patient's sick-role, negotiating and implementing some form of treatment. Since such episodes are usually limited in time the medical solutions are mostly concerned with medication and other types of interventions.

The concept of 'sick role' is a very important aspect of the doctor patient interaction, especially in the case of acute episodes. It has been developed by medical sociologists as a means of explaining how a society deals with people who are ill with minimum disruption of the normal workings of that society. A society faces the problem of integrating sick people into a social order, where they will have a recognised status and be able to perform a legitimised role. If, for example a person does not feel well (state of ill health), to be able to stay home from work and not lose the wage, he/she will have to change from the "state" into the "status" of being ill. This means that the status is a social position, legitimised by a recognised agent (doctor) and has a specific role (sick role) attached which has a certain number of rights and obligations for the incumbent.

Consequently each "state" can have a corresponding "status" with a specific role, and people can move from a state to a status and back by meeting the necessary requirements. These are the acquisition and relinquishment of a status through legitimation by a recognised professional.

Thus the movement of individuals from one state or status to another will depend on their actions, which define the distinction between a state and a status. Therefore, the decision to undertake an action or not will form the core of the system. This action will follow the stage of receiving the information, the stage of making a choice followed by a decision, with possibly the action to follow or not, depending on the decision made. The information may take different forms such as noticing a symptom, learning about a potential risk, hearing the results of a test etc.

Each status has a role attached, or in other words the status and role are two different aspects of the same thing. Whereas the status denotes the social position within the social structure, the role denotes the expected behaviour or actions associated with that status. One can, therefore, more often hear the expression "sick role" than "the status of being ill", where both describe two aspects of person's position in the society in case of being ill.

It has been recognised that the sick role has a certain set of rights and obligations attached to it which are: (a) a sick person is exempt of certain social responsibilities; (b) he/she cannot be expected to take care of themselves; (c) he/she should cooperate in becoming well as soon as possible; (d) he/she should seek medical help and cooperate in the prescribed treatment.

These rights and obligations form the basis for the process through which a person goes in acquiring a sick role. The process can take the following path: a person notices symptoms; after assessing the meaning of the symptom he/she will test the reaction of the social environment to the idea of him/her taking on the sick role; if the reactions are positive and if the symptom persists he/she will decide to see a doctor, who may confirm the existence and seriousness of the symptom and in this way will legitimise the sick role; when the patient is cured, he/she will be discharged by the doctor, will relinquish the sick role and will again take on the role of a healthy person.

A similar process occurs with the legitimation of the at-risk and chronically ill roles. The difference is that both of these roles are of long duration and a person cannot easily, if at all, relinquish them during the life time. In case of an acute episode as in the case of an accident the first phases will be collapsed with imminent acquisition of the sick role with the arrival of an ambulance.

This classification is valid for simple cases where the illness can be diagnosed and the risk is medically recognised. There are, however, cases where the situation is not clear cut and simple. A person can only acquire a status if such a status has been recognised and institutionalised by the society. In case of smoking, people are aware of the risk from lung cancer, but the status of being at risk is not formally recognised, and people can smoke without any sanctions being applied. If such a smoker comes to see a doctor, the latter will not be able to legitimise a sick role, since the person is not yet ill, nor will he be able to legitimise an at-risk role, since such a status/role does not formally exist. The only way open to a doctor is to legitimise a quasi sick role, which implies the risk and treats the smoker as if he/she is already suffering from the disease from which he/she is at risk. Such a quasi sick role will have a similar set of rights and obligations as a legitimised sick role. The need for legitimising the quasi sick role arose from the fact that the status of being at risk from smoking does not exist and the state of being at risk does not have any rights attached but only obligations for the incumbent. By legitimising a quasi sick role this balance is again established and a person may activate all the rights that a sick role would have.

Health promotion and education is mostly concerned with health hazards or risks, many of which have not been formally recognised or institutionalised. This means that health promotion and education deal with raising people's awareness of dangers to health in the hope that they would recognise these dangers and see themselves in the state of being at risk. If this state is not matched with an appropriate status/role, the chances of an individual changing behaviour, undertaking an action or modifying his/her lifestyle are low, and especially for a long term duration. This is why we hear people going on a diet to drop out after a certain time, revert back to smoking after giving up, etc.

The implications for health promotion and education are numerous: it can influence the kind of information available to the population at risk as well as the general population, it can influence the choice within the decision-making process by making desired decisions more attractive and reducing the fear from negative consequences, and by evaluation of such processes may find out how effective the intervention has been and what needs to be done to remedy any mistakes.

Finally, one should realise that social roles associated with certain statuses are governed by norms or expectations which define the role-performance and may invoke sanctions in case of deviance. It is because of this, that the role performance of an individual will depend not only on the decision making process and its outcome, but also on the social support that individual receives in the form of supportive norms and more general social reinforcement from his/her social environment.

Behavioral practice

There are numerous behavioral problems which can require a medical solution, as for example a whole range of mental diseases which manifest behavioral symptoms and require medical treatment. There are, however, other behavioral patterns, like those associated with smoking, obesity, hyperkinesis etc., which are readily interpreted as mundane occurrences and have also attracted medical solutions.

Management

The health care system is involved in providing services concerned with the management of illness or being at risk. The medical measures concerning management can include provision for handicapped, mentally ill, chronically ill etc. According to the requirement management will include:

At-risk status

People can live in areas with an increased risk from a certain disease or may be involved in occupations which have an increased risk for their health. Management of people with an at-risk status may include protective arrangements in the working environment or for personal use. Here one would also consider the constant monitoring of workers exposed to danger of radiation, or to other noxious substances;

Sick role

Once a person has acquired a sick-role, a number of measures will be necessary concerning the management of this status to enable people to fulfil successfully their sick-role. Here one could think of post-operative management of patients, as well as the process of rehabilitation.

Health promotion solutions

The health promotion solutions will be closely related to the way a problem has been defined in health promotional terms. This will usually include the manipulation of societal factors and adjustment of individual reactions to those factors. In this way, health promotion solutions are concerned with:

Environmental interventions

A successful application of a medical solution will require a conducive and supportive social environment. This will include:

Physical environment

The solution of many problems originating on a societal level will require governmental intervention and community participation in policy planning and execution. Norms are social expectations which will define the provisions made by the social environment in support of medical solutions. We can differentiate between the following types of norms:

1. *legal norms* express the provisions including rights and duties defined by law and supported by legal sanctions. Legal norms cover a whole range of rights and duties of the individuals, their family, as well as the community in which they live;

2. *professional norms* define the rights and duties of members of different professions engaged in prevention, management or treatment of disease and health risks;

3. *social norms* reflect the general culture and value system of a certain population group or community. They are reflected in individual attitudes to acceptance and utilisation of services provided.

Social environment

Services available for the solution of certain health problems represent an important aspect of societal factors and will influence the success of any intervention. They will depend on 'healthy public policies' and appropriate provision made on an organisational and administrative level. This will be reflected in social expectations predominant in that community. The type of sanctions will differ, but may have as strong a coercive power as legal or professional sanctions and may activate a strong social support. The services to be considered are:

1. *medical services* which will reflect the type of health care system in the country, the geographical distribution of hospitals, clinics, GPs, and the proportion of health personnel for a given population;

2. *social services* play an important part in helping people to overcome the social effects of their at-risk or sick role. They can contribute in the form of professional support, financial support, as well as temporary or permanent placement in special institutions;

3. *lay support systems* are an important form of societal service that is usually initiated by individuals or groups, and plays an important part in prevention, management and treatment of diseases. The role of this system is increasing with the realisation that it is the only way of achieving self-reliance and reducing over-dependence of individuals on the medical system.

Individual reactions

In cases where there is a positive and supportive social environment, individuals may still have problems in utilising it or adjusting to it. The health promotional activity will be concerned with:

Physical environment

Even in cases where there are positive and supportive norms related to utilisation, compliance and management of a disease, individuals may not fully use these services due to their wrong perception of existing expectations. This can be expressed in the form of:

1. *conformity* to certain norms which are perceived to exist but in fact do not exist or do not exist in that specific form;

2. *variance* which may go beyond the accepted limits or may take harmful forms in cases where the existing norm is not precise enough;

3. *deviance* from existing expectations or norms may have many reasons and in some cases, the return to conformity may require, in addition to medical treatment, also an increased amount of social pressure supported by social sanctions.

Social environment

Individual reactions on an organisational level will be concerned with the willingness of individuals to participate actively in planning and decision making on a community level. Even where the services do exist, are accessible and available, the general image may be such that people may not want to use them. It may be necessary to change the image or individual perception of that image. The services involved include:

1. *medical services* which for a number of reasons may have a stigma attached to their image such as cancer hospitals, lunatic asylums and clinics for sexually transmitted disease;

2. *social services* may also carry a stigma for certain population groups. It is a fact that quite a large proportion of the population does not make use of different kinds of benefits which they have a right to claim. There is, however, also the problem of over-utilisation of other social services which involve waiting queues;

3. *lay support systems* in the form of different self-help groups have been in existence for some time and have provided help and support to a number of people. There are, however, certain groups of people who for different reasons do not use this support system, although they could benefit from it. Increased utilisation of existing systems the and creation of additional new ones may greatly improve the health of a community.

Health education solutions

Even within the best social environment and with the best medical care available, the health of individuals will depend on their competence to deal with health problems that face them. To increase the competence of individuals in dealing with health problems, health education has to address the following areas:

Knowledge (awareness)

There may be cases where individuals are healthy and live a long life without any accurate knowledge about causes, prevention, treatment and management of certain diseases. This situation is, however, rare in industrialised societies, with a certain overall level of minimum education where people are exposed to information through mass media and where they want to know the reasons for, as well as methods of dealing with a health problem. In this sense awareness about the existence of a health problem supported by knowledge about its characteristics becomes an important aspect of individual competence to deal with it. Health education interventions aiming at raising this competence through knowledge will concerned with the following:

Acquisition

The acquisition of new knowledge will depend on the learning process, communication networks and understanding the language, which will have to be taken into account in any health education intervention;

Modification

This represents a more difficult task for health education, since it has to deal with the existing (false) knowledge and supplementing it with new (accurate) knowledge. This will involve a number of processes which may include acceptance of innovation as well as changes in subjective reality based on previously existing knowledge;

Operationalisation

This means translating the existing accurate knowledge into action. Here health education is dealing with positive resolution of cognitive dissonance, motivation for a positive action, assertion training and acquisition of other social skills, all of which should enhance the probability of a desired action taking place.

Attitudes

If one interprets attitudes as internalised social norms then the general orientation towards a health solution will influence individual attitudes. The following aspects of attitudes are important to be considered by health education:

Severity

It is necessary to consider a health problem as being sufficiently serious or severe to merit a positive action. The perception of severity in health education has been shown to be associated with fear and is motivational only at an optimal level.

If it is too low it may not merit an action or if it is too high it may inhibit an action. The question of optimal severity for each specific health threat is of special interest to health education;

Susceptibility

The belief that a person is susceptible to a health threat i.e. that it can happen to him or her, is an important aspect of a general attitude to a health threat. The feeling of susceptibility is closely related to the problem of locus of control and will influence whether an action will take place or not;

Utility

The probability that existing positive knowledge and attitudes will result in an action will depend on the cost benefit analysis associated with the required action. This will be expressed in terms of the subjective expected utility, an individual anticipates from an action and the anticipated cost involved.

Skills

A number of health actions related to prevention, treatment and management of a health threat or disease will require certain competence associated with specific skills to cope with the problem. The role of health education is to enable individuals to learn those skills and to achieve this it will be necessary to utilise the following:

Communication and learning

The process of communication is very complex and includes a number of approaches out of which the most appropriate for a specific problem will have to be selected. The same applies to the learning capacity of the individuals and the learning processes which will have to be activated to achieve the best possible results;

Coping and modification

In certain cases modification of knowledge, attitudes or behaviour may produce the desired results. In other cases when this is not possible the individuals will have to learn to cope with the existing problem in terms of management and coming to terms with the unavoidable outcome. The role of health education in this area is very important and needs to be developed further;

Decision making and operationalisation

The ultimate aim of most of health education intervention is for an individual to operationalise the accurate knowledge, the positive attitudes and the acquired skills in terms of an action aimed at prevention, treatment or management of a disease. Health education has a role to provide the necessary cue which will trigger off a desired action.

Competence

The recent shift of emphasis from risk factors to healthy life-styles and the emphasis on self-reliance has required a new approach in health education. Its aim has been to raise the general 'competence' of individuals to look after their health and not be too dependent on the health care system. In this sense, health education is a part of the general education for life and survival as well as for taking on the responsibility for the improvement of one's quality of life.

Numerous programmes exist which are concerned with increasing a person's competence and a variety of technologies which enable people to carry out a more accurate diagnosis or to be able to monitor their health and to discover early any signs of increased risk from a health threat. People are encouraged to acquire scales to measure their weight; there are simple-to-operate gadgets to measure one's blood pressure and levels of blood cholesterol; there is a test to check on blood sugar, a gadget to monitor one's biorhythm and alpha waves, even a do-it-yourself acupuncture set, etc. Also commercially available are all kinds of equipment for exercising at home (stationary bicycles, rowing machines, weight lifting equipment, mobile running tracks).

A very popular technological development is the production of video tapes with programmes for practically every aspect of one's health. There are regular TV and radio programmes concerned with health issues. All these developments have resulted in people's willingness to accept the responsibility for their own health and to increase their competence to deal with health issues on their own in the privacy of their home.

People feel the need to increase their competence and another popular way is to either establish or to join a self-help group. There are at present a great variety of such groups and some of them are highly successful and have been in existence for a long time. This form of social support has been found to be very important for maintaining certain health enhancing behavioral patterns such as not smoking, dieting, controlling drug intake and avoiding alcohol abuse.

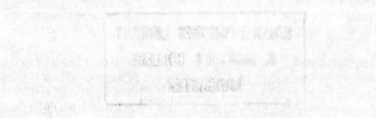

UNIT 3:Available methods and approaches

Introduction

The success of health promotion and education depends on the methods the agents use in achieving their aims. Depending on the status of the agents the methods will be different: the informal agents (such as parents) will use methods that are implicit in bringing up their children and which have been described as a part of the socialisation process of the child; the formal agents will use methods that have been developed for the achievement of specific aims and will largely depend on the type and the location of the consumer or client population.

The study of methods has been carried out within the framework of different "models" developed by health promotion and education practitioners and formalised for the purpose of research an evaluation. In the past one could differentiate between two groups of models: the cognitive models which have been concerned with transmission of information and increase of knowledge in the client population and the social intervention models which have concentrated on the changes of the social environment in which the client population lives and works.

The cognitive models have been using the personal or group approach and have concentrated on the development of methods aimed at the improvement of the processes relevant to the transmission and acquisition of knowledge. The social intervention models have been using the mass media approach and have been concerned with the improvement of advertising methods aimed at changing social values and norms in a population. This differentiation has become obsolete due to developments in communications technology (transistor radios, television and satellite). Whereas before the transmission of information was usually limited to individuals or groups (at lectures or as readers of certain newspapers), with the wide-spread access to new technology (nearly everybody in England has access to TV, and some programmes are seen simultaneously by hundreds of millions of people throughout the world), the transmission of information has been able not only to increase individual knowledge but also to influence the value systems and social expectations (norms) in many countries.

It is because of this blurring of boundaries between the effects of different methods that the notion of models has been abandoned and each method is being considered in terms of its own characteristics and processes and as a part of a more general or "ecological" approach. Within this general approach, it is still useful to look at who does what to whom and with what effect.

The **aim** of Unit 3 is to acquaint the participants with the methods which they could use in planning and executing a health promotional and educational intervention and enable them to acquire appropriate skills necessary for their practical work; to achieve this aim, the Unit has the following **objectives**:

1. to provide the participants with knowledge and skills related to a personal approach when carrying out health promotional and educational work;

2. to provide the participants with knowledge and skills related to group work;

3. to provide the participants with knowledge and skills in planning and carrying out a community programme based on community participation.

The **method** used in Unit 3 consists of written material, individual studies, task work, group discussion, lectures and reports by the students.

The achievements of students will be measured by continuous **assessment** and written reports.

The personal approach

The *medical* definition of the problem should provide information about relevant risk factors and health threats, their characteristics and the ways of prevention, management and treatment on an individual level.

The *health promotional* definition should include information about the environmental factors necessary to support an individual decision about health protection and improvement, and also include the description of mechanisms which will enable the individuals to influence and change their environment.

The *health educational* definition should indicate the areas of improvement necessary for individual decision-making and actions. The outcome of such definitions could influence the choice of methods and contents as a part of interventions based on the following theoretical assumptions:

Learning and communication

Education is becoming a most important growth industry, labour intensive and attracting large capital investments from a whole array of sources. Its importance has been appreciated for a long time and has spawned many research and development projects. The underlying interest has been to understand the ways and means of people's learning, improve it and capitalise on the most effective and efficient methods of teaching. Since a learning situation mostly involves a person's interaction with other people, communication has been also in the centre of interest associated with learning.

Learning

Most health education interventions are based on an explicit or implicit theory (Jehu,1967) which provides the rationale for the chosen approach and explains the processes involved and the expected outcomes. Most of health education "cognitive" models are based on some aspects of learning theories and utilise them in carrying out a health education intervention. For the purpose of health education the existing learning theories can help us to understand how people learn, unlearn and relearn certain facts which are related to their habits, routines, behaviours, actions, decision-making and choices in the field of health and disease. These theories form a part of a number of health education models and approaches and are the basis of health education interventions.

Learning can be defined as relative permanent changes in behaviour potential occurring as the result of past experience (Lieberman,1974; Bandura,1968). It is important to note that learning affects the 'behaviour potential' and not necessarily the behaviour as such. There are different types of learning processes which include:

1. *conditioning*

This type of learning has been made famous by Pavlov and his dogs. He is considered to be the originator of the theory of classical conditioning. The theory is concerned with modifying the 'unconditional stimuli' and 'unconditional responses', such as a dog seeing food and salivating. By introducing a new stimulus (conditional stimulus) such as a bell together with food, the dog was made to salivate (unconditioned response) even when the unconditioned stimulus (food) was removed, and the dog was exposed only to the conditioned stimulus (bell). A higher order conditioning can occur if a conditioned stimulus (bell) is continuously accompanied with another stimulus (a black square) which subsequently may become a conditioned stimulus in its own right. Translated into human learning situations, one could assume that some learning, especially in early childhood, takes the form of 'classical conditioning' as in the case of the meaning of the word 'bad' which can be associated with certain actions and will evoke distress in a child.

The idea of 'conditioning' as a means of learning has been developed further by Skinner, who became famous for his 'black box' approach and the performance of his pigeons. He is being associated with operant conditioning as a means of learning. He placed pigeons in a box and observed their pecking behaviour. He introduced a number of levers at which the pigeons could peck, one of which when pecked produced a food pallet. The pigeons soon stopped pecking in a random fashion and learned to peck the lever which produced food. Even when the lever was changed, they soon learned to peck the right lever. While in the box, the animals performed a number of behaviours, one of which was pressing the right lever which was rewarded by food. It can, therefore, be assumed that the crucial element in learning is reinforcement by means of reward. This idea can be translated to human beings who also learn by means of operant conditioning. The example usually quoted is that of a child presenting a number of facial expressions one of which is smiling which is rewarded and reinforced by eliciting mother's positive reaction. The more the child smiles, the more the mother reacts and reinforces this kind of behaviour. The same could be said for a child who emits a number of sounds, one of which may be 'dada' which is immediately interpreted by parents and positively reinforced, which will elicit a child's repetition of that particular sound. With the introduction of teaching machines, the principle of reward is used to reinforce pupils in their learning process.

2. *social learning*

From these first simple steps in understanding the process of learning in humans by initially studying animals, further developments (Bandura et al.,1969) have taken into consideration the complexity of human responsiveness to different stimuli, at different times, in different situations and in performing different social roles. This has resulted in theories related to *social learning* of which Bandura is one of the recognised exponents. This development was the result of applying more stringent rules to testing 'theories', one of which is their power of prediction. Developments in learning theory shifted the focus of causal analysis from hypothesised inner determinants to detailed examination of external influences on responsiveness. Human behaviour was extensively analysed in terms of the stimulus events that evoke it and the reinforcing consequences that alter it.

Traditional theories depicted learning as a consequence of direct experiences, whereas, in real life people learn at least as much by observing others as from experiencing something themselves. The importance of modelling became recognised as a part of *observational learning* which includes attentional processes (identifying the behaviour that one wants to model), retention processes (observation will be effective if the observer commits it to memory), motoric reproduction processes (reproducing the models behaviour will depend on the available skills of the observer), reinforcement and motivational processes (reproduction of learned behaviour from a model requires positive reinforcement which will result in observer's motivation to actually perform the desired behaviour).

If one tries to translate this into a practical learning situation, then it will be soon realised that just providing a 'model' is not enough to create similar behavioral patterns in others. On the other hand, a model who repeatedly demonstrates desired responses, instructs others to reproduce them, physically prompts the behaviour when it fails to occur, and then administers powerful rewards, will eventually elicit matching responses in most observers. The crucial factor in this process is "repeatedly', which may mean anything from few to hundreds of demonstrations.

Reward is, however, only one of the many reinforcers that affect the outcome of a learning experience. Often, the negative reinforcers are as effective, such as punishment for the absence of a certain behaviour. Reinforcement control plays an important part as a behaviour modification technique, based on the assumption that behaviour is controlled by its consequences which can include direct experiences or symbolic social reinforcements. Some of the symbolic social reinforcements include approval of others, money, social success, etc.

It is not, however, possible to explain all human behaviour in terms of external stimulus conditions and response consequences. A number of *cognitive* factors play an important part in deciding what one observes, feels, and does in certain situations and at certain times. Cognition plays an important part in recognising the links between stimuli and responses, and between the responses and the consequences as reinforcements.

Another aspect of cognitive control is the role *belief* plays in the interpretation of experiences or observations. Very often the belief about a consequence overrides the actual experiences or observations of a consequence. One can, therefore, modify the statement that behaviour is controlled by its immediate consequences and replace it with 'anticipated' consequences. Belief and actuality do not always correspond and this is an area in which learning can produce important results. Social learning is a dynamic process based on a continuous interaction between behaviour and its controlling conditions. It is a two-way causal process between the environment and the individual where one forms the other and is in return formed by the other.

Communication

There are many different ways of defining the concept of communication depending on the branch of science involved (engineering, sociology, psychology, linguistics etc.).

More recently a new approach in the study of communication has been based on some developments in the field of communication engineers, which resulted in the recognition of a new concept of 'information theories'. In terms of the latter " *communication is said to occur when a source of messages transmits signals over a channel to a receiver at the destination. The transmitted signals usually have representative function and are combined according to rules agreed upon in advance by the source and the destination"* . This explanation can include not only human but other types of communication as for example a tracking system which located the position of an object and transmits information to a missile for its destruction. This approach also forms the basis for the more recent developments in computer sciences and computer-based information-processing systems (McQuail,1976,1981; De Sola Pool,1973; Hovland,1973; Smith,A.G.,1966).

In terms of health promotion and education, communication is interpreted as meaning an interaction between an individual with another individual, a group or a whole society. In this sense it is a part of human behaviour and social interaction and encompasses both the verbal and non-verbal means of communication and the relevant theories developed in these areas.

The simple approach of telling people what is best for them in the hope that they will heed the advice is no longer sufficient. This complexity is also reflected in the analysis of the communication process as one of the central factors in health promotion and education.

To understand the different ways the concept of communications has been studied, it will be useful to examine some of the models researchers have developed and which have been used in planning health education interventions.

1. The engineering model

Studies of communication have been closely related to the development of communication technology. The earliest formal model of a communication system was an engineering one, consisting of such parts as the sender (coding) the channel (decoding) and the receiver. This approach was later adopted by social scientists in their studies.

The engineering model was designed to answer such questions as: who sends the message, why has it been sent, how has it been sent, what has been sent, with what effect and to whom. It takes as the basis the situation where A sends a message to B using a channel of communication. Laswell (1948) described this model as providing an answer to the question "Who says what to whom, by what means and with what effect". Shannon and Weaver (1949) were the first to develop an underlying theory and an explanatory model:

```
SOURCE
(MESSAGE)
TRANSMITTER
SIGNAL              (SENT - RECEIVED)
RECEIVER                 NOISE
(MESSAGE)
DESTINATION
```

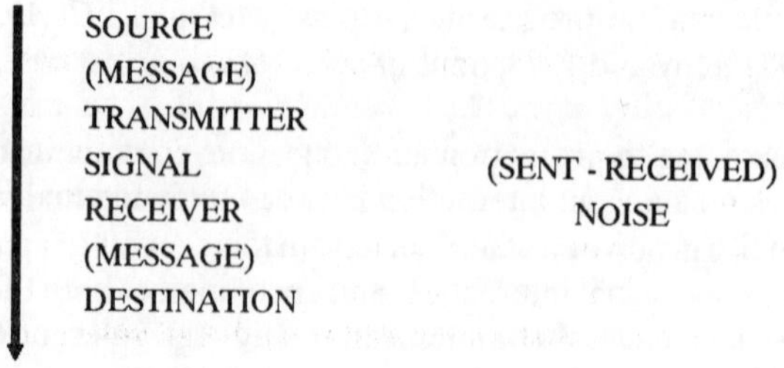

Diagram 3 Engineering Model of Communication

fect". Shannon and Weaver (1949) were the first to develop an underlying theory and an explanatory model:

The appeal of this model was in its contribution to the rapidly growing interest in the effects and effectiveness of communication, using as its theoretical basis the then popular stimulus-response model of behaviour control and learning, and providing a basis for the development of a new scientific discipline of communication.

For a long time this model was considered satisfactory because it took into consideration a whole variety of problems which could occur in any part of the system and cause a breakdown in the communication process.

As a result of such an approach one becomes sensitised to such problems as the social distance between the sender and the receiver, as for example due to their parochial as compared to cosmopolitan orientation to health care. The postulated difference is the social group orientation compared to individual orientation to medical care. The model postulates that the patient (parochial orientation) can be characterised by a high level of ethnic exclusivity, friendship solidarity, family tradition and respect for authority, whereas the doctor (cosmopolitan) will score low on each of these characteristics. On the other hand, the patient as opposed to the doctor will score low on his/her knowledge about disease, and will score high on scepticism of medical care and dependency in illness.

One has also become aware of the role of noise or confusing issues in reducing the effectiveness of communication. The message that A sends to B may differ from the message that B receives from A about a subject X (the A-B-X model of noise). The distortion may be due to noise which can be described as follows:

a. *syntactic noise*, such as electrical distortion on the phone, a torn page in a book, etc., or in more general terms any structural difference between the message sent and the message received;

b. *semantic noise*, or the different meaning given to the message by the receiver as compared with the intentions of the sender (a statement about age can be interpreted as a compliment or an offence).

c. *pragmatic noise*, due to conflicting messages such as simultaneous news of a war and a peace movement, or in general terms anything that appears in a message or its environment that was not produced by the sender and that decreases the probability of the receiver responding in the way intended by the sender.

In this way, noise can be considered as a negative factor hindering successful communications.

On the other hand a contributing factor that came to light when applying the engineering model is the role of "redundancy" or repetition of the message or its parts. One can again differentiate between:

a. *syntactic redundancy,* characterised by signs and symbols which are included in the message although they could be anticipated or the message could be understood without it (IOU or "I owe you"; a saying such as "A stitch in time..."etc.)

b. *semantic redundancy,* which arises from the use of synonyms and it has been shown that the more different expressions on uses for the same thing, the better will the message be understood;

c. *pragmatic redundancy,* which has so far been neglected as a research topic and which examines the proportion of signs and symbols that can be omitted without changing the receiver's response.

In addition to this more mechanical approach, studies have also been concerned about the beliefs and meanings as a part of the communication process. The questions of whether the sender chooses to send a message to the receiver, what kind of message he/she will send, as well as the response of the receiver have been examined by using the P-O-X model (where P is the sender, O is the receiver and X is the message). The model postulates that the sending of the message will depend on:

- P beliefs about X (structural and functional properties of the message)

- P attitude towards X (the feeling and the value placed on X)

- P beliefs about O (how will the receiver react to the

message).

The response to the message by the receiver will depend on:

- O beliefs about X

- O attitude towards X

- O beliefs about P

- O attitude towards P

To determine to what extent the message as such influences the effectiveness of a communication process one has developed special techniques, such as content analysis, which enables an objective and systematic identification of specific characteristics of the message. Studies using content analysis have explored, for example, the effects of knowledge of facts about cancer as a part of a message on the reduction of fear experienced by the receiver, the fear being a recognised inhibiting factor in the utilisation of preventive services in the cancer field. The terminology used became recognised as an important factor in the effectiveness of a message, and to analyse it more objectively one has also developed semantic differential testing of the text.

2. The two-step flow model

Whereas the engineering model has been found useful in describing the two-person communication, it was not very useful in describing the processes involved in mass media communication. Katz and Lazarsfeld (in McQuail,1981) developed a two-step flow model to explain the processes involved in mass media communication. They found that the engineering model was inadequate to represent accurately the social reality of a mass audience and the process of opinion formation. They produced a two-step flow model based on the concept of opinion leaders. From their research into political opinion formation during a presidential campaign in which the main emphasis was on the use of mass media, they concluded that the *flow of information was from the medium (radio) to the opinion leaders and from them to the less active section of the population.* One can summarise their findings, that according to this model, mass media do not operate in a social vacuum but have an input into a very complex web of social relationships and compete with other sources of ideas, knowledge and power. Subsequently the idea of opinion leaders has been changed into gate keepers, or people who hold the key into a community and are influential in forming the social norms of that community.

3. Other models

As can be seen, the engineering model has been pushed as far as it will go, developing specific theories for the interrelationship between the various parts. With the expansion of the scope of research into communication and the shift from engeneers to social scientists, one can say that today the engineering model cannot be considered sufficiently general to explain all the problems entailed in the process of communication.

More recent studies have concentrated on the language as one of the prerequisites for successful communication. This resulted in the further development of the study of different aspects of human communication: (a) *syntactics*, or the way the signs (words) are related to each other (by position, expression and the direction the message travels); (b) *semantics*, or the study of how the signs (words) are related to objects, including the study of the meaning of words in different cultural settings; and (c) *pragmatics*, or the study of how people react to and interpret different signs (words). All these aspects are closely inter-related and cannot be treated separately.

As the form of language became one of the focal points in communication studies one gained new insight into the problem area. Studies concerned with language acquisition have drawn the attention to the possibility of a restricted period in human development during early childhood (Piaget,1973; Oates,1979; Pride&Holmes,1972; Dittmar,1976), which is optimal for language acquisition with consequential speech difficulties in later life if there is some developmental disruption during this period.

Other research studies have highlighted the differentiation in the type of code (elaborated or restricted) transmitted during socialisation according to the social class and school environment of the receiver.

Some studies have been concerned with the acquisition of language by trying to establish the existence of an universal "language acquisition device" (LAD) inherent in every human being, which would account for underlying similarities of different languages and explain the process of the child's speedy language learning, a fact that cannot be explained satisfactorily by behaviorist learning theories.

The advent of computers suggested new models such as the cybernetic model which is characterised by its feed-back mechanism. Following this model, communication has been considered as an interaction process instead of the unidirectional transmission of messages.

Even more recently zoologists and ethologists contributed to this field with the studies of animal communications (from insects to primates) in the hope that this might provide some better understanding of this process among human beings.

Socialisation

A birth of a child can be considered from two different points of view: from the point of view of the society into which the child has been born and from the point of view of the child itself. For society is implies providing ways and means of integrating the child into the existing social system with the fewest possible disruptions and threats to the system, whereas for the child it implies activating all the inherited biological and psychological attributes for the purpose of understanding the surrounding world and adjusting to its demands as well as learning how to cope with it, for the sole reason for survival (Berger&Luckman,1967; Dager,1971; Danziger,1970; Denzen,1977).

Although there is no generally accepted single definition of society, for our purpose it will suffice to describe it as an "aggregate of human beings of both sexes and all ages bound together into self-perpetuating group and possessing its own more or less distinctive institutions and culture...." (Gould & Kolb, 1964, pp.674). *Culture* consists of patterns of behaviour, constituting the distinctive achievements of human groups, including their embodiments and artifacts, as well as ideas and their attached values. *Value* denotes the shared cultural standards according to which the objects of attitudes, desires and needs can be compared and judged.

1. *Institutions*

Because society is a self-perpetuating system, ways and means have been evolved to ensure continuity. The social environment, with its stability, is man-made and not based on any biological determinants. Because of the instability of the human organism it becomes imperative to provide a stable social environment with a well defined *social order*, which is again the product of men's activities and not based on any 'natural laws'.

To explain the 'social order' into which a man is born, and which he considers to exist outside him as an *objective reality* in spite of the fact that it has been created by man in the first place, it will be necessary to trace the way an activity becomes institutionalised.

When a human activity is repeated frequently and produces desired results with an economy of effort it becomes *habitualised*. Although man has drives which if not satisfied create tensions, he must learn the way of satisfying them and thus relieving such tensions. Habitualisation provides the direction and specialisation of activity which can reduce the accumulated tensions that result form *undirected drives*. By following habitualised behaviour, the need for *decisions* is reduced because of preset patterns of behaviour for certain standard situations. Habitualisation also implies that the same pattern of behaviour can be applied in any future situation. By reducing tensions and the need for decisions, habitualisation supports the stability of the external world, frees man for experimentation with new solutions bringing about innovations, and creates the basis for the *predictability* of human behaviour. When habitualised behaviour becomes a part of a social interaction and when there is reciprocal typification of habitualised behaviour between several actors engaged in a social interaction, then such habitualised behaviour becomes *institutionalised*.

Institutionalised behaviour in a society deals with some basic problems of that society. In this sense reciprocally typified behaviour represents the institutions of that society. Some of the most common areas of institutionalised behaviour in any society include language, work, sexuality and territoriality. Institutions involve the regulation of an individual's behaviour according to some definite pattern, including a normative ordering and regulation, upheld by sanctions which support these norms.

Thus, by definition, institutions *control* human conduct by setting predetermined patterns of behaviour. Control raises the problem of an individual's compliance or deviance from the existing norms. The mechanism of sanctions in case of *deviance* is generally described as the system of *social control*.

2. Aims of socialisation

The aim of an ongoing social system is to integrate new members in the most efficient way and to ensure that they fit into the existing structure without any danger of disruptions.

Human drives can give rise to undisciplined behaviour which ignores future consequences in favour of immediate and possibly transient gratification. Since one of the main prerequisites for harmonious and successful social interaction is predictability, the main aim of socialisation is to inculcate basic *disciplines*, which will result in disciplined behaviour, which includes the restriction of immediate gratification by postponing, foregoing or modifying actions for the benefit of future gains. These disciplines include a wide range of behaviour from the toilet training of small children to future orientation with new respect to education and employment.

Discipline in itself is limiting and cannot be sustained without some future goals. It is, therefore, necessary for socialisation to instil *aspirations* which will reflect these future goals according to the openness of the society. Aspirations instilled through socialisation will be related to a whole set of characteristics such as sex, social class, religion, etc.

For the individual to be able to relate to certain aspirations it will be necessary for socialisation to provide him with a sense of *identity*, which will either encourage or discourage him in trying to achieve the goals set for himself. The rigidity and limitation of choice concerning future aspirations according to a person's identity will depend on the social system in question. Industrialised Western societies are characterised by a large degree of choice for the individual, which weakens his sense of identity because of less securely fixed aspirations. It also means that since socialisation lasts longer, complete identity is achieved later in life than in some simple societies. The time until this identity is achieved can be troublesome, as is the case with teenagers in our society.

A person activates his identity in societal terms by taking over certain *social roles*, the performance of which he learns through socialisation. Together with roles he acquires accompanying *attitudes*. Attitudes provide the individual with inwardly felt emotions and sentiments which provide internal constraints and a conscience about what is right and what is wrong. Often social roles require more than just the right sentiments. In that case socialisation teaches the individual *skills* necessary for the fulfilment of his role without which he would not be able to fit into the society. In complex societies, characterised by division of labour, these skills are inculcated through formal education.

In this way socialisation represents the important instrument of social control, by means of which societies ensure that the newly integrated individuals conform to social norms inherent in the institutions of the relevant society.

Furthermore, to ensure that the socialised individual internalises the right meaning attached to the relevant behavioral patterns, as well as to counteract any questioning on his part, if he deems it appropriate, the social system includes *legitimation* as a device to maintain the taken for granted reality of the society. This means that the fundamental structures of a society within which the social experiences take place are not questioned but are accepted as seemingly natural and self-evident conditions of everyday life. This is achieved by the legitimising of the explanations and justification of social institutions. This need arises because of one of the main characteristics of institutions, which is their *historicity*. Institutions exist before a person is born and will be there long after he dies. They are handed over in terms of a tradition, without the person's awareness of how and why they were evolved. For him to understand and accept this, it is necessary to provide him with an interpretation which is approved or legitimised by the society. Although the "legitimised" version of the explanation of an institutional order is based on theories, the individual need not be aware of any theoretical basis and accepts it as a part of his general "knowledge". This pre-theoretical knowledge is very often expressed in terms of "what everybody knows" or commonsense. And this is what differentiates an ordinary person from a social scientist: although both live in the society and are acted upon and in turn act on the institutions of that society, the ordinary person takes it for granted, whereas the social scientist is interested in the theories that lie behind it or develops new theories that explain it better.

3. *Reality*

Institutions - evolved through interaction of individuals - for every new member born into that society, become the *objective reality* that confronts him as an external and coercive fact. Such a world becomes a 'social world' in terms of comprehension and firmness it achieves in a person's consciousness. For a child it becomes the 'real' world and is not easily changed by individual efforts. By internalising such an objective reality the child develops his *subjective reality*, which represents his personal interpretation of the world around him.

The adjustments between the objective and subjective realities is the central part of the process of socialisation. Because the objective reality of the outside world undergoes constant changes, and because human biological development continues after birth and represents a long-term process, every viable society must develop procedures for reality-maintenance to maintain the symmetry between the objective and the subjective reality.

Because of new marginal experiences, new knowledge and new interpretations of existing knowledge, the maintenance of objective reality as inevitable is being constantly threatened. Since society cannot rely on the chance that the individual will be successful in adjusting the balance between the objective and subjective reality, it had to develop more reliable procedures. These can be differentiated as routine and crisis maintenance procedures.

Routine in general terms is considered to be the process by which something is made to be everyday. The sociologist Weber (1970) used it to explain the role of a charismatic leader in a society. Once a charismatic leader achieves recognition, status and material gains as well as a set of followers, the tendency is for him to have his position 'legitimised'. Genuine charisma opposes it and rests upon the legitimation of personal characteristics. And yet, through the routinisation of charisma, this personal aspect diminishes, and ensures the opportunities for the successor of such a charismatic leader. In this way the charismatic aspects of leadership are lost, to become part of the structure of the new social order.

In terms of socialisation, when certain habitualised activities become widely shared among a large number of people, they become taken-for-granted routines. Each action stops being a source of speculation and astonishment and becomes a part of everyday life. Generally speaking, people only stop to think when, for one reason or another, the routine of their life becomes interrupted by something they consider to be a problem. Because of this we can say that most of man's thinking is devoted to problem-solving.

Routines remain functional in supporting the objective reality only as long as they enjoy social *support*. This support is mediated through *significant others* with the help of 'less important' others acting as a 'chorus'. Both play an important part in a person's everyday life by re-affirming his subjective reality and its conformity to the objective reality of his social world. By providing social support for routine reality-maintenance, a society makes provisions for preventing major upheavals of the system and insures smooth running of the everyday life.

There are, however, situations when this smooth running can be disrupted by some unforeseen event. To avoid undesirable repercussions for the whole system, society makes provisions for *crisis maintenance* of reality. The social processes are the same as in routine maintenance except that reality confirmation has to be explicit and more intensive. In some cases *rituals* come into play, and if the crisis is extensive enough, the whole society, and not only individuals, may participate in activities aimed at reality maintenance. Collective rituals for reality-maintenance can become institutionalised for some specific crisis as for example in case of a war.

If the objective reality has undergone drastic enough changes, which do not allow readjustments through routines or rituals of the subjective reality, then the society must make provisions for *resocialisation* of the individual. The process resembles that of primary socialisation since it has to readjust the subjective reality. It is different from that of primary socialisation, since it does not start from nothing and involves relearning with all its inherent problems. To be effective, resocialisation must include the affective aspect of primary socialisation. The new reality can be successfully mediated by significant others with whom the individual must establish strongly affective identification. This implies that the subjective reality can be transformed either partially and gradually or totally. Total transformation is called *alternation* and can only be achieved by including both social and conceptual conditions.

4. *The process of socialisation*

In simple social systems of 'primitive' societies, the objective reality internalised during early childhood does not change much. As the child grows up, the skills and knowledge acquired during childhood usually suffice for its future roles in that society. In the complex systems of industrialised societies, the period of acquisition of special skills and knowledge extend into adulthood. Because of this we can differentiate two qualitatively diverse aspects of socialisation: primary and secondary or formal socialisation.

Primary socialisation takes place within the family into which a child is born, lasts from birth through early childhood and includes learning sequences which are socially defined. These learning sequences are based on biological growth and are differentiated according to sex and various social characteristics of the family.

Through primary socialisation the child internalises the values and norms mediated through significant others, who in this case are parents or parent substitutes. The first institution with which the child comes in contact, and is aware of, is language, without which socialisation would be greatly limited. (Although the family is the first institution the child comes into contact with, it does not become aware of this until much later). For the child there is no choice of significant others or of the social world it enters, and at first the family represents the totality of 'his world'. The main characteristic of primary socialisation is the child's identification with significant others with whom it develops very strong affective relationship. This is the period when attitudes are formed. The values, norms, routines, attitudes and habits internalised during that period, because of their affective aspect, are of a lasting nature and can be changed in later years only with great difficulty and by means of special processes. *Secondary or formal socialisation* takes place during later parts of childhood and adolescence as well as early adult years.

Because of the division of labour and differentiation of social roles, there is a need for social distribution of skills and knowledge in a society. In this way an individual acquires role-specific skills, knowledge and specific languages, and is able to take his place in that society. The main characteristic of secondary socialisation process is the lack of emotional involvement (with certain exceptions) with the agent of socialisation who has usually a socially recognised and formally legitimised role in that society. The process is characterised by formality and anonymity, and usually includes a ritual aimed at legitimising the new status acquired by the individual. The best example is the child's schooling, carried out in formally recognised schools, by teachers, transmitting special skills and knowledge for the fulfilment of future roles, and including examinations and formal ceremonies of graduation on completion of the process.

Sometimes an important aspect of secondary or formal socialisation is anticipatory socialisation, which can also be described as the positive orientation of individuals to non-membership groups. Individuals who adopt the values of a group to which they do not belong, but to which they aspire, are considered to be undergoing *anticipatory socialisation*. The system may make provisions for anticipatory socialisation as in the case of medical students. They spend some time during their formal education in hospitals, stay with general practitioners and, generally speaking, learn how to act and behave like the doctors with whom they identify.

In this case anticipatory socialisation is considered to be functional, whereas, in a closed system, where the individual cannot gain acceptance of the new group and loses his place in the old one, it would be dysfunctional. This is the case of the marginal man who does not fully belong to any specific group. From the standpoint of the group which the person is aiming to leave, anticipatory socialisation can be dysfunctional, whereas from the point of view of the society, it is functional, because it recognises the structure and a positive orientation to certain out-group norms.

5. *The biological basis*

Darwin's theory of evolution has had repercussions in many other fields in addition to biology. One of them has been sociology, where the concept of instincts has been used to account for human behaviour. The existence of societies was explained by a herding instinct, property by an acquisitive instinct, competition and wars by an aggressive instinct, etc. After a while the emphasis changed from instincts which could not explain many complex patterns of human behaviour to the concept of drives. Today the concept of instincts is mainly used to describe animal behaviour, and it is considered to contain both the impulse and the programmed behavioral pattern of satisfying it. (A bird has an instinct to build a nest as well as a biologically fixed behavioral pattern of how to build it.)

Humans have a number of reflexes (eye blinking) and certain needs expressed in drives (sex, hunger, shelter, etc.) but no programmed behavioral pattern of how to satisfy them. Human biological drives are considered to be organic tensions that are felt as discomfort or impulses but which do not direct behaviour towards specific goals or touch off a predetermined sequence of coordinated activities leading to that need-satisfaction (Broom and Selznick, 1973). In other words a drive implies activity but does not include a predetermined way of carrying it out.

Because of this, humans have to rely on his learning capacity and the process of socialisation does just that. Once this was realised, the idea that man is infinitely plastic became dominant, especially after certain experiments (Pavlov) showed that some basic animal instincts could be manipulated. The idea that expressed needs, except those related to survival, are a product of socialisation, as for example in the case of a baby in distress, where the need was considered to be hunger and not the contact with the mother. However, more recent experiments with Rhesus monkeys (Harlow & Harlow, 1965) have shown that there is a need for social contact as a strong biological imperative in monkey infants. Lack of satisfaction of this need can result in behavioral aberrations and in adults can be manifested as the inability to mate and take care of the offspring. Not only is there a biological need for social contact with a mother or mother substitute, but also for infant-infant contact, the lack of which can destroy the ability for adequate adult heterosexual behaviour. These findings of studies with animals are supported by findings in the studies of certain cases where the child was found to have been deprived or sustained human contact. In addition, a 'development quotient' has been established which can be used to measure the level of social adjustment of a child. Human infants have a relatively long period of dependence and sexual immaturity compared with most animals, and this characteristic provides the necessary time for socialisation to take place. However, the basic preconditions for socialisation are his ability to learn, the capacity to use language with an accompanying high level of intelligence, together with the biological drive for social contact.

There is, however, a certain amount of disagreement between psychologists and psychoanalysts in their interpretation of human drives. Levine (1973) summarises different approaches, starting with Freud who postulated that human drives are potentially disruptive to social life and the aim of socialisation is to tame and channel them into socially useful forms. The cost of harnessing various drives can be seen in various neurotic symptoms. Freud sees few compatibilities between the individual and the society. Hartman and others present a more complex view of socialisation, allowing room for neutralising drive energy in ways which need not be disruptive for the social organisation, and the socialisation of the child is seen as including the development of adaptive qualities that will serve himself as well as the society. Psychoanalytic behaviorism is an even more complex version of that basic idea. It has had the greatest influence on the study of socialisation: the child's primary (innate) drives form the basis for his later social adjustment by acting as reinforcers for socially valued habits and for the acquisition of secondary (acquired) drives that reinforce a wide variety of positive social behaviour, including the internalisation of models for the appropriate fulfilment of different social roles. The emphasis is on drives as reinforcers and not only as the cause of conflict.

6. *Internalisation of norms*

Cook (1973) reviews various theories developed with the aim of explaining the ways in which a child internalises the social order into which it has been born. He begins with Durkheim's model of internalisation of cultural norms and social controls: the conduct of society could only be achieved through its ability to exert an incontrovertible force on the shaping of its component individuals. This implies that people do not comply with social norms out of choice but out of necessity. He cites Wrong's concept of the 'oversocialised man' as a warning that the postulate: "adequate socialisation is achieved when society's requirements become the socialised man's requirements" could be a dangerous oversimplification, since a perfect fit can never be achieved. Because of this, socialisation continues throughout a man's life and is never complete. Based on Durkheim's basic idea a number of different theories of the child's acquisition of the sociomoral order are reviewed:

a. The Freudian theory of child development is the oldest and had most impact on research in child-rearing carried out by psychologists and anthropologist. Freud provided an answer to Durkheim's problems of how the moral regulations of the society become constituent parts of the individual psyche. It is based in the constant conflict between the individual's instincts and the demands of the society. There are two features of Freud's theory that have been most influential for studies of socialisation: the concept of identification which can be equated with the process of learning, and the critical stages of personality.

b. The social (reinforcement) learning perspective has contributed most in the last decade towards research into the child's acquisition of morality. The concept of identification has been reinterpreted in behaviorist terms, and most of the studies have been concerned with the influence of differing environmental conditions for learning provided by different parental practices. One of the most influential approaches for the explanation of how a child internalises social norms has been by means of role theory, social reinforcement theory, the frustration-aggression thesis and from other child development theories.

c. The cognitive-developmental perspective is based on Piaget's theory (1959) of the child's moral judgment and has been influential in increasing concern with cognitive socialisation. It is based on studies of moral development, and postulates that for a child to develop internalised moral standards it is necessary for these changes to be accompanied by cognitive growth. The theory has been criticised from several points of view, one being the problem of differentiation between the child's ability to understand behaviour, rules and principles while not being able to reproduce them, which has been the critical question for research in child socialisation in general. The research, following Piaget's theory has been mainly concerned with testing the suggested stages of moral development and with examining the more complex social relationships and their meaning for morality. Piaget has not been happy with the direction recent research, based on his theory, has been taking especially the emphasis given to verbal methods, since the child learns practically all the social rules through verbal means.

d. The social competence (role theory) perspective differs from other theories by focusing on child's ability to perform social roles with approval. Brim has suggested that there are two aspects to child's role learning: he must understand the focal statuses of the society so that he can understand his position vis-a-vis them, and he must learn how to perform his roles, including both the required actions and accompanying feelings. The problem for researchers lies in the definition of various roles, which must precede any investigation.

In Cook's opinion, nearly all the theories mentioned are characterised by their underemphasis of the importance of language for socialisation, and the need for exploring this wide are is being suggested.

7. The agent

Most children in our society are born into a family and, therefore, the family is one of the main agents of primary socialisation. The parents, who compose the primary family together with the children, create the social environment, represent the significant others, creating in this way the child's outside world. The parents create the framework of values and norms which the child internalises to become his own.

Because of this, the position of the family within the social structure of the society is significant, since it will to a great extent, decide the future of the child. It will influence the kind of values, norms, attitudes and behaviour the child will internalise during its successful socialisation.

One of the most influential factors concerning the position of the family will be its socio-economic status. It will be reflected in the values and norms, and it will influence his future orientation, career, education, peer groups as well as his attitudes and personality traits. It will also influence the way the child will present itself and interrelate with the outside world. The socio-economic group of the family is included in the social class to which the family belongs. It is closely linked with the occupation of the head of the family and represents a sub-culture with specific values and norms. The differences between social classes affect the way the child is nourished, brought up, the kind of relations it will have with its parents and siblings, with whom and in what way it will fear and respect and in particular the language in which the process of socialisation takes place.

There are, however, certain differences in socialisation of children, even within one family. Some differences are obvious, such as defined by the sex of the child, whereas others are more subtle, such as between the first born and subsequently born children. In this way a family, as the most important agent of socialisation, has its own particular set of values and norms, which it filters through to its children in a selective and differentiated way.

Interviews and counselling

Interviews

If investigators are used to carry out a survey, they will be expected to interview a population sample (Atkinson, 1967) and it will be necessary to brief them about a number of issues:

     1. *familiarity with the instruments* - the investigators should be familiar with the instruments that they are expected to use in a survey

in terms of the way they should be completed, how far they should enter into discussion, and which comments they are allowed to make;

2. *gaining entrance* - once the population has been chosen and the addresses distributed among the investigators the actual survey will start by visiting the respondents. Before actually knocking on the door of a family or an individual it will be useful to find out certain things about that community, such as: what are the working hours, i.e. when can one expect the husband to return from work and when will the meal take place; what is the general pattern of work in a household; when do mothers spend most time with their babies; when do they do their housework, go shopping, visit friends etc.

One should not forget that an interview of this kind represents a relationship, the conditions of which should be negotiated. This means that the respondent should know what the interview will be about and should have a possibility to decline participation in it. It is important to bear in mind that the privacy of the respondent will be to a certain degree violated and that the respondent should have a feeling of some gain if and when allowing such an intrusion.

It helps if the investigator is recognised as an expert in the field of investigation (i.e. a health visitor in uniform) and can provide certain help and advice in addition to gaining information. The respondent should also be reassured about the confidentiality of the enquiry, anonymity of the respondent and the valid purpose of the study. In short, the respondent must get the feeling of certain gain from participation, of the right to refuse certain information and the value the investigator will give to the answers provided, respecting the integrity of the respondent's person and family.

In some cases the sex of the investigator will be of importance. This can be due either to gaining entrance into a home where the female respondent may be alone which in her case is not culturally acceptable, or because of the topic of investigation which may be offensive if presented by a male investigator to a woman or vice versa.

In such cases, one can either choose the appropriate sex of the investigator or ensure that the investigator is accompanied by a person of the appropriate sex.

The success of the interview will depend on the ability of the investigator to speak the language or use the terminology which is the respondent understands. One should also bear in mind that embarrassment could be caused due to the poor conditions in which the respondent lives, in which case the interview should take place on neutral ground and ensuring sufficient privacy;

3. *conducting interviews* - once the acceptance has been achieved the interview can take place.The important thing to look out for is the maintenance of continued interest of the respondent. Once this interest is lost one should either try to rekindle it or, if it does not work, one should stop and arrange for another meeting.

The best guarantee for the maintenance of interest will be the feeling of reciprocity on the part of the respondent. It will, therefore, be of great importance to encourage as many questions on the part of the respondent as there are answers expected from him/her. If there are no questions raised, this can be remedied by interrupting the interview from time to time and prompting for questions by the respondent.

There can be certain areas of enquiry which can be taboo or too sensitive for the respondent to discuss. The general areas of enquiry can be negotiated at the beginning of the interview. It should not, however, be taken for granted that a general agreement at the start will ensure full participation to the end of the interview. The respondent may not understand what is involved, may change his/her mind halfway through the interview or simply become bored and lose interest. This may be awkward, since this may involve several visits and one should be able to judge the sincerity of excuses given for pulling out on the part of the respondent. If the excuse is not serious one can discuss the continuation, but if it is serious, too great a pressure may create a feeling of guilt or intimidation with the respondent, thus creating more damage than the exercise is worth.

It can be envisaged that during the study of an individual respondent or a family a certain degree of dependence is being created, especially if the respondent is made to feel inadequate due to ignorance, poor conditions or lack of available resources.

It will be of greatest importance to introduce each topic tactfully and limit it to the level of the respondent without indiscriminately asking questions for which the answers are obvious.

When interviewing mothers with children, it could easily happen that a child will be present at the interview. The child should not be disregarded and the interviewer should not show impatience with any possible interruption, nor make the respondent feel that the interview is more important than the wellbeing of the child. If other members of the household are present, their contribution should be taken into account as well as the answers of the respondent, because they will influence those answers. In that case such additional contributions should be noted on the questionnaire.

If a return visit is planned the interview should be conducted in such a way that it does not endanger the willingness of the respondent to be visited again.

4. *conclusion of interviews* - it is as important to take care about the way an interview is concluded as about the way it is started and carried out. One should bear in mind that the visit of the interviewer could represent an exciting event which will be discussed among friends and relatives. The impression made and the conduct of the investigator will be critically assessed and success of one interview will possibly affect all the other interviews if one works in a close knit community.

In addition to influencing the chances of success of the study as whole the conclusion of an interview will be of importance for each family or individual and great care should be taken that one does not leave the respondent with a feeling of inadequacy, guilt, shame, resentment or feeling that they wasted time due to the way the interview is conducted or the behaviour of the interviewer. The respondent should be left with a feeling of satisfaction and sense of gain, stimulated sufficiently to be willing to participate in any future health education or health promotion programme.

At the end of the interview the respondent should be reassured about the privacy and confidentiality of the information. No doubt should exist about the possibility of the information given being misused or discussed with unauthorised persons. There is sometimes doubt that the information could end in the wrong hands since most of the studies are sponsored or carried out by some official organisation or institution. The respondent should be reassured that no one will have access to the answers of any individual case and that only the aggregated answers will be published, which excludes the possibility of identifying the respondent.

Counselling

The usual context of a doctor-patient interaction is that the patient notices certain symptoms which usually mean the presence of a disease and seeks medical help. The doctor is usually in the situation to treat the patient and cure the disease, or in rare situations, where there is no cure the doctor may be able to alleviate the condition. The division of labour was more or less clearly defined with the medical profession treating the disease or alleviating the condition, and the social workers dealing with ensuing social and emotional problems of the patients.

With the advent of AIDS this demarcation line has been blurred and the medical profession finds itself increasingly in the position of entering into the "counselling" relationship with the patients and their families. Once this need has been identified, it became clear that the medical and paramedical professions need to acquire the skills of counselling, which is a professional activity.

1. *General aspects*

The definition of behavioral counselling: *it is a process of helping people to learn how to solve certain interpersonal, emotional and decision problems* (Krumboltz & Thorsen ,1976). The key word in the definition is "learning" which implies that counselling is about helping the clients to learn. The clients can learn certain skills or how to acquire certain competence in dealing with problems.

The word "behavioral counselling" indicates that the result of counselling is a change in behaviour. Another key word is "how to solve" which implies that the aim of counselling is to enable the clients to become independent and self-relient problem solvers.

The clients' independence will be manifested in their ability to give up their dependence on the counsellor. In this way the clients can become more self-reliant and independent, able to solve their own problems. The other key words are "certain....problems" which implies that the clients must learn to accept that not all the problems can be solved, or solved by clients alone.

The counsellors can help clients in a number of problem areas such as improving their interpersonal relationships, solve some emotional problems, learn about problem solving and decision making. They can learn to change some habits such as smoking, overeating and taking better care of their bodies. They can learn how to overcome shyness, stress and depression, sexual dysfunctions, alcoholism, compulsive gambling, drug abuse, as well as fears and anxieties. Because of the great variety of the problems, counsellors must specialise and in that way will become experts in a narrow field of problems presented by clients.

The counsellors can be involved in helping people to solve problems which they present, or they can help people to prevent certain problems before they occur. They learn from their remedial work about the variety of problems which could have been avoided, and can become engaged in preventive counselling.

The main aim of counselling is twofold: the client should learn to make decisions wisely and to be able to change his/her own behaviour to produce desirable consequences. In this way the client will assume control over his/her own life.

One is faced with the question, why so many people do not have those skills and need help. The main reason is that these skills are a part of the socialisation process and have to be learned. The environment in which some people have grown up does not provide opportunities for learning such skills. For example, there are environments that do not provide individuals with sufficient rewards for certain kinds of behaviour.

Without such a reinforcement it is doubtful that a person will learn how to take control of his/her own life, and how to avoid feelings of powerlessness, depression and alienation.

The other reason is that in certain environments some forms of negative behaviour are accepted and reinforced. The consequence for a person is, that being "deviant" as far as the rest of the society is concerned, is normal and a person may not realise that there is a problem at all. In other environments excessive punishment may be used as a form of social control which can affect people with certain phobias or some form of deviant behaviour. The result may be hardening of such problems and increasing difficulty to ameliorate it. Some people may not have had the opportunity to learn to recognise signals or cues from the environment, indicating whether certain behaviour is appropriate or not. Without the sensitivity to read and react to social cues, a person may continue with a behaviour without realising that there is a need to change it.

One of the most crucial skills that a counsellor needs is to help the client in developing decision making skills, for which an eight step model has been evolved:

- Formulate the problem by specifying the client's goals and values;
- Commit time and effort;
- Generate alternative solutions;
- Collect information about the alternatives;
- Examine the consequences of the alternatives;
- Reevaluate goals, alternatives and consequences;
- Eliminate the least desirable alternatives until a tentative choice is made;
- Generalise the decision-making process to new problems.

In general terms one can define three main areas where counselling is being widely employed: in altering maladaptive behaviour (behavioral deficit or excess, inappropriate behaviour, fears and anxieties and physical problems), decision-making and prevention.

To deal with this range of problems, counsellors have at their disposal a great number of methods (over 30) which range from information-giving and relaxation to counterconditioning and token systems.

Some recent developments in counselling methods include: treating fears through experience as well as imagination, managing fears rather than avoiding them, coping models rather than mastery models, self-control rather than external control, covert and cognitive behaviour as well as overt, observable behaviour, prevention as well as remedial, etc. One of the main difficulties encountered in counselling is the formulation of goals from the problems presented: the problem is someone else's behaviour, the problem is expressed as a feeling, the problem is the absence of a goal, the problem is that the desired behaviour is undesirable, the problem is that the client does not know his behaviour is inappropriate, the problem is a choice conflict, the problem is a vested interest in not identifying any problems.

There have been situations in which people have helped others by talking to them and listening to their problems. Once this activity became formalised, the profession of counsellors was born. Since then a number of developments have occurred and the counselling activities have been shared among a number of professions such as social workers, doctors, nurses, dietitians,etc.

The main characteristics that all of them need to have include empathy, acceptance and genuineness. They need professional conduct and taking responsibility for the consequences of their work by keeping in touch with the clients until the solution of the problem is achieved. Since the counselling became recognised as a professional activity, people engaged in it needed special training.

There are a number professions that find themselves in the situation of being involved in counselling and there are a number of courses offering them such skills.

With the coming of AIDS, where the medical profession can offer, practically, very little help and hope, the main approach in dealing with potential or actual sufferers has been counselling. This resulted in a great increase in the number of people engaged in counselling and in a close cooperation between the medical profession and the social workers. More recently the counsellors have not been recruited only from the ranks of social workers and a number of voluntary workers have taken on this job, as well as members of specially created self-help groups.

This upsurge in the number of counsellors made counselling as a method of solving certain problems very much in demand and there are other areas of commerce or industry where the use counselling as a part of looking after the health of their workers. The most recent example of preventive counselling has been introduced by an industry as a service to employees who are facing redundancies and job loss. It was found that the fact of loosing a job is less stressful if the person in question can be adjusted to this fact with the help of a counsellor.

2. *Practical application*

The starting point in the counselling interaction is when the client presents his/her 'problem' which can be an undesirable habit, a crisis, an anxiety, a frustration, or any other kind of concern. This, however, is not a problem in the classical sense with an attached solution. It is more of a 'problem situation' which can be either changed or which demands that the client learns how to cope with it. This situation is often due to the missed opportunities or to unused potential of the client. In other cases, where there is no possibility of solving the problem, the helper will help the client to manage the situation better. In practice one can differentiate between stages through the helping process must pass in the process of finding a solution (Egan, 1986).

Stage I is concerned with identification of the problem by the client. It consists of a) telling the story; b) screening, focusing and clarifying the problem which is done by the client with the help of the helper; c) development of new perspectives on the problem.

Stage II is concerned with setting new goals based on the new action oriented understanding of the problem, selection of one of them as the result of the previous process of screening and focusing, and the development of a preferred scenario for action.

It consists of a) the choice of a new scenario; b) critical assessment of that scenario; c) choice and commitment to specific actions.

Stage III is concerned with the development and implementation of strategies for reaching the agreed upon goals. It consists of a) brainstorming possible strategies for the chosen action; b) formulating a plan for the implementation of these strategies; and c) the action or implementing the decisions and commitments made by the client.

This model is cumulative, since the success in stage II will depend on the success in stage I, and the stage III will depend on the successful completion of stages I and II. In other words, the stages are integral parts of a dynamic process of interaction, which should be considered as a whole and where the stages are differentiated for easier monitoring of the processes and the evaluation of outcomes.

It is important to bear in mind that the stages of the model presented should be treated as guidelines along which an interaction could progress. They should not be applied rigidly, since this could destroy the spontaneity of the clients involvement in solving his/her problem. The counsellor must have skills which will enable him/her to show empathy and explore the problems in greater depth; to confront the client with different aspects of the problem; and to move the client towards undertaking the agreed upon action.

The training of counsellors in the application of this approach includes the understanding of the procedure, observation of a skilled counsellor applying it in a real life situation, step-by-step supervised practice, and extended practice in real life situations.

Summary

As one can see, there are different ways knowledge can be transmitted and/or acquired, all of which include to a certain degree the process of communication between the source of information and the recipient. One of the main functions that communication performs is to enable people to learn. The content may be different, such as learning to survive in a physical and social environment, how to perform a job, bring up the new generation etc. This learning potential is the basis of any health promotion and education intervention as can be seen from a summary of the following facts:

1. Health education is concerned with various factors which can affect people's health and disease. It uses "medical models" to define the state of health and disease, and "psycho-social" models to define health edu-

cation interventions concerned with improvement of health and management, prevention and treatment of disease.

2. Health education interventions are usually aimed at increasing people's knowledge and skills relevant to the improvement of health and prevention, management and treatment of disease as far as it can be achieved by educational as compared to medical methods.

3. The educational methods are, therefore, concerned with actions and behaviour which are conducive to improvements in the state of health of individuals and populations. These actions and behaviours can be seen as a part of a life-style or can be dealt with specifically.

4. People's life-style is defined by the physical, social and cultural characteristics of the environment as well as by the individual's potential, his/her habits, routines and choices concerning the issues of health and disease.

5. One of the basic mechanisms in the acquisition, maintenance and changes in a life-style is due to human capacity for learning which is defined as "relatively permanent changes in behaviour potential occurring as the result of past experiences".

6. The first exposure to learning is described by theories related to "primary socialisation". They describe the processes a new-born baby activates to learn how to survive in a physical and social environment into which it is born and in which it grows up. This is followed by formal processes of education which is defined as socialisation for future roles and is also known as "secondary socialisation".

The changing "objective" reality in which a person lives may require certain readjustments which have been described as "resocialisation" and "anticipatory socialisation". In this way the socialisation theories describe the individual potential for learning and the social opportunities for this potential to be activated.

7. Psychologists have been continuously interested in the process of learning and have carried out a great number of experiments (on animal and human subjects) resulting in numerous theoretical explanations of this process. The approaches used cover classical and

instrumental conditioning, discrimination learning, serial learning, paired-associate learning, free recall, concept formation, problem solving and language acquisition.

8. Others (psychologists, sociologists, anthropologists and linguists) have been interested in factors which describe and underlie the commonly shared human potential for learning. They examined the processes of language acquisition, sensitive periods for specific learning, motivation, memory, as well as a number of medical conditions which impede the learning process or affect the existing knowledge and skills.

9. There is also a whole field of research concerned with behaviour modification with special emphasis on methods and outcomes of achieving modification and reinforcing its retention.Most of this work is based on learning theories supporting various methods of behaviour modification.

10. Health education is primarily interested in the early stages of learning during the process of primary socialisation when the basis for future life-style is laid and the existing objective reality is internalised as a person's subjective reality. This is expressed in numerous health education interventions concerned with improving family competence in bringing up their children and helping them to acquire knowledge and skills relevant to a healthy life-style as well as knowledge and skills related to prevention, management and treatment of disease.

11. The next phase of learning of interest to health education is during the process of secondary or formal socialisation when children learn among other things also the legitimised body of knowledge concerning health and disease based on rational explanations. This is expressed in numerous school health education programmes.

12. During a life-time a person is faced with a number of new situations and problems for which he/she must make rational choices as a part of their decision-making process. Health education programmes in this area are concerned with enabling people to make rational choices by minimising the cost and maximising the benefits of every action or decision.

The Group Approach

Most human activities take place in group settings. Health promotion and education can utilise group processes and mechanisms for the attainment of goals related to health improvement and disease prevention, management and treatment (Douglas,1970,1976; Klein,1963; Cartwright & Zander,1953; Dean&Rosen,1955; Thelan,1954; Moore,1987; Pfeiffer & Jones, yearly). There are different ways of classifying groups for the purpose of better understanding of group potential for health promotion and education: according to type of groups one can differentiate between

1. *existing groups* - such as families, school classes, professional groups etc; and

2. *created groups* - such as learning groups, decision and action groups, self-help groups, therapeutic groups, etc.

There are several important characteristics which should be taken into account when using a group method for the purpose of health promotion and education:

1. *group cohesiveness* - which denotes the attraction of its members and the possibility of member's identification with group values and goals;

2. *group pressures* - which influence members conformity to group values and norms and enable changes in attitudes and acceptance of group goals;

3. *group goals* - which can be imposed or shared and which will depend on members' commitment and actions;

4. *group structure* - which will help in understanding the power structure within the group, the communication processes and the role of leadership within a group.

Most social interactions take place in groups and a number of social and behavioral sciences have studied groups, resulting in the development of methodologies and a whole set of theoretical explanations concerning the structure, processes and outcomes of group interactions.

Large groups

People very often find themselves as members of some large group or gathering which meets for various reasons. Some of the most common reasons are:

Information

One aim of a large gathering or meeting can be to transmit information to a group of people about some issue, problem, event or topic of general interest. It usually takes the form of a meeting with a speaker as in the case of political gatherings; or it can take the form of a lecture given by a speaker on a specific topic. The advantages of this kind of interaction are the possibility to reach a large number of people in a limited space of time and with using only one speaker.

Knowledge

The transmission of knowledge in large groups is a very common occurrence. Most of the learning that takes place in schools is done in classes which represent a large group situation. The methods of transmission as well as assessment form the basis of our educational system.

Entertainment

Most entertainment which includes a live audience is performed in large groups. The processes involved are well known and tested by many entertainers who can measure their success by immediate feedback from the audience.

Sometimes, a large group can have all the three elements present: transmission of information, acquisition of knowledge and being entertained at the same time. This aspect is very important in evaluating large group performance and has to be reflected in the definition of the aims of that group to include all the three aspects. It could well happen that the success of a group aiming to transmit knowledge is assessed on the basis of its entertainment value.

Summary

Most large meetings do not produce decisions or commitments of the participants since they do not have a built in mechanism for member participation which is the basis for a decision making process. They also rarely have built in mechanisms for interacting and receiving feedback from members. The chairman can be the expert or can be accompanied by an expert who provides the contents of the lecture. The feed-back is usually restricted to inviting the members to 'ask questions' or 'give comments'. The response is limited to those who feel secure enough to stand out in a large meeting, or who feel that they know more than the expert and want to show it to others.

One way to enable the members of a large meeting to provide feedback is a method of participation known as 'Phillips 66'. The chairman asks the audience to form groups of 6 members sitting together, who turn to face each other and have 6 minutes to discuss the lecture and agree on the most important point they would like to make. The chairman then invites a representative of each group to present the point or raise the question from the group. In this way the chairman can ensure the feed-back from most of the audience, who will have a feeling of active participation in the meeting.

Another way to capitalise on the potential in the audience is to invite members with specific interest or expertise to form a sub-group or a sub-committee and thus ensure the continuation of work on the issues raised at the meeting.

In the past, large meetings gave way to group work as the method of preference, and were avoided by 'progressive' health education. Their importance is now realised, although for different purposes. They need to be seen as an important part of a selection of methods, especially for health promotion, and should be evaluated in that context.

Small groups

A person living in a society cannot avoid being a member of a number of small groups where the interaction between the members is more intense and the group membership can be of a lasting duration. Because of its pervasiveness, small group research or the study of group dynamics has been one of the major interests in social sciences as well as health education. There are a number of publications reporting the findings of such research and dealing with the group processes and mechanisms, as well as the behaviour of group leaders and members.

The leadership role has attracted special attention because the way a leader acts will reflect on the 'social atmosphere' in which the group members operate. One of the classic studies of leadership (White and Lippit, 1943) consisted of two experiments with three different types of leadership: democratic, authoritarian and laissez-faire. It showed a number of advantages of the democratic leadership in terms of group productivity and member satisfaction and was accepted as a model for the desired form of leadership. It may be of interest to note, that the two experiments were carried out on a very small number of subjects: the first experiment was carried out in two boys' clubs (each 5 members) and the second on four groups of ten year old boys, each having 5 members who met after school to engage in hobby activities. Although the value of the findings could be questioned because of small numbers, the idea caught on and for decades dominated the group work method by emphasizing the advantages of 'democratic' form of leadership. Since then many other studies have examined the role of the leader and recognised the complexity of processes which depend on leader's actions or lack of them.

Other studies have examined the different types of behaviour of members and classified it into constructive, destructive and nuisance types. Studies have also looked at the level of group productivity, at groups as means for attitude change of its members, and the advantages of group discussion with commitment as compared to discussion without it. One can experience the latter at any large conference, which must include obligatory group sessions. At the end of the conference, before the final report, group 'rapporteurs' are invited to present group reports which they have prepared with great personal sacrifice (while other members have an evening out) and in a record short time. These reports become a part of the conference document, have no influence on the conference as such and mostly represent an exercise in paying lip-service to the democratic procedure. There are few conferences where the group reports form the feed-back to the organisers, and where the organisers have the flexibility to change the programme to accommodate the new ideas or demands raised in groups. In practical terms the success of a group will depend on the leader and the members, and their interaction on the road to reaching the agreed upon goal(s).

1. *The role of the leader*

A successful leader of a group will be aware of the important processes that can enable or hinder group work and should endeavour to facilitate them. The activities that help in organising group thinking include the leaders task to initiate new ideas or new approaches to the problem under discussion; the leader should help the members to clarify the problem so that everybody shares the same understanding of the topic under discussion; this can be enhanced by elaborating on the topic by raising some possible problems or aspects of the problem that nobody mentioned so far; and finally the leader should be able to summarise the discussion so far, bring the members back on the main track and review any decisions already made.

There are some activities that will improve the understanding of the problem or topic under discussion. These include fact-seeking or asking questions which enable the members to provide the group with relevant facts; getting below the surface of the problem by analysing the finer details which will be relevant to the expected actions; activating members of the group to bring out their knowledge and experiences.

Some activities are important for the maintenance of group solidarity and progression towards the set goal. They include encouraging the members to participate not disregarding the shy and quite members; appreciating the contributions and praising the constructive members;

encouraging self-discipline among the members which will prevent them from dominating, attacking or disregarding the needs of other members.

2. *The role of the observer*

In some groups a person is allocated the role of the observer, who usually withdraws from participating in the group work and observes what is going on. The observations will include the performance of the leader, the participation of the members, the progression towards the set goal, as well as the processes which have been activated during the working of the group. There are lists which include different facts to be observed and which the observer fills in during the sessions. At the end of each session, before the leader's summing up, the observer is invited to produce the observations made. They should be constructive, even if in some cases they may be critical. The aim of such observations is to contribute to the improvement of group work.

3. *The members*

One assumes that the people that find themselves as members of a group, want to be there and are motivated to participate actively in the group work. Not everybody is in a group for the same reason and the concept of 'hidden agendas' is important and should be taken into account by the leader. Some members may genuinely want to solve a problem, whereas some others may use the group for therapeutic reasons and try to solve some personality problems in that group situation.

The contribution of the members will depend on the roles they play within a group. These may differ according to personality traits of each individual. One can recognise certain typical characteristics (Strauss,1957) such as: the "pigeonholer", who is trying to bring order to group thinking by classifying and stratifying ideas and suggestions; the "hair-splitter" who is orderly-minded and must know the exact details of where everything fits; the "eager beaver", who is full of enthusiasm and comes up all the time with new enthusiastic suggestions and ideas; the "explorer", who is interested in every new idea, whether he/she knows anything about it or not; the "talker", who needs a lot of words to say something very simple; the "fence-sitter" who does not commit himself or herself to any ideas during the discussion but agrees with the winning one at the end; the "superior being", who has no patience with others and thinks he/she knows it all; the "doubting Thomas", who does not believe that anything could work; the "wise-cracker" who interrupts the discussion by telling jokes; the "dominator", who hogs the limelight and must be in the centre of group attention; the "manipulator", who flatters one side to gain advantage for an idea or attacks the other side by belittling their contributions; the "always vulnerable", who takes everything personally and defends himself/herself from any suggestion; the "blocker", who for some special reason does not want the group to succeed in a particular task and distracts the discussion with side issues.

Dealing with all the different types is the role of the leader who must find a balance between all the different personality traits and working styles to maximise the productivity of the group.

Family groups

Everybody is born into a family and in most cases creates a family of their own in later life. Family group is a situation where primary socialisation occurs and children learn how to survive in a social environment and acquire values, knowledge and skills relevant for their immediate and future roles. Because of this the competence of a family to raise a healthy new generation is very important and has been the target for health promotion and health education for a long time.

The studies of family groups have developed a classificatory system which differentiates types of families according to a number of dimensions: membership, cycle of family development, role relationship between members, social class, geographical location, income, education, etc. Most of those dimensions have been found to be associated with the health of the members of a family and have been used by health promotion and health education in planning their interventions.

A special aspect of studying the family group relationships has been their interaction with the health care system and especially with their family practitioners. The existing literature related to group aspects of this relationship has concentrated on social support and diffusion effect of various experiences shared by family members.

There are considerable cross-cultural variations in the composition of the family unit and in the expectations governing the relationship between family members. There are families where the dominant member is a grandparent or an uncle as compared to the more common patter of father being the dominant member. There are also differences in the role of women as brides and mothers and their authority over the children or over the family income. This great variation is also expressed in the way a family is established or dissolved. There are different legal and cultural norms associated with courting and marriage as well as with obtaining divorce. Many of these norms are purely religious depending on the dominant religion in the family and the social group of which the family belongs.

One should realise that family groups are linked to other groups through their keen and social networks. Their keen relationship can be defined as close-knit or loose-knit according to the intensity and proximity of kin members to a family unit.

There are also differences in ways children are brought up in different cultures. Social norms regulating the way children are brought up may range from completely permissive to a rigidly authoritarian approach.

All these elements play an important part when planning a health promotion and education intervention based on a family unit instead of an individual. Different methods have been developed concentrating on raising family competence in dealing with health problems and bringing up a healthy new generation.

Adolescent groups

A specific aspect of Western industrialised societies is the recognition of a special status given to adolescent groups, resulting in the development of the concept of adolescent culture. A number of studies looking at peer groups have explored the relationships between the members of such groups in many areas of their social activities such as, consumerism, fashion, pop culture, sexual relationships, deviancy etc.

Health studies concerned with this population group have been mainly concerned with the specific problems characteristic for that group, like smoking, drug abuse, teenage pregnancies, gang wars, crime, road accidents, etc.

More recently a new form of health education and health promotion has been taking place with this population group, resulting in creation of a number of self-help groups dealing with health and social problems. The framework within which these problems occur is either home, school or work and each will have certain specific characteristics for consideration in a health promotion and education intervention.

Adolescent groups show the three main forms of social structure i.e. informal hierarchy, sociometric structure and norms, but each in a special and characteristic way. There is no central task activity and no marked hierarchy of power or leadership. There can be leaders for specific activities and the leadership role rotates between the members according to their special talents or abilities.

Adolescent groups are of interest to us because of a number of special processes which one cannot find in other types of groups: (a) there is no specific task, but joint activities are devised which entail the kinds of interaction which meet the needs of members; (b) one of these needs is the establishing of an ego-identity, independent of the family of origin which is reflected in the emphasis on clothes, the great self-consciousness and the concern about acceptance by members of the group; (c) sexual motivation is a major factor in adolescent groups, and is partly responsible for the intensity of attraction to the groups and for their paring structure; (d) there is, however, a common group task of acquiring together the social skills of dealing with the opposite sex and dealing with adults.

All these characteristics are important when planning a health promotion or education intervention, which will have to consider very specific mechanisms and processes as well as interests and motivation characteristic for this population group.

Work-groups

In our society most adults, especially males, are expected to work for their living and the present high rate of unemployment has created a new under-class of people who cannot or do not meet these expectations. Even the people at work are exposed to high levels of stress due to the insecurity and danger of losing their job. A large proportion of the female population works in the home which is not recognised as a legitimate occupation and creates a different range of problems and stresses.

Health care at work is mainly concerned with reduction of accidents and absenteeism from work. There are specific organisations using specific methods to carry out health promotion and health education at work. There are a number of opportunities for workers to undergo health check-ups and have regular monitoring of their health in case of being exposed to some health hazards within the working environment. More recently there have also been instances where the workers and employees have had access to counselling services because of high levels of stress or conflict situations.

Contrary to adolescent groups, the work group is primarily concerned with carrying out a task. To do this the group has a formalised structure with norms regulating the relationships between people occupying different statuses in a work-group. The assessment of the success or failure of a work-group is usually expressed in terms of cost-benefit analysis or levels of productivity.

The members of work-groups are characterised by having special knowledge or skills and undergo a process of training or education to be able to meet the expectations at work. This preparatory period is characterised by anticipatory socialisation where people learn what is expected from them in terms of performance and behaviour. That is when they learn about the norms governing relationships as well as the ways of entering and leaving a working group.The social environment within which work-groups operate is usually clearly defined in terms of legal, economic and social norms. One of the problems due to the social environment can be that a work-group, internally assessed as highly successful, can disintegrate or be dissolved due to economic conditions in the environment.

It has been established that most successful work-groups are those which are characterised by a high level of cohesion which is reflected in the high group moral. Some other groups, such as apathetic and erratic show low cohesion and are also less successful in achieving the tasks. There are some highly cohesive groups, such as strategic groups which are related to union activities and are not necessarily constructive in relationship to production since their main task is to protect the rights of their members. Conservative groups manifest high output and are moderately cohesive. They can have a sufficiently cooperative attitude and can be highly productive. They are mainly characteristic for men in high status jobs who find it easier to perform joint tasks within an atmosphere of cooperation.

Studies of work-groups have looked at the structure and the power distribution by applying sociometric methods. They have looked at close relationships within sub-groups, the problem of identity with the group or with the product and the security levels for members of the group. The role of leadership acquires special meaning in terms of informal group structures as well as formal management structures.

There is some evidence that the introduction of special topics or tasks into the existing groups in work situations have beneficial effects on productivity. The classical example is the 'Hawthorne' effect which affects the productivity no matter what one does with a group as long as one does something. The experiment was concerned with changing working conditions to increase productivity. It was found that improvements in working conditions positively affected productivity, but to the surprise of the experimenters, the productivity continued to improve even when the working conditions were not only returned to the previous state, but even were made worse. The explanation was that the experiment as such represented a motivational force by singling out a group of workers, increasing their cohesiveness and strengthening their group identity, and that the changes in working conditions were less important.

Health promotion and education interventions have to take into account the complexity of the group structures, the symbolic importance of group identity and the traumatic consequences of leaving a group. There have been some attempts at preventive counselling, not only in the case of planned redundancies but also for people leaving the group due to retirement. In some high-stress occupations this can have very dramatic consequences and an exceptionally high death rate was for example noticed among airline pilots within the first five years of their retirement.

Committees, problem solving and creative groups

Most decisions in public life are reached as a result of committee work. The members are formally nominated, their tasks are regulated and the procedures are set out. The work is done by means of discussion which is aimed at taking decisions and solving problems. Being a member of a committee adds prestige to individual standing in a society and that is one of the main motivational forces for constructive participation in the committee work.

Interaction in committee is unlike interaction in most other groups. Although it is primarily verbal, nonverbal language plays a very important part. As for example, when one has to catch the eye of the chairman to be allowed to speak. The interaction is highly regulated with set rules according to the language used in addressing the chair and other members, the duration and the frequency of speaking, as well as in terms of contents governed by the agenda.

The understanding of the working of committees is very important especially for health promotion, where one of the methods i.e. lobbying will depend on using this knowledge to attract the attention and get a problem on the agenda of a committee. This method has so far been greatly neglected in health promotion and education training programmes, which have disregarded the fact that in some countries (i.e.USA) there is a "professional" group of lobbyists for hire with a high level of skills in performing their job.

Although committees are basically problem solving groups there can be some other kinds of such groups which need not have the highly formalised aspects of a committee. The problem solving process within groups is advantageous in comparison to individual decision making because of the shared responsibility and social support.

When problem solving groups are concerned with new ideas or new products they then manifest a creative character due to the innovative nature of their tasks. One of the characteristics of such groups is the risk taking behaviour and "selling" of new ideas to other members of the group. The members of this kind of group can be involved in creative work individually or as a group. In the latter case, a high degree of cooperation is necessary for the successful achievement of the group task.

T-groups and therapy groups

The existence of these groups is due to psychologists and psychiatrists discovering that people when treated in groups can show higher levels of cure than when treated individually (Whittaker,1965). There is a difference between T-groups and therapy groups, with the former being concerned with specialised training and the latter with the treatment of some mental disorders. The processes and mechanisms involved in these groups are highly specialised and require a professionally qualified leader. The rules are a part of the teaching and treatment methods developed by psychologists, educationalists and the medical profession.

Health promotion and education contents can be a part of the training programme of such groups depending on the professional skills involved in training or health problems presented in the group. Health promotion and education related to mental health is increasingly becoming a specialisation in its own right and the practitioners require special qualifications to practise it.

Self-help groups

Most recent trends in health promotion and education have placed great emphasis on developing self-reliance among people and communities (Hatch & Kickbusch,1983; Gartner & Riessmann, 1977). This trend reflects the existing developments in the self-help movement in industrialised societies.We are witnessing a real explosion in the number of self-help groups, a phenomenon which has been attributed to the growth of technology, complexity of institutions, depersonalisation of services, increased professionalisation of everyday life, alienation of individuals from society, community, other people and even from themselves.

Self-help groups have made a significant contribution towards dealing with problems which could not be or were not solved by other institutions. They provide a mechanism whereby individuals in a group setting can assume responsibility for their own bodies, psyches, and behaviour, gain back a feeling of competence and self-respect, and help others to participate in solving of mutual problems.

Their numbers have grown to enormous proportions and according to a rough estimate there are virtually hundred of thousands of self-help and mutual aid groups in the world. They range from Alcoholic Anonymous (membership 750,000) to groups for parents who abuse their children, groups for older citizens, for parents of twins, for cancer patients, for people on diet, for drug abusers, parent education groups, Gamblers Anonymous, Overeaters Anonymous, etc.

There is a self-help group for nearly every major disease listed by the World Health Organisation. The self-help health groups cover among others addictions, blood disorders, endocrine conditions, health maintenance groups, intelligence problems, infant mortality, mental illness, neuromuscular disorders, obesity, physical disabilities, sensory disorders, skin disorders, surgery, etc. Some of the self-help groups have developed into whole movements such as environmentalist groups, energy conservation groups, community groups, not to mention the whole range of consumer protection and political groups.

Since grouping of individuals can take many forms and can operate in many different ways, it is necessary to define the main characteristics of self-help groups as distinct from other groupings:

- they mostly originate spontaneously and are not imposed from outside;

- they involve person-to-person interaction and active participation of all the members;

- the decisions for actions are based on agreement among the members;

- the groups start usually from a feeling of powerlessness and fulfil a need of the members jointly to solve some problems which they could not solve alone;

- in this way the group fulfils the need for a reference group, identification with other members and a common cause, and as a means for ego reinforcement.

Sometimes, self-help groups operate within a defined ideological framework or for certain specific groups such as women's groups, gay groups, some minority groups, etc. This variety is reflected in the many definitions of self-help groups, such as: it is a social movement; it is a spiritual movement and a secular religion; a phenomenon of the service society; an alternative caregiving system; a supplementary community; an agency of social control and resocialisation, an organisation of deviants and stigmatised; a vehicle for coping with life transitions, a therapeutic method, etc.

A simpler classificatory system differentiates between groups that focus on self-improvement (Alcoholic Anonymous, etc.) and those that focus on changing social norms (gay liberation groups, etc.). This reflects the distinction between how the group feels: whether it is the problem of the individual or of the social system.

Another way of differentiating between self-help groups is whether the aim is self improvement, self-fulfillment and personal growth; groups that undertake the role of advocacy; groups that aim to create alternative patterns of living; groups that represent 'outcast havens' or refuge for desperate people who are trying to achieve protection from the pressure of life and society.

The intrinsic assumption in the self-help group movement is that it is composed of lay people (in the context of group aims) and the main question is what if any is the role of professionals in the working of such groups. This problem is highlighted in health promotion and education where an accepted method is for health educators to initiate the creation of 'self-help' groups for the solution of a number of health problems. Their role in this area has not been defined, nor empirically tested, so that at present there is a variety of ways of health education professionals acting within this movement. In some cases, such as with community workers, there is a conflicting trend for them to reject the dependence on the formal system (although paid by that system) and identify with the community groups and their members. This raises a key question: will the professional attempt to dominate and socialise the self-help group to existing professional norms, or will the self-help group be independent, relating cooperatively with the professional structure? The danger is that a successful self-help movement may provide the authorities with the justification of cutting down services and reallocating resources, as for example in the attempt to return old people 'into the community'. Another danger is, that members of a self-help group, in seeking independence from the system, become overdependent on the group, which means that they have only replaced one type of dependency for another.

Any systematic research (observation or experimentation) concerning the self-help movement would contaminate the spontaneity and affect the processes in such a way that the findings would not be valid. It is, therefore, that most of insight into group work has been gained from anecdotal sources in a descriptive form. There are, however, some generalisations that can be made about the group processes:

1. *helper-therapy principle* :   means that in helping others one helps oneself most. In other words, within an Alcoholic Anonymous group, when one alcoholic helps another one, he will help himself most to avoid temptation of taking a drink. This is a basic principle in certain types of self-help groups where the 'reformee' must perform the role of the 'reformer' and may gain most by playing this supportive and helping role. Thus, the most effective way for exsmokers to avoid starting to smoke, is to take over an active role in helping others to stop smoking and thus reinforcing their own nonsmoking behaviour.

2. *learning by teaching* :   it is a well known fact that one learns most if one is committed to teaching others. This is true for academics as much as for children who are recruited to teach other children some hygienic habits.

3. *the group process* :   the success of any self-help group will to a large extent depend on the processes that are being activated within the group. A successful group will provide peer support, identification with other members; will give aims, objectives, limits and norms; will

provide feed-back and reinforcement; will help to integrate individuals and will help the individuals to combat stigma and change the perception of self.

4. *consumer as producer* : the role of consumers in the field of human services has been recognised and it is well known that the productivity of the producers will depend on their interaction with consumers. It is because so much of the essence of human services (health care, education, etc.) depends on the involvement of the consumers. To be successful in learning, the pupil must be fully involved in the learning process; to be healthy a person must be fully involved in preventing and managing illness and maintaining health. This consumer involvement is one of the main characteristics of self-help groups.

As was stated earlier, the number of self help groups is rapidly increasing, although it is also very variable. There are a number of new groups which outnumber the groups that are of a short duration and fold up after fulfilling their aims and objectives. As an example one could mention the various self-help groups in the field of cancer. They range from support groups helping women to cope with mastectomies, to groups which gradually turn into voluntary organisations. An instance of one such organisation is the Women's National Cancer Control Campaign, which is at present highly formalised and organised with many important personalities as sponsors and a highly structured managerial system. Their work on screening women at work for cervical cancer is efficiently organised and supported by evaluation studies of their mobile units, which provide screening jointly organised by the WNCCC and the various commercial enterprises. The WNCCC is extending its coverage with a number of branches covering a wide area of the country.

Other types of groups in the field of cancer are concerned with helping women to control their own health as in the case of groups that are concerned with breast self examination. They promote the most advanced techniques as well as provide support and relieve uncertainties which are usually connected with any medical measure carried out by people on their own.

One could also mention a number of consumer groups which follow the most recent trends in public interest. For example, there are at present a number of groups concerned with the 'green' issues and environment protection and preservation. The interesting development is the recognition of the power of 'green consumers' and 'green investors' who can indirectly control the production, sale and the investment policies by means of their choices and preferences.

Behaviour modification clinics

One of the areas where health promotion and health education is becoming increasingly active is dealing with problems which can only be solved by creating a special environment for the clients. As a result of this, a number of specialised behaviour modification "clinics" have been established dealing with such problems as dieting and weight loss, giving up smoking, increasing exercise, changing lifestyles, managing stress, etc.

Behaviour modification methods

It would be wrong to limit oneself to diagnosing a behavioral problem only in terms of internal response-producing agents; the more appropriate approach examines interrelated control systems in which behaviour is determined by external stimulus events, by internal information-processing systems and regulatory codes, and by reinforcing response feed-back processes (Bandura, 1969).

This holistic approach allows for the complex definition of the problem and requires a treatment regimen which may include several methods. This does not mean that the treatment disregards some of the conventional methods of behaviour modification such as higher level conditioning and various aspects of social learning. It, however, means that the number of available methods has been considerably increased and allows for better outcomes.

The first step in contemplating behaviour modification treatment is to define the aims and objectives in terms of the expected outcomes. Since one is mostly dealing with concepts that are theoretical constructs, they will also need to be defined. There is no such thing as a 'trait', a 'personality' a weak 'ego strength', 'self-awareness', 'emotional maturity', positive 'mental health', etc. They are words that are meant to help in dealing with certain problems, and can be only understood and measured if they are clearly defined. In other words, each of the concepts is what the measurement of that concept produces. This is an important factor to be taken into consideration and any attempt to evaluate an intervention or assess the outcomes of a treatment will have to consider the definition of the aims and objectives.

As was stated earlier, the treatment will include a number of methods and it will be important to organise them in a hierarchical order in terms of learning experiences. Because of this it will be necessary to establish in the first place the necessary components and order them according to the chosen treatment.

The methods mostly in use in behaviour modification include certain aspects of social learning, such as modelling and vicarious processes, as well as positive control and reinforcement of the changes in behaviour, aversive control (still in dispute), extinction, desensitisation, etc. All these methods are complex and costly in terms of time and involvement, and will require a professionally trained person to implement them.

There are, however, simpler methods which have been used by trained lay persons and which have shown a certain degree of success. They have been used, for instance, in running anti-smoking clinics, weight reduction clinics, and clinics for pregnant women and mothers with small babies.

Training the trainers

People who run these clinics are usually partly trained lay persons with a medical, nursing, psychology or social work background. The training courses last from few days to several weeks or months. They may be for practitioners or trainers of practitioners. There are attempts to professionalise such activities, because at present there is very little control over the procedure or the outcomes. There are, however, a number of reputable educational institutions which are entering into this field of training and there is every possibility that the practitioners in the field of helping others will become professionally accountable.

Health promotion clinics in general practice

The new contract which the UK General Practitioners had to sign, includes as part of their duties, establishment of various health promotion clinics for their patients. There are conditions in terms of number of patients, which the general practitioners must meet before they can be paid for their work in these clinics. It is because of this that the interest in the working of such clinics has increased and forms a part of the general training programmes in health promotion and education.

Health Promotion Clinics take the form of situations of interaction between the health care personnel and the patients, for the purpose of health promotion and health education. Although they can consist of discussions with individual patients (counselling), they are also meant to be carried out in groups. A "clinic", therefore, to qualify for payment within the contract implies a set of individual or group meetings during a session in a general practice. In this context Health Promotion Clinics are considered to be using the group setting.

Although the contract covers the running of clinics in general, it is necessary to realise that according to the subject matter, each clinic should be considered as a special case. It is also necessary to develop indicators and criteria for the assessment of each clinic before the payments can be approved by the Family Practitioner Committees. At present there are no criteria for the assessment of health promotion clinics and work is in progress to define the following areas:

1. *Aims and objectives*

The general aim of clinics should be to provide patients with an opportunity to join a clinic dedicated to their specific problem and benefit from behaviour modification methods which should help them to learn how to cope with or solve their problem.

To achieve this aim the objectives of the clinics should include provision of an acceptable organisational structure, trained staff, the use of appropriate methods, and the evaluation and auditing of the outcomes on a short and long term basis. Each clinic according to the problem should define its own aims and objectives which should be within the framework of the general aims and objectives.

2. *Staffing*

According to the problem, each clinic should be run by staff that is trained in the topic as well as method most appropriate for that problem. A basic qualification requirement should be stated for running specialised clinics since different problems will include different methods which again will demand different types of qualifications.

3. *Patients*

There should be a defined way for the recruitment of patients for different clinics. In general the procedure should include an offer from the GP based on the medical opinion about the advantages or necessities for attending such a clinic instead of being treated individually. The patient accepts the invitation and signs a form committing himself/herself to the treatment offered and to the attendance of the clinic. In this way the relationship between the patient and the clinic is on a contractual basis, which in case of private clinics is achieved by patients paying for the treatment.

4. *Methods*

The patients should have the benefit of the most appropriate and effective methods in dealing with their problems. These can include among others: positive or aversive control, extinction, desensitisation through counterconditioning, aversive conditioning, as well as other forms of group therapy.

5. *Assessment*

The reasons for the assessment may be to establish the progress of the patients or to satisfy the requirements for financial reimbursement. In either case it will be necessary to establish for each type of clinic the required indicators, the acceptable criteria and the documentation procedure which will provide data for the assessment.

In addition to general assessment procedures, it will be necessary to establish a body responsible for auditing clinics against some generally accepted or defined standards.

The Community Approach

The concept of "community" implies a larger number of people living together and sharing certain values and interests as well as interacting for a certain purpose or a shared goal. In health promotion and health education the community approach has a long tradition and can be better understood if one examines the following:

1. *Historical development:*

There is a difference between traditional community "organisation" and "development" approaches compared to the new community "participation" approach as recommended by WHO.

2. *The new "ecological" approach:*

The steps in implementing the new "ecological" approach include:

a. need definition - which can be defined on scientific or epidemiological data, or on awareness and realisation of the community members (felt needs);

b. enabling process - which includes the selection of leaders, their training and support in achieving their goals;

c. monitoring and evaluation - which ensures the achievement of set goals and through the feed-back mechanism enables corrections of any negative side-effects.

Working with communities

The methodology of working in communities or with communities has been mainly developed by social workers, as part of their approach in dealing with social problems. Other methods used by social workers are the case study approach and group approach (Henderson & Thomas, 1981; Porterfield, 1966; Scherer, 1972; Minar & Greer, 1969; Rapoport, 1960; Catalano, 1979; Fagence, 1977; Baric, 1985).

The criticism of the community approach as practised by some social workers has been mainly concentrated on the manipulative aspects and the lack of cooperation with other agencies or even community members. There seems to be a 'cultural lag' between the agents of change and the consumers which affected the benefits to the community.

On a social level the improvements have been planned in a way that lacked the participative elements. The criticism has been that the changes were either, induced or forced and on a personal level, the interventions have been aimed at changes in people's attitudes and behaviour, adjusted to social changes.

Social workers do not accept the manipulative aspects of community change and do not disregard individual efforts based on other approaches. The most important innovation has been the emphasis on the advocacy role of social and other community workers and the striving to ensure full community participation in the achievement of desired changes.

Classification according to LOCATION:

There are different ways one can classify community work. One is to differentiate between 'development' and 'organisation' with the special application according to the location of the intervention.

1. *Community development*

This term is used for interventions in developing or "backward" countries and has following characteristics:

- Programmes established by external agents;

- "Multiple" approach;

- "Inner resources" approach;

2. *Community organisation*

US interpretation meaning community planning and action, mainly in the welfare field, and mainly the responsibility of social workers. The characteristics of this approach are:

- "specific content" objective;

- "general content" objective;

- "process" objective;

3. *Community relations*

This defines the methods and ways an agency, association or council relates itself to the geographic community, or a relationship of a "functional" community to the wider community. The characteristics of this approach are:

- public relations;

- community services;

- community participation.

Classification according to the APPROACH:

1. *Locality development*:

This approach includes general development leading to solutions of local problems; one can differentiate between the problems which a community can solve alone, the ones for which it will need partial help from outside, and the problems that can only be solved by outside interventions;

2. *Social planning* :

It includes an approach to solution of social problems through rational deliberation and controlled change;

3. *Social action*:

The disadvantaged segment of the population needs to be organised to be able to make adequate demands on the larger community for increased resources or services in accordance with social justice or democracy. (See diagrams 4 and 5.)

A new approach to community participation

Introduction

Most professionals working in or with health promotion and education would agree that the health problems facing them are caused by or are dependent on the interaction between external and personal factors influencing health and disease. They have no difficulty in accepting the "ecological" approach to the endeavours directed towards the improvement of health, they recognise the need for a "multisectoral" intervention within the framework of a more general concept of "health promotion", and they accept the empirical evidence supporting "community participation" within primary health care as the most promising way of achieving self- reliance and self-determination of people in taking the responsibility for their own health.

There are, however, certain problems in interpreting an ecological approach which are mainly due to the historical development of the "discipline" of health education. In the past the attention was concentrated on models and methods which were concerned with individuals (alone or in groups) and their health behaviour. They were useful in providing a theoretical framework for the definition of the problem, whereas the solutions were based on past experiences, tradition and common sense. Although some of the models recognised the importance of environmental (physical and social) factors in defining the problem, practically none used these in planning their interventions. Even the "community organisation" as primarily a social intervention method has been used to influence individuals within communities, and evaluation used individual indicators and criteria to assess the outcomes.

The concept of community organisation is undergoing a constant reassessment since in the past it was mainly developed and used by social workers and for social problems. Applied in the field of health, the reinterpretation of the concept of community participation moved away from the existing health education "blame the victim" approach and has placed new demands on the methodology of health education interventions. One is forced to accept the fact that the presently available health education methods cannot fully meet these new demands. Due to the historical developments, there are well developed and tested health education methods for influencing individuals, but practically none effective on a community level as indicated by the ecological approach.

This problem is faced not only by the practitioners but also by the teachers of health education. Some of the teaching institutions that are at present engaged in developing and providing health education training programmes on different levels, try to use learning processes which include the community-based experiential learning method and the exposure of students to practical field experiences. The problem is, however, that in the present situation sending students into communities with the available knowledge helps them to identify and experience community problems but does not enable them to see and learn anything about the way communities go about solving these problems. (See example).

Concepts of community participation

Any teaching programme depending on a community based and problem oriented method of learning needs an outlet for students' fieldwork experiences. Although this approach to teaching has been for a

SUMMARY OF APPROACHES: MODELS ACCORDING TO SELECTED
PRACTICE VALUES

	MODEL "A" Locality development	MODEL "B" Social planning	MODEL "C" Social action
1. Goal categories of community action	Self-help, community capacity and integration (Process goals)	Problem-solving regarding common problems (Task goals)	Shifting power relationships & resources (Task or Process)
2. Assumptions about community structure and problems	Com. eclipsed, anomie lack relationships, democratic decision-making	Substantive social problems; mental, physical health, housing	Disadvantaged populations, injustice, deprivation
3. Basic change strategies	Broad cross-section of people determining and solving problems.	Fact gathering about problems; decisions on rational courses of action	Crystallization of issues; action against enemy targets
4. Characteristic change tactics & techniques	Consensus: interests; group communication & group discussion	Consensus or conflict	Conflict or contest; direct action, negotiate
5. Salient practitioner roles	Enabler-catalyst; coordinator teacher of skills and ethics	Fact-gatherer & analyst, programme implementer, facilitator	Activist-advocate; agitator, broker negotiator
6. Medium of change	Manipulation of small task-oriented groups	Manipulation of formal organizations and data	Manipulation of mass organizations and processes

MODELS ACCORDING TO SELECTED PRACTICE VALUES (CONT.)

7. Orientation towards power structures	Members of power structure collaborate in common venture	Power structure as employers and sponsors	Power external target for coercion & overthrow
8. Boundary definition of client system or constituency	Total geographic community	Total community or com. segment (including "functional")	Community segment
9. Assumptions about interests in community support	Common interests or reconcilable differences	Interests reconcilable or in conflict	Conflicting interests; irreconcilable; scarcity
10. Conception of the public interest	Rationalist-unitary	Idealist-unitary	Realist-individualist
11. Conception of the client population or constituency	Citizens	Consumers	Victims
12. Conception of client role	Participants in interactionist problem-solving	Consumers or recipients	Employees, members, constituents,

Diagram 4   Summary of Approaches

SUMMARY OF APPROACHES: MODELS RELATED TO PERSONNEL

	MODEL "A" Locality development	MODEL "B: Social planning	MODEL "C" Social action
Agency type	Settlement houses, OCD, Peace Corps, Friends' service cttee, Model cities, health assoc. consumer groups	Welfare councils, planning boards, fed. bureaux, environmental planning bodies and groups	Minority power, welfare rights groups, womens', black, consumers' radical, reform, movements
Practice position	Village worker, neighbourhood worker, consultant to comm. organization teams, agricultural ex- tension worker	Planning div- ision head; planner	Local organiser
Professional analogues	Adult educator, non-clinical group worker, group dynamics leader, professional agric. ext. worker	Demographic, social survey specialist, public administration, hospital planning specialist	Labour organiser, also minority group welfare rights or tenants' association

Diagram 5 Models and Personnel

number of years a part of the curriculum of a number of Universities, the community based learning has been and still is the main obstacle to the achievement of the set educational goals. There are few if any communities which could serve as examples of how one can solve the existing problems through community participation including self-reliance and self-determination.

In practice, after diagnosing community needs, the students are expected to initiate and produce a solution as well. Providing solutions is considered to be their task as initiators, enablers and organisers, whereas, communities are considered to be recipients. This represents the extension of the philosophy underlying the doctor-patient relationship to the "health care - community" relationship. The community is expected to assume a dependency role similar to a "sick role" and comply with the recommendations of the professional experts.

Even the traditional expectations concerning the doctor-patient relationship have been changing in recent years. Now the patient is expected to play an active role, taking responsibility for his/her own health, decide on the first contact with the health care system, and cope adequately with the new situation after relinquishing the "sick role". This represents a general shift in responsibilities from the health care system onto the people themselves. Although this shift concerning the doctor-patient relationship is widely recognised, there is no noticeable shift in the health care - community relationships. The roles of initiation, enabling, advocacy and action are still firmly in the hands of the external agents who are members of the health care delivery system, and often health education specialists. This paper represents an effort to critically assess the requirements for active community participation in the sense of WHO documents. The existing approach to community participation depends on the interaction between "external factors" and the "community forces". The external factors can be the services available, the initiation of a new programme or any similar activity coming from outside the community. The process of community participation as envisaged at present can be divided into three phases, as Diagram 6 shows.

1. *Initiative and Diagnosis*

a. Diagnosis of the community problems still depends on the medical model and is influenced or carried out by the members of the medical and/or paramedical professions;

b. Once the problems have been defined and ranked according to priorities based on the extent of threat to life, there is a need to initiate certain activities within the community;

2. *Community Acceptance and Action*

a. The "community development" or "community organisation" methods are used to achieve a positive response from the community to the external initiative and to accept it as a part of their own endeavours for improving health;

b. This acceptance is materialised in the form of a "community programme" for action, developed by external agents, and accepted and carried out by members of the community (or sometimes the external agents as well);

c. The construction and practical application of the programme requires professional expertise and service support from outside;

3. *Evaluation*

a. In exchange for support the external agency will expect to be allowed to evaluate the programme alone or with the support from community members;

b. The findings are then being fed back into the planning and execution processes, resulting in adjustments of the initial community programme.

This process seems logical and has been applied often in the past. The problem, however is that there is no clear definition of the relationship between communities and the external agents, especially as far as the community dependency role is concerned.

This method of using external agents limits the activities to a few selected communities. The selection is usually based on mortality, the presence of an interesting medical problem, interest of local health services, political influence, etc. It is also the result of a "crisis management" situation with limited chances of becoming a more permanent venture and a part of community's "life style".

The advantages of this method are in the motivation that is provided for the communities to participate in such programmes. They gain prestige from participating in a national or international programme, receive outside help in expert knowledge, services and technology and all the publicity associated with such a venture. The long term benefits are, however, limited and once the outside support dries out, the community reverts back to its old ways. The expert services, on the other hand, gain important experiences and can mount a similar programme in another community with similar outcomes.

The emphasis WHO gives to community participation in taking care of their own health indicates the shift in responsibility from the health care system to communities. The logical consequence has been the development of new approaches which is based on the concepts of self-reliance and self-determination. The health activities should be integrated into the everyday life of a community and should be guided by available community resources. The external support should be mainly in raising community competence in dealing with their own problems and should represent the support system for community endeavours in the improvement of their own health and management of diseases. It should be part of primary health care within the framework of health education as a part of a wider concept of health promotion.

The new approach is based on the interaction between "external factors" and the "community" forces. It consists of two phases: the activities of external factors and the activities of the community, as Diagram 7 shows

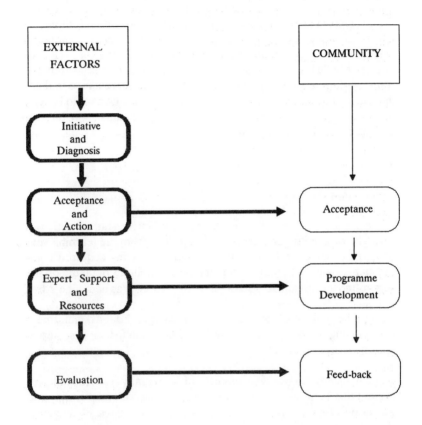

Diagram 6 Phases of Community Participation

1. *External Factors*

a. On a country or provincial level an appropriate agency (health education, health promotion, health service, etc) develops the "movement" aimed at popularising the concept of "healthy" cities or communities by using the media and gaining the support of important political representatives.

b. Once the idea becomes familiar and generally accepted, the appropriate agency creates and popularises the fact that certain training facilities or workshops are available for the interested community leaders where they can acquire competence in carrying out such programmes in their own communities. The contents should be within the framework of health promotion and will include competence in dealing with different community problems of which health should be only one. The outcome should be that a number of leaders show interest and attend such learning ventures.

2. *Community Forces*

a.The second teaching phase is characterised by the shift of activities from the centre into communities. On return from the learning venture, the local leader(s) or representatives, having acquired competence, discuss with other members the possibilities of taking on the commitment to nominate their community (or city) as being "healthy".

b.Once the general agreement has been reached and the commitment has been made, the preparations should be made for the first step in their own programme.

c.The first step will be the assessment of community resource in terms of a multisectoral approach to the diagnosis of needs and planning and execution of solutions. The competence for this kind of diagnosis should be a part of the training programme and should allow for the necessary outside help and support.

d. The second step will be the development of an intervention programme including role definition of the participants, distribution of resources, development of indicators for evaluation and a plan for action. There should be a set of short and long term aims and objectives which will form the basis for evaluation. In addition to acquired knowledge, outside help may be mobilised.

e. Evaluation should be a part of the intervention with feed-back mech-

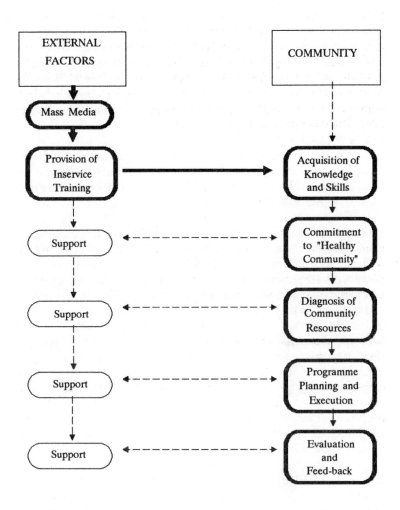

Diagram 7 External Factors and Community Forces

anisms allowing for the adjustments of the intervention. In addition to acquired knowledge, outside help may be mobilised.

This new interpretation of community participation in promoting their own health is characterised by two types of activity which are clearly visible: that of the external factors and that of the community. The roles of both are clearly defined and the actual work is done by the community within their own limits of available resources. Outside help is mainly concerned with raising competence of community members to deal with their own problems.

Although the definition of health problems is still within a medical model, the general needs of the community are much wider and the competence includes the ways of dealing with all of them and not only the health problems alone.

This approach does not usually have the benefits as some externally organised intervention, and the question of motivation is often raised. If, however, the movement towards health improvement becomes a part of the national policy and is widely publicised, then participating in it and excelling in the achievements will provide sufficient recognition and prestige for the leaders as well as the community.

This type of community movement is much wider than the existing concepts of health education activities, and should be considered as a part of health promotion. This should be taken into account when planning workshops for community leaders and be reflected in the contents provided.

The "Healthy City" Approach

When one looks back at the historical events that mark the main turning points in the conceptualisation of public health and the health care delivery, two events stand out : the Alma Ata Declaration (1978) producing the Health for All by the year 2000 (HFA) commitment, and the World Health Organisation (WHO) endeavour to implement the HFA principles on a local level. The new developments initiated by the World Health Organization, which followed these events, resulted in the differentiation between health education and health promotion, in encouraging a multi-sectoral approach and community participation, created the idea of a New Public Health and created a new movement which became known as "The Healthy City Project" (WHO 1984, 1988a, 1988b, 1988c; Duhl & Hancock, 1988). This new conceptual framework is the direct result of the changes in the World Health Organisation's approach to the fulfilment of its responsibilities: "That (i.e. 'going local') means to move beyond the production of guidelines and recommendations into practicality and implementation.....to bring HFA from the shelves of the health bureaucracy into the streets of European cities. To start, there where health is created in everyday life - where people live, work, love and play..."(Kickbusch,1989).

Within this new conceptual framework, based on the redefinition of the WHO role, new ideas have been developed, backed up by policies and strategies. These new ideas are based on the primary care approach, are concerned with people's life styles, and depend on a multi-sectoral approach within the framework of a 'New Public Health'. They have forced a redefinition of the role of health education and have brought in the concept of health promotion. In this way they represent a 'paradigm shift' and a very important new development in the prevention of disease and the improvement of health in general, even under very difficult conditions, such as are to be found, for example, in the inner city areas.

The WHO Healthy City project represents the action component of the Health Promotion Programme and the Environmental Health Programme at the WHO Regional Office for Europe. It is based on the Ottawa Charter for Health Promotion (Ottawa, 1986).

The movement

Historically speaking, the 'Healthy City' movement started with a workshop organised by the City of Toronto in 1984 and called 'Healthy Toronto 2000'. The potential of an approach based on a whole city were soon recognised and the idea was pursued in a number of meetings and workshops resulting in the formal acceptance of the WHO sponsored 'Healthy City Project'. At the Lisbon conference (1986), the representatives from 21 European cities came together to explore the application of the 'Healthy City" concept, which resulted in the acceptance of a new definition of health as "a social rather than a narrowly medical concept, which meant that the improvements can only occur from a partnership of all the institutions and organisations, as well as the inhabitants, in a city.

The formal structure of the Project includes 25 cities (the core group) and there is a great number of other cities throughout the world which have started similar projects and benefit from the experiences documented and evaluated in the Core Cities. It is becoming a world-wide movement for the improvement of health and the achievement of HFA targets. The idea of such a holistic approach has been extended to include the 'Healthy Community' programme adjusted to rural areas, and the 'Healthy Enterprise' programme, which is developing in commercial and industrial institutions. The principles of the movement can be summarised as including:

- the process of enabling people to increase control over and to improve their own health;

- the process of advocating for conditions favourable to health;

- the process of mediating between different societal interests for health.

These are completely new skills in the context of public health and include the following new areas for public health action:

- building healthy public policy;

- creating supportive environment;

- strengthening community action;

- developing personal skills;

- reorienting health services.

The achievement of these aims is based on three strategies: enabling, mediating and advocating. The main strategic principles include:

- 'retrofitting', which means starting with existing re-sources and potentials, moving in   small steps, and aggregating small changes, thus avoiding, large scale and unrealistic   programmes;

- long range planning, beyond the usual politically defined cycles and short term   development plans;

- continuous process of consultation and negotiation with city forces and institutions and   ensuring that health issues are at the forefront of any planning.

One of the consequences of this movement has been the rethinking of the existing public health and creating a 'New Public Health' concept, which has resulted in the creation of a number of Schools of Public Health in this country.

Existing programmes

Although there is a number of cities in UK which have adopted this new approach, there are four which are included in the Healthy City Project as core cities: Belfast, Bloomsbury/Camden, Glasgow and Liverpool. The experiences of these core cities are being publicised and are being applied to a number of other cities in the country.

Project Cities are designated by WHO on the basis of following criteria:

1. Cities with a strong commitment towards the overall principle and targets of the European Health for All strategy;

2. Cities with a specific political commitment at top city level to develop and implement a Healthy City strategy;

3. Cities which are prepared to secure the necessary resources to pursue and implement their Healthy City strategies;

4. Cities which are prepared to participate actively in the exchange of experiences within the European Healthy City network;

5. Cities which are prepared to actively support the development of a national Healthy City network.

The 5-year programme for action developed by WHO and starting in 1988 provides a framework for focusing yearly activities in the City programme:

1988: Inequities in health;

1989: Strengthening community action and developing personal skills;

1990: Supportive physical and social environments;

1991: Reorienting health and environmental services and public health;

1992: Healthy policies for healthy cities.

The definition of a Healthy City: It is one that is continuously creating and improving physical and social environments conducive to health and that creates and expands those community resources for health which enable people to mutually support each other in performing all the functions of life and developing to their maximum potential.

The parameters of a Healthy City are:

1. A clean, safe, high quality physical environment (including housing quality);

2. An ecosystem which is stable now and sustainable in the long term;

3. A strong and mutually supporting community with a high degree of participation and community control;

4. The meeting of basic human needs (food, water, shelter, income, safety) for all the cities' people;

5. Access to a wide variety of experiences and resources with the possibility of multiple   contacts, interaction and communication;

6. A diverse city economy which is innovative, import-replacing and both self-reliant and actively exchanging with other cities and its own hinterland;

7. Encouragement of connectedness with the past, with the cultural and biological heritage and with other groups and individuals;

8. A city form that is compatible with and enhances the above parameters and behaviours;

9. An optimum level of appropriate health care services accessible to all;

10. High health status.

The assessment of the Project examines two main components, i.e. the assessment of the process of the project itself, and the assessment of what is happening in each of the nine separate components of the project.

The assessment of the process of the Project examines who started the Project and how they started, what is the vision of that particular city about what a healthy city is, who are the people and organisations engaged in the Project and what kind of organisational structures have they developed, what kind of funding is available, how is the communication with the public and the participation of the public ensured, and what barriers have been encountered.

The assessment of the progression towards the changes in the nine components of the strategy includes questions related to each component. The nine components are:

- Values;

- An ecological systems approach;

- Personal control over health;

- Inequalities in health and its prerequisites; Healthy ublic policy for urban areas;

- Environments supportive of health;

- Strengthening community action;

- Developing personal skills;

- Reorienting health and other urban services.

The formats of the questions concerning each component include:

- What is your impression of what has worked well in this component and to what extent is this unique to the city or generalizable to other cities?

- What is your impression of what has not worked well in this component, and again, is this unique to the city or is it generalizable?

- Are there particular problems in this component that seem to need attention?

- Does the city have indicators to measure change in this area, if so what are they and do hey use a mixture of both health and non-health measures, process and outcome measures, etc?

- What is your assessment of the level of commitment to action in this component?

At present efforts are being made to develop a set of indicators which could be used for the assessment of progress of a 'Healthy City' project. So far an agreement has been reached about the criteria for the selection of indicators, one of which is that the indicators must be simple and relatively easy to collect. The others are, that they should be sensitive to change; be capable of analysis at the small-area level; be related to health, HFA, health promotion and the 'Healthy City Project'; and that they carry social and political "punch".

Further developments

One of the aspects of the yearly conferences is that the cities give a progress report from which one can see the type of developments achieved and the future trends. From these reports about the processes which have been involved in the creation of the movement and the structures involved, one can recognise some common patterns which include:

- the establishment of an intersectoral Healthy Cities committee as a decision-making committee of the city;

- the establishment of an inter-sectoral officer group (technical committee to implement a city health plan;

- the appointment of a health ombudsman to develop the health advocacy function;

- generation of a broad-based public debate;

- the establishment of an agreed minimal data set;

- the carrying out of population surveys of at least the most disadvantaged subgroups of the population;

- the definition of a clear set of research questions;

- the development of action strategies and activities for implementing projects for different target groups;

- the development of dynamic working links with the local media;

- the production of a review of public and private sector health promotion activities;

- developing cooperation with local institutions, such as museums and theatres as vehicles for mass public education;

- promoting a new approach in environmental health operations taking into consideration the need to provide jobs in time of unemployment;

- organising a forum of Nongovernmental Organisations and extensive networking and coalition building.

Following these patterns of development it becomes obvious that the Project use the conventional community organisation approach which gives emphasis on the definition of the problem, creation of organisational structures which take over the Project management, and an optimistic hope that it will all end in improving people's life and health.

There is an inbuilt problem as far as the evaluation of such movements (which is what the Projects are) is concerned. Very often the movement is of a social nature and the indicators are based on individual changes and improvements. Since such a movement involves complex processes and multi-sectoral agents, it becomes difficult to know which of these have resulted in what kind of improvement. At present (1990) this is the main concern of the organisers who are trying to develop an acceptable, reliable and valid system of indicators and criteria for the evaluation of the 'Healthy City' achievements.

The whole movement is at present exposed to a critical assessment due to the political changes in Europe. With the demise of the doctrinal and traditional socialist values, the whole ideological basis for the movement is questioned. The movement is still respectable since it uses a holistic systems approach and recognises the interdependence of various external and personal factors in the process of health improvement. By taking into account the local resources (which may have changed in the meantime) it will be able to shift the emphasis in accordance with the changes in the social and value system of the local situation. By doing this, the movement will evolve into new forms of intervention following the local developments.

Here one should differentiate between the developments in the Core Cities and the great number of new cities which have jumped on the band wagon and declared themselves a 'Healthy City' without the rigorous controls and monitoring procedures which are characteristic for the Core Cities. It will be necessary to develop some standard monitoring, evaluation and auditing procedures which will be suitable for all similar developments and will ensure the protection of citizens.

Mass Media Approach

Making use of mass media in health education has, in historical terms, been one of the first methods used by formal health education. The early decades of this century have seen not only the use of mass media, but also attempts to improve the effectiveness of this approach by means of research and evaluation (Leather et.al,1981; Ogilvy, 1983).

The theoretical framework

The theoretical basis for this method includes a number of theories and models, all of which have been used explicitly or implicitly by the health education agents. Some of these can be summarised as follows:

1. *Models: KAP and Social Marketing*

In the early years of this century, formal health education has been concerned with health improvements among the underprivileged population groups in developing countries as well as developed countries. The initial fact-finding surveys showed that one of the most common characteristics shared by these groups was ignorance. Considering the size of populations in question and the limited number of health education agents, the efficient as well as effective way of spreading knowledge was by mass media. Since this did not produce desired improvements in health, the approach was extended to include the development of positive attitudes to accompany the newly gained knowledge.

After the Second World War, the researchers looking at health education practices developed the Knowledge-Attitude-Practice Model (KAP) as a framework for their research. The findings from studies of the application of this extended KAP model were not encouraging and further developments followed. One of the side-effects of research into the KAP model, however, has been an improved insight into the use of mass media. This research is well documented and includes comparative studies of lecture vs. group discussion, effectiveness of posters vs. live lecture, prerequisites for an efficient and effective exhibition, etc.With the further developments in health education, the KAP model fell into disrepute and was more or less abandoned. From time to time, someone came up with the idea of using the KAP model, to be soon labelled as 'uninitiated' or even worse 'ignorant' in terms of health education methodology.

Gradually new models were developed stressing the advantages of the individual and especially group approach, which meant that mass media fell into disrepute as an effective health education method. Everyone who was anyone in health education knew that knowledge does not mean action. This lasted for quite a while, until more recently, with the introduction of the Social Marketing Model, mass media came back into fashion.

The Social Marketing Model is in fact an approach based on the developments in marketing techniques as a part of the 'new' subject of business studies. Meant for commerce, by analogy it has been applied in health education under the assumption that health could also be treated as a marketable commodity.

Tones (1990) gives a very good description of this approach and quotes Solomon on the ten key marketing concepts having relevance for health promotion through public health campaigns. These are *the marketing philosophy* which is based on the idea of 'exchange' and the prime role of satisfying consumer needs; *the four P's* (product, price, place, promotion) which is also known as the 'marketing mix' and which deals with the characteristics of the product, its price which should be affordable, attractive and accessible, and places importance on advertising; the *'hierarchy of communication effects'* implies that one should take into account the fact that certain interventions can have short and long term effects and that the indicators should be chosen to to cover the whole range of the change process; the *'audience segregation'* principle is based on the assumption that targeted messages will be more effective than aiming at the whole population which is composed of different groups with different needs and characteristics; *'understanding of the market'* is obviously a necessary precondition and implies that in addition to the consumer, other market forces may be present and affect the campaign; *'feed-back'* is a part of the evaluation process and should be used to adjust the programme during its development; *'interpersonal and mass communication interaction'* is concerned with the need to support mass media campaigns with personal educational programmes; *'commercial resources'* utilisation means that the field of health can benefit from the experiences of the commercial expertise; *'competition'* is an important fact of marketing and with the new developments in the National Health Service it is acquiring a very important role in the health field as well; it is necessary to define *'expectations'* if one wants to evaluate a campaign, as is regularly done in commerce, where accountability concerning expenditure and outcomes has always had a high priority.

One of the most important aspects of the Social Marketing Model, which is obscured within the 'hierarchies, steps and rules' of the model, is the reintroduction (indirectly) of mass media and advertising into health promotion and education.

Spending money on advertising is now again respectable and is expected to be carried out, as can be seen in the comprehensive advertising campaigns related to AIDS in recent years. Not only is advertising a required part of health promotion, it is also permitted and expected to employ advertising agencies to sell the product 'health' or at least 'prevention' of certain risk factors.

2. *Decision-making theories*

The coexistence of a number of different models and approaches resulted in the attempts to revise one's knowledge and understanding of the decision making processes in this new situation (McGrew & Wilson, 1982).

According to current knowledge, the decision making processes depend not only on the method of transmitting information abut to a large extent on the contents of the message. It is because of this, that the health education messages had to be carefully adjusted to the felt needs of the receivers so as to maximise the probability of making the desirable choice. It was because of this that the advantages of recommended actions were overstressed, as well as the disadvantages following the rejection of the offered solution. A number of studies have been looking at the effects of using fear as an instrument in frightening people into desirable actions. It was soon realised that there is no such thing as 'optimal' fear and that people are either frightened or not. If they are frightened too much, fear acts as an inhibitor and the process of rationalisation takes place, with no action taking place. The validation process has been found to play an important part and the role of immediate social network as well as the professions has been found of greatest importance. Since any decision is usually followed by a feeling of regret or uncertainty, it was found that any message transmitted by mass media needed a follow-up reinforcement to counteract the effects of cognitive dissonance, which is a result of the conflict between attitudes and actions and which can be resolved in many different ways.

The understanding of the decision-making processes is closely related to the type of decisions involved in maintaining health and preventing and managing disease. These are linked to the desired behaviour and actions enhancing the chances of a parson leading a healthy life-style and being healthy. Decision-making is dependent on the information a person has regarding his/her own health, about the potential health risks and about the influences on maintaining health and preventing disease.

In more general terms, decision-making has been of interest to many professions and to different branches of science. One can differentiate between two kinds of models mostly in use to understand decision-making: the *static* and the *dynamic* models.

The static models have been based on the postulate that individuals will attempt to maximise the utility of a decision (SEU) or *subjective expected utility*. Another model of great importance has been the deterministic *transitory model* which postulates that if a person prefers A to B and prefers B to C, then he will automatically prefer A to C. These models have not been sufficiently general to explain every combination of a decision-making process and have been gradually replaced by stochastic models where a person calculates the probability for each stage of the process, and which is characterised by inconsistency and intransitivity.

Dynamic models consider decision-making as a function of the interaction of the environmental and personal factors, where the environment may be stable and the information changes, or the environment changes and the information is stable.

The basis on which most of the decision-making models have been based is the assumption that the process can be only studied if one uses the ideal situation as the base-line and then examines the differences in the actual process. The base-line assumption has been that a person is represented by *"economic man"* who is characterised by total rationality and controls total information about the subject related to making a decision. In practice this would mean the this ideal person would be rational in the sense that he/she would try to maximise the benefits and minimise the cost involved in a decision (*minimax* theory) and that the information he/she has would in every case influence the decision within the minimax framework. The studies of deviation from this ideal state have, therefore, concentrated on the emotional or other influences which affect this total rationality, or the amount and quality of information that has coloured the decision in question. Since the available information is concerned with alternatives on offer, the studies have also included the assessment processes in the light of preferences and constraints.

There are many ways a person can obtain information about a health matter. For example, a person may learn about the harmful effects of smoking cigarettes either from a friend, from his doctor, by reading about it in the paper, by attending a lecture or in a number of other ways. The common factor in this is that he receives information and he is faced with the decision of whether to act or not. Therefore, the decision-making process will form the core of the system within which an individual operates with regard to illness and health.

To better understand the decision-making process, a model has been drawn up in a greatly simplified form. It shows three main stages: receiving information, making a decision and undertaking an action:

    a. *Pre-decision process*: We start with the assumption that a person is faced with several mutually exclusive alternatives. Because each has certain attractiveness, a state of conflict exists. He must make a choice with two possible decisions: if the conflict is not resolved, no action will follow and the person will continue to assess different alternatives which are facing him; if the conflict is resolved, then he will undertake an action. The more similar the attractiveness of choices, the greater will be the conflict. To resolve it, he will carry out an evaluation of each alternative, which one can assume is an objective or unbiased process. It will result in collecting additional information and building of divergence between the alternatives to make the choice easier.

b. *Post-decision process*: The decision made is equal to a commitment and will be based on the alternative chosen. If the decision is negative, then there will be no action, and the person will continue to evaluate various alternatives or just give up the whole idea. If, however, the positive decision was followed by an action, then the person has entered a state characterised by the existence of dissonance.

The concept of cognitive dissonance was introduced by Festinger, who postulated that every individual strives towards consistency within himself. This relates to consistency of opinions and behaviour. When inconsistency or dissonance exists, being psychologically uncomfortable, it will motivate the person to try to reduce it and achieve consonance. It can be reduced by changing one of the two elements between which dissonance exists, by changing the environmental influence or by changing the opinion through additional information. The process of reduction is considered to be biased and subjective: a person will try to reduce the dissonance by re-evaluating the alternatives and by the spreading apart of their attractiveness; he/she may not be able to reduce it and then he/she may reverse the decision, or if that is not practical he/she may continue to have a feeling of regret about the choice he/she made.

3. *Behaviour in uncertainty*

There are many diseases that have been found to be related to human behaviour or dependent on a human action. A certain pattern of diet can result in undernourishment or even rickets; a timely recognition of a lump in the breast as a serious symptom may result in timely seeking of medical advice and reduce considerably the adverse outcome. In the former case we talk about behaviour and in the latter about an action, which may be defined as behaviour that is just not a response but has a specific meaning or intention. The behaviour-action continuum illustrates a set of processes and influences derived from institutionalised or new knowledge about illness and health threats. Institutionalised knowledge is reflected in social expectations or norms about the preservation of health and the prevention and cure of illness. These norms are internalised by individuals as routines or habits, and become a part of the role performance that accompanies a specific social position or status. New knowledge reaches the individual either as a part of new or modified norms or as a set of new alternative choices which may form the basis for a decision about the preservation of health and prevention or cure of a disease.

There are many examples of institutionalised knowledge about health and illness being transmitted as a part of the socialisation process and resulting in routines or habits of the recipient. Most of the hygienic habits of cleanliness, avoidance of accidents, preference for specific foods prepared in a specific way, the exercise-rest sequence, etc., are internalised by a child during the process of primary socialisation as routines and habits to be carried out throughout his adult life. This institutionalised knowledge, reflected in social expectations of norms, reinforces routines and habits that form a part of health -related behaviour serving to maintain health and prevent disease. Institutionalised knowledge is, however, undergoing constant changes due to the incorporation of new discoveries in the medical field. These discoveries either modify the existing norms or create new ones. The discovery of the importance of fluoride in the preservation of dental health modified the existing routine of tooth-brushing by introducing this substance into toothpaste or water, or as tablets to be taken by children. The discovery of the dangers of overweight in early childhood for the health of children when they grow up brought about a new norm concerning our image of a healthy baby and changed our emphasis on weighing of babies and equating a fat with a 'bonny' baby.

Institutionalised knowledge, updated and modified by new medical discoveries, is also reflected in norms concerning a person's role-performance according to a recognised social position or status. Disease represents a social as well as personal dysfunction. To minimise and regulate the disruptive consequences, such dysfunctions are integrated into the social structure as specific statuses with appropriate roles. We can distinguish among the statuses of being healthy, ill or at risk. A person's role performance for each specific status is defined by a set of norms or formally recognised social expectations, and can consequently be classified as conformity or deviant. There is, however, usually a grey area where the performance does not quite match the expectations but is still within the limits of accepted tolerance and is classified as variant. The willingness of a person to acquire a status implies his willingness to conform to the norms defining his role behaviour. This willingness is influenced by the coercive power of a norm which is based on supportive sanctions. In other words, the acquisition of a status followed by deviant behaviour will invoke sanctions imposed by the society. The recognition of the societal aspects of different health states with matched statuses and roles has had a great impact on recent developments in health education. Because of the realisation that health messages do not always produce the desired results, health educators have been considering other possible approaches. This has resulted in a critical assessment of the advantages of a societal approach compared with influencing personal choices (Baric, 1978).

New insights into the causes of some health threats as a result of some medical discovery may take some time before they become integrated into institutionalised knowledge and formalised norms. In such a case the individual will find himself in a position of assessing the evidence, with a freedom of choice when deciding whether to undertake a specific action or not and without any threat of sanctions or other forms of social coercion.

The usual sequence of events has been that a research discovers a statistically significant association between a personal characteristic or behavioral pattern and the increased risk from a disease. This was the case when Doll and Hill (1950) substantiated the existing suspicion of an association between cigarette smoking and lung cancer. This triggered off a whole spate of research to support or disprove it, and became an issue of public concern. Some people used it for fund raising purposes and the establishment of public associations, whereas others used it as a reason for starting numerous health education projects to stop people from smoking. The strong feelings of health educators about the desirability of the recommended behavioral change have not been matched by the willingness of the client population to comply with the advice received. Because of this failure an enormous amount of money and effort has been spent in finding out why the majority of smokers do not give up the habit in the face of the evidence linking smoking to such a dreaded disease as cancer.

Health education has been so far mainly engaged in transmitting to people information about new discoveries related to the prevention of diseases together with the recommended measures for the reduction of the attached risk. So far it has had relatively little success in spite of the obvious logic of the arguments used. New insight into this problem has been gained by studies of decision-making and of choice between several existing alternatives.

An important contribution to the understanding of these problems has been made by Cohen (1972). It provided an insight into the assessment of the subjective or 'psychological' probability attached to statistical evidence about a health threat as perceived by an individual when confronted with a health education message recommending a behavioral change. It also contributed to the understanding of problems related to receiving, understanding and acting upon a message received by the introduction of the concept of thresholds: the information threshold, the psychological probability threshold and the action threshold.

     a. *The information threshold*: The first question to be faced is what kind of and how much information a person must receive before even starting to relate it to himself and start assessing the utility of the recommended change against the disutility of the discomfort accompanying such a step.

It is a well-known fact that knowledge as such is not in most cases sufficient to initiate the desired action. A study concerning the influence of knowledge about the stages of the development of a fetus *in utero* on the opinion whether and when an abortion should be legally allowed (Baric and Harrison, 1977) showed that there was no direct relationship between the two. Even when health education as a part of the study was carried out and subjects" knowledge was increased, no change in the respondents' opinion was observed.

This was also confirmed in a study of smoking habits, comparing medical with non-medical students (Baric, MacArthur and Fisher, 1976). In addition to knowledge, the study also explored the relationship between students' attitudes to smoking and their actual smoking behaviour. There was no significant difference in smoking between the two groups, although the medics had a higher level of knowledge and fewer positive attitudes to smoking.

Following the interpretations given by Cohen (1972), various people would appear to need different amounts of information before they reach their information threshold. Some may, however, make their decision 'instantaneously' as Fellner and Marshall (1970) found when investigating the response to an appeal for kidney donors; 14 out of 20 donors reported making their decision 'in a split second'. In other cases more information may be needed, or information with certain 'weight' before the threshold is reached.

    b. *Psychological probability threshold*: Once the information threshold has been passed, a person will start to assess the possibility and the probability of a threat affecting him and what the consequences might be. Cohen (1964) has drawn a clear distinction between the objective or mathematical probability of an event's occurring and the subjective or psychological probability a person gives to that event. This problem has been largely neglected in health educational studies and Cohen's work in this area represents a major contribution to health education. Most health education activities have been and still are limited to the transmission of information in the hope that people, as 'rational' beings, will heed the advice. Since this does not always follows, an insight into personal interpretation of information about a risk to health is very important.

One of the clues to the way people assess information about a probable risk to their health can be derived from the description Cohen gives of a person's translation of a population probability to his own personal (or sample) probability. According to probability theory, this cannot be done, since by definition a population probability can never be attributed to any specific event or individual in that population. We can say that the probability of a positive smear in a cervical cancer screening test is 7 in 1000 but we cannot say which seven it will be in that population or even how many thousands of women must be screened before we get this level of probability. And yet, this is exactly the argument used in many health education programmes to influence individual women to come for a test. This is based on empirical evidence that people daily try to guess what their chances are, when deciding about an action.

How do people make such interpretations, and could the understanding of this process help health education? Cohen gives a very
plausible explanation in describing a trial of children at different ages
given the task of guessing the number of yellow and blue beads in an
array of beakers from the information about the whole population of
beads. The guesses were not solely dependent on information about
the population but were governed by people's ideas about the population (macrocosm), which they then translate to apply to themselves
(microcosm). These ideas can be coloured by different influences such
as ethical and aesthetical beliefs as well as by one's own image. One
can overestimate the probability of something that is considered to be
beautiful or good, or if one is an optimist. The translation of a person's
image about the macrocosm in interpreting the events concerning his
microcosm has also been described by Suchman (1965), although in a
different context. He related people's behaviour to their orientation:
parochial or cosmopolitan. People with a parochial orientation
showed a low level of medical knowledge; their knowledge was based
on popular beliefs and personal experiences, and was acquired through
informal sources; in illness they showed a high level of dependence on
their immediate social environment (family and friends): they also
showed a high level of scepticism about medical care system and its
agents. The cosmopolitans showed a high level of medical knowledge
based on scientific evidence and acquired through formal sources such
as the educational system or scientific literature; in illness they showed
a low level of dependence on family and friends, and they were not at
all sceptical about the health care system or their agents. When health
education information is transmitted through public channels and
bases its arguments on scientific concepts such as probability, the cosmopolitans are more likely to accept it than the parochials. This has
been supported by studies of utilisation of health services and modification of behaviour.

Lack of willingness to accept the arguments presented by health educators in favour of a change in behaviour may also be due to the mis-
interpretations of the probabilistic statements made. People in general
have difficulties in differentiating between the 'possibility' and the
'probability' of an event occurring. This may be because it is usual for
people to reason that something may or may not happen, i.e. that they
will become ill or will stay well. This 'either-or' approach is treated as
a 50 : 50 probability. The fallacy, however, is that these two events need

not be equiprobable. The realistic interpretation would be, that although they can become ill or not, if they smoke their chance of becoming ill is twenty times higher than for non-smokers.

Another common fallacy is to treat discrete events as a sequence of events instead of each one separately. When told that smoking in pregnancy may harm the fetus (Baric and MacArthur, 1977) women who had smoked during their previous pregnancy and had a healthy baby in general disregarded such information. They believed that since it did not happen before, it 'cannot' happen now. On the other hand, it is known that parents with one baby suffering from the 'Dawn' disease find it very difficult to believe that the next one will not be a mongol too.

An interesting story was reported in *The Times* (23.9.1977) from Bucharest, about an air crash in which the aircraft was split in two and half of the passengers were killed. A survivor from Turkey in describing the accident concluded "Having survived the accident I think I am now 'insured' against tragic happenings like this and won't be fatally involved in other aircraft crashes. I travel a lot by air". In Cohen's terms, the person must have obviously been an optimist, since if he had been a pessimist he could have equally logically reasoned, that since he survived one crash, in the next one he would most certainly be killed.

      c. *The action threshold*: Whether a person will undertake an action, after passing through the information- and psychological probability-thresholds, will also depend on passing through the action-threshold. Even then it will still not be certain what kind of action will follow.

The first question, therefore, will be what makes a person undertake an action? Becker (1974) in his review lists a number of models applied by various researchers in an attempt to find this answer. A popular and probably most widely used model in health education has been the Health Belief Model described by Rosenstock (1974). It postulates that a health action depends on a person's belief in his own susceptibility to the health threat; that the occurrence of that disease would at least have a moderate severity on some component of his life; and that taking some action would in fact be beneficial by reducing his susceptibility to the condition, or if the disease did occur, by reducing its severity and that it would not entail overcoming important psychological barriers such as cost, pain, convenience and embarrassment. This model has been used in a number of retrospective, prospective and intervention studies and was found to be descriptive value rather than predictive. Later an additional factor was included, i.e. a 'cue', which seems to be most important in triggering off an action even if all the other factors are present. There have been several criticisms of this model: it does not include motivation as a factor; each person will provide his own cue if he decides to act; the factors in the model have not been standardised; they do not represent discrete units, etc. Becker also discusses other models related to this problem (Lewin, Toeman, Rotter, Edwards, Atkinson and Feather) some of which employ the notion of behaviour in uncertainty and psychological probability related to making a choice. It seems, however, that the complete understanding of the psychological mechanisms which prompt a person to undertake an action still eludes us, and that each of the models mentioned explains only a part of the process without providing a complete answer.

Once a decision has been made and an action follows, we are faced with the problem of what kind of action it will be. An intervention study carried out among pregnant women (Baric, MacArthur and Sherwood, 1976) with the aim of informing them about the dangers of smoking during pregnancy illustrates this point. A doctor in an ante-natal clinic talked with a number of pregnant women about the dangers to their unborn child, in an attempt to persuade them to give up smoking during pregnancy. In an interview in their homes ll weeks after the intervention it was found that 52% of the women had reacted and did undertake some action. Although all of them received the same kind of information, supported by similar kinds of arguments, the range of their reactions was considerable: 10% stopped smoking, 7% stopped but started again, 24% reduced and 11% increased the number of cigarettes smoked. The rest (48%) reported no change.

From all the studies cited, as well as from other literature, it seems obvious that the problem of making a decision which will result in a recommended action is much more complex than would appear from the existing models currently in use. It has also been shown that there is no such thing as a 'health action' or 'health behaviour', but that we are dealing with specific reactions of individuals to specific health threats or disease symptoms. One person may make up his mind 'instantaneously' when confronted with the facts, whereas another may need a long time and a vast amount of information before even considering the possibility of acting. One individual may react negatively to too little information about one health threat and also negatively to too much information about another threat. It is also known that a low level of perceived susceptibility may inhibit one kind of action (vaccination), whereas too high a level of perceived susceptibility may inhibit or delay some other action (breast examination).

4. Mass communication theories

Telling people what is best for them is not sufficient to reduce the prevalence in a population of a health threat due to behaviour. The examination of various attempts to find an effective way of achieving this reduction supports this assumption. It has been shown, following Cohen, that it is not theoretically correct to translate a population probability of a risk to its individual members. It has also been shown that, although individuals tend to do this all the time, the translation will depend on individual characteristics, value orientation, cultural and social background, etc. This indicates that it cannot be used as a practical tool for planing a health education approach aimed at individuals. It has been furthermore, shown that individual perceptions of probability of a health threat differ to such an extent that no individual-based approach to a population could cover all the necessary variations. This has been supported by findings from mass health education campaigns, most of which have been effective only for a small proportion of a population. It should not be forgotten that nearly everybody in England knows about the risk smokers run from lung cancer and some other diseases, and yet only approximately 20% of smokers give it up in any one year. Even if smokers have attended some smoking clinic where more intensive methods are being used, only a similar percentage give it up for at least one year.

The studies in communication at the time, produced a new insight into the reasons why the transmission of information via mass media does not always work. The development of the 'two step' communication model explained the process of acquiring, internalising and acting upon information received by means of mass media. The model postulates that the crucial role in this process is played by 'gate keepers' or 'reference persons' or 'opinion leaders' in a certain field and in a certain community. These mediators serve as testing board for new ideas, as models in adoption of innovations, and legitimisers of new social expectations. The outcome of this insight was that the mass media were considered as only one element in behavioral change with the social support element playing a crucial role in activating the gained knowledge.

5. Implications for health promotion and education

This brings us back to the various ways health knowledge is transmitted and internalised. It would appear (Baric, 1976) that the most economical procedure for health education would be to influence routines and habits through the socialisation process and at the same time to institutionalise at-risk statuses with accompanying norms for each health threat. This is the way in which health education can operate successfully on a population level. Individuals who do not conform to social expectations (deviants) and other special cases can then be approached on an individual level by specially trained health educators and other professionals. In the case of new medical discoveries, it will also be more economical for health education to concentrate on the integration of this new knowledge into new norms with sufficient power to act as a cue for individual action. In this way people could conform to well-defined social expectations related to health instead of making haphazard individual choices which may produce unexpected and undesirable results.

As far as the mass media are concerned, it has been shown that they have a limited value in transmitting information on an individual level as a means of producing an action or a change in behaviour. Their main advantage lies in the fact that they act on a 'mass' level and affect whole populations simultaneously. In this way the mass media become vital in creating and affecting social norms since this can only be achieved by transmitting information to whole populations at the same time.

The invention of printing and the production of the first newspapers started the mass communication revolution. The following technological developments such as radio, telegraph, telephone, photography, films, television, satellite communication and computer technology, have brought about a radical change in the assessment of the impact of mass media on human behaviour, their value system and their sharing of expectations. It resulted in a more personalised awareness of cultural differences and produced a system of instant information and the possibility of conceptualising earth as a planet with limited resources and humans as living in a 'global village'.

This new situation makes it difficult to apply the existing and relatively simplistic theories on mass communication (especially those developed in the field of health education) to a world in which, for example, hundred of millions of people could watch the horrors of a war in their sitting room every day, hear the noises and count the numbers of dead and wounded, not to mention witness the suffering of the civilian populations. The existing theories dealt usually with one medium operating on a mass level (newspaper, TV, etc.). The fact is that in the present situation we are part of a 'multi-media on a mass level' culture. The models and theories need to be much more complex to be able to account for the cultural differences within which multi-media mass communication operates.

Advertising

Advertising is a part of health promotion and education aimed at selling the commodity called 'health'. Some people seem to confuse the concept of advertising with that of mass media communication and mass campaigns. The best way of learning about advertising is to see what the people do who grew reach in the advertising industry or who grew rich by using successful advertising for selling their products.

One of the top ten advertising personalities in the world wrote a book on advertising, in which he gives simple and streigthforward advice to people interested in the business of advertising. His main advice is to spend proportionally most of the time on research and learning about the product. If at the end of that period, one starts to believe in certain aspects of the product which are favourable and could be used to influence others to buy it, one has the basis for a promising advertising approach (Ogilvy, 1983).

One should bear in mind that good advertising need not be 'creative' but interesting enough to sell the product. This interesting aspect means that the successful advertisement uses the right 'appeal'; and the appeal is 'right' if it prompts the consumers to buy a specific and not any product of the kind advertised. This means that in advertising one is concerned with 'brand images' and 'brand loyalty' of the consumer. One should also bear in mind that any advertising that does not succeed in increasing the sales, need not be just 'unsuccessful' but could be actually harmful.

When one has learned everything that is to be known about the product, the next decision is to 'position' it, which means to decide which aspect of the product one will use in terms of 'what the product does and for whom is it'. Positioning means choosing the right audience as the target for the advertisement and the right characteristics which will sell the product. If one stops and thinks, one will realise that the images one has of many different products have been created by the advertisers: the Volvo car as a 'winter' car, the VW Beatle as a reaction to vulgar big American petrol-guzzlers, the Marlboro as the macho cigarette. These are all examples of successful positioning of the product and creating a niche in the market for it.

The next step is to decide on the 'brand' image. This is equivalent to the 'personality' of the product. It is an composition of its name, its packaging, its price, the style of its advertising and finally the nature of the product itself.There is an advantage in the continuation of the same image, although this is often impossible because of the change of the marketing director, the advertising agency or because the existing brand does not produce the expected results. There are situations in the market place which require a change in the brand image. For example in selling of cars one can follow the change in brand image from a 'cheap' car to a 'cheap to run' car, to a 'reliable' car, to a 'green' car (using unleaded petrol with a catalytic converter). There are also new scientific discoveries which can influence the brand quality as in the case of sun lotions from 'you will tan easily' to 'it protects you from skin cancer' with the whole supportive system of giving the protective value in numbers.

It is important to realise that a brand carries with it and sells an image. The image is created by advertising, and once it is created it sells the product. One does not question the product but the image that it represents. A very good example is the great success of certain firms selling water. It seems impossible to make a fortune by bottling and selling ordinary drinking water. It has been known for quite a while that there is a lucrative market for 'mineral' water which is sold because of some 'health' property. But now we are witnessing the success of selling ordinary drinking water, such as the water from some undefined highland spring. It goes to show that one can sell anything with the right brand image. The macho image of Marlboro cigarettes has been going for 25 years and is still successful in making the brand the most popular in the world.

The next thing is to have 'a great idea', which will be proven great only if it sells the product. This is, what the advertisers call the 'creative' part of work, which differentiates between those who earn hundred of thousands of pounds from those who loose their jobs after few attempts. It is easy to recognise retrospectively a good idea, but very difficult to know in advance which idea is good. Long experience helps, although even the most successful advertisers remember those 'which got away'; and it does not help to rely solely on one's own feelings and instincts: the consumers may react quite differently to the same image. One's own feelings do help if one asks oneself, whether one wishes to have thought of it oneself, and whether it will be still good in 10 years.

The product should be made the 'hero' of the advertisement. There are no dull products, only dull writers. The problem with the writers is that in addition to ideas they must have sufficient time to think out, test and produce an idea. This includes a considerable period of testing within the advertising agency as well as within the organisation that commissioned the advertisement. There is a tendency for writers to become professionals with emphasis on background knowledge in addition to ideas.

There is some dispute about the possibility of evaluating an advertisement. The story goes that there are too many factors involved in selling a product that it is not possible to measure the contribution of the advertisement as such. There are some cynics who say that advertisers are only good in selling themselves and the idea of advertising to the customers, without any great impact on the selling of the product. One can measure people's awareness about the product, their opinions about the advertisements and one can even ask them whether the advertisement influenced them in buying the product. People may say "yes", but in fact they themselves do not exactly know why they bought something and what part the advertisement played.

One of the questions that is often raised is associated with the selection of appeals to be used in selling a product. Great emphasis has been placed on the appeal of sex and the role of fear. There are books written on the advantages of certain appeals and the preferential images such as children, young animals and nudes. The most recent experience has shown that anything can be acceptable if the purpose is right, as was the case in the use of condoms in advertisements about AIDS on TV and other mass media.

Another way of learning about advertising is to see what the opposition does and after a critical assessment, learn from their successes. Health education and promotion has been for some time in direct competition as far advertising is concerned with tobacco manufacturers in their fight for abolishing smoking. There have been numerous studies and publications based on the examination of cigarette advertisements, a number of laws and voluntary codes of practices have been adopted, and smoking is being banned from an increasing number of places. To find out whether smoking is becoming less acceptable, one needs to look at the advertising agencies and their willingness to take on tobacco industry as their clients. In general this not the case and even the top advertisers proudly display their successes in selling cigarettes, thanks to their advertisements. In general, one can say that reduction in smoking is mainly a Western European and in parts American occurrence, and that there is very little evidence of reduction in smoking in Africa, Asia and Eastern Europe. Since most of tobacco industries are multinational, they can still spend millions on advertising and sponsorships of world events, including sport.

It seems wrong to speak in general terms about advertising in health promotion and education. Advertising is concerned with selling a product (cigarettes) and health education is concerned with preventing people from buying and using it. This seems to be the main reason why it is difficult to translate the experiences from advertising and marketing to health education. There are some exceptions, as in the case of selling the idea of condoms for safer sex. Here the problem is, however, that the topic is delicate and subject to so many taboos, that it is not possible to exploit all the experiences from other types of advertising, such as selling make-up. The latter is a very good example of selling images and illusions, supported by glamorous images and carefully phrased claims for the products. If one could use such tactics to sell condoms, maybe the use of condoms would increase and thus contribute to the prevention of AIDS. In recent years the AIDS campaigns have had a very high profile and large amounts of money have been spent on advertising. As was stated earlier, it is impossible to link any changes in behaviour or in the prevalence of the infection with the existing advertising campaigns. The question is whether the advertising has benefited more in promoting the institutions that spent the money on advertising, than to the prevention of disease which should have been the main purpose.

The media

The time we live now may one day be labelled as the 'post computer' era since the advent of the microchip revolutionised the way we communicate, interact, work and play. The first attempt at mass application of the new technology was in the field of education, starting with TV programmes as a part of the Open University 'education for the masses' approach, and followed by the distribution of computers in classrooms and the spread of 'computer literacy' among the new generations of children in this country.

Health education, and later health promotion, followed this 'information technology' revolution and tried to keep abreast of the new developments. It started with the 'Radio Doctor' programmes as a special feature aimed at informing people about new medical developments, later to become a true 'multisectoral activity', with everyone jumping on the bandwagon and using health as news items, scientific topics, political issues, contents of soap operas, advertising appeals, etc.

The combination of TV, video recorders and computers resulted in the development of probably the most effective learning methods in the

form of 'multimedia technology', which is a combination of technologies which allows the mixture of computer-generated text, graphics
and animations, live and still video images and sound. As a new technology it will provide new and cheaper tools for video production,
video-graphics, music, animation, advertising and business presentations. The most recent development in this field is interactive videos.
These are now increasingly used for training purposes, from teaching
workers technical skills to training managers how to manage multi-na-
tional corporations. There are some new programmes for training professionals such as doctors in various skills related to medical diagnosis
and interventions and some very good programmes for learning foreign
languages. Interactive videos are considered to be the next most promising development in multimedia technology.

Although health education and promotion have not as yet been able to
make use of interactive videos on a large scale, the didactic videos have
been highly successful in enabling people to learn about various health
topics, such as first aid, looking after your baby, reducing weight, exercising, relaxing, etc.

The whole concept of 'mass media' has changed from media which
transmit messages on a mass scale to media which are being used by
masses of people on an individual basis in their homes or as part of individual learning programmes in schools (every student with his/her
own computer).

The multi-media revolution has had as a consequence the growth of
new professions or experts for different media and different use of
same media. There are an increasing number of specialist firms that
deal with the preparation and production of the new media or the programmes for the new applications of the more conventional media. An
important development is the growth of 'in-house' experts, as in the
case of 'desk-top publishing' which is a part of many health promotion
and education units.

Another important aspect of the availability of the new technology is
the software that is being developed in the fields of data collection (da-
tabases), analysis (spreadsheets) and communication (word process-
ing) for existing personal computers. Various data-base programmes
enable the storage of whole libraries of information with an easy and

immediate access; there are statistical packages which enable in-house analysis of survey data from quite large samples; there are other management programmes which allow for the analysis of future trends and can accommodate simulation models; there are graphics animation programmes, as well as programmes which enable networking and direct links with other computers and access to their data as in the case of access to different libraries in the world. All this technology represents, in fact, a qualitatively jump in the performance of health education and promotion units once its potential is fully exploited.

It is becoming increasingly obvious that the life-style of people is changing due to the developments of information technology. People learn, think , make decisions, and are entertained differently from the outset of the technological revolution, and health promotion and education must take these developments into account if it does not want to lose touch with reality.

UNIT 4:   Planning an intervention

Introduction

This unit brings together the various aspects of the preparatory work required for planning and carrying out an intervention.

The **aim** of this unit is to enable the participants to operationalise the knowledge gained and apply the skills for their future practical work.

To achieve this aim, the unit has the following **objectives**:

1. to acquaint the participants with the process of planned change;

2. to provide them with necessary skills for planning, execution and evaluation of a health educational and health promotional intervention.

The **assessment** of Unit 4 will be based on the intervention programme the participants are expected to produce at the end of the Workshop. This assessment will use as indicators the level of practical value of the planned intervention and the scope of the intervention planned.

The **method** includes knowledge input and task work.

Planning an intervention

After defining a health problem and choosing the best solution, this part deals with planning and evaluating an intervention. In other words, it is concerned with the execution of the intervention. Since the conceptual framework differentiates between health promotion and health education this part deals with planning interventions for both, treating them as linked and complementary aspects of a complex intervention.

Here are some basic ideas about the requirements for planning an intervention which should be born in mind when considering which methods would be appropriate for achieving a specific aim. These ideas can be summarised as follows:

1. *Establishing a base-line:* this will include the data about the external factors, personal and family characteristics and the level of competence; the way these data can be collected has been described in great detail in previous chapters;

2. *Existing needs:* whatever the situation and the level of competence is, it will be necessary to find out whether the needs, as defined by professionals match the needs as felt by the target population; in some cases the health needs may be latent or of secondary importance, compared to more immediate problems such as poverty, bereavement, imminent wedding or an unwanted pregnancy; in such and similar situations health education is faced with a crisis which will have to be taken into consideration during the planning process; if one, however, finds that the needs of families correspond to the problems as defined by professionals, normal planning procedure will take place;

3. *The planning process:* the initiative for an intervention or action can originate at different levels (national, intermediate or local) and can come from politicians, health workers or people themselves. The scope of an action or intervention will depend, therefore, on the level at which it originated. If it is a national initiative, the scope will be much greater than if it originated on a community level. This will have important consequences on who will be involved, what kind of resources will be needed and available, and who will be the target population.

The type of problem that triggered off an initiative for an action or an intervention will also have important consequences for the planning process. The problems can be differentiated in terms of a crisis, short and long term problems. A *crisis* can occur due to natural causes (draught), social causes (migration), health causes (epidemic)., personal causes (bereavement) or due to the unexpected intensification of already existing problems such as an increase in road accidents, a lung cancer epidemic, mass migration etc. In case of a crisis there will be a number of agents, professions and institutions involved trying to alleviate it or solve it. Health education has usually not been a part of such an intervention in the past. Recent experiences, however, have shown that an important part of resolving a crisis situation can be played by health education intervention aimed at improving the coping abilities of the stricken population. For example, in the present famine in Africa it was found that the distribution of food was essential but not sufficient and the people needed help in learning how to prepare the food received, how to cope with social disruptions due to migration and how to take over the task of planning their future in the new situation and environment. In the case of a *short term problem* which has a recognised start and ending, such as an immunization campaign, the planning procedure will include all the usual steps in planning, such as the definition of the problem and solution, the resources, the methods and the evaluation. Most planning, however, is concerned with *long term problems*, which have been present for some time and will continue in the future. The aims of health education in such a situation will be to reduce the incidence and prevalence of the enabling and contributing factors and to monitor the progression towards a possible solution in the future.

Once a problem is identified, the first step will be to decide which parts of it can and should be dealt with by health promotion and which by health education. At this stage the differentiation between the two is of greatest importance, since according to their role definition, their tasks will be allocated and the appropriate agents mobilised. At the same time it will be of greatest importance to realise the interdependence between the two and the need to include both in planning a successful intervention. There are many examples which support this statement from our experiences in the field of family planning and in case of a number of preventive measures, demanding actions which were against social norms and cultural values. At present, most of the efforts are devoted to drawing the boundaries between health promotion and health education and only few attempts have been made to define the ways their interdependence can be taken into account in planning a solution to a recognised problem.

4. *The choice of methods*:   according to the type of problem and the role allocation of the agents, the expected outcomes will include a number of options among the available approaches, such as legislative measures, provision and/or improvement of services, reduction of communication barriers between the agents and the consumers, changes in social norms, strengthening of social support, raising family and individual coping competence in recognising and solving their own problems. Each approach will use different methods, such as lobbying, political action, economic measures, consultations, mass media, community actions, self help groups, increase in knowledge and skills and counselling. Although there are at present many books written on the use of different methods, such as the principles of counselling, or preparation of a TV programme, production of posters, conducting interviews and improving communications skills,etc., there is a great need to specify the appropriateness of each of the methods for a specific aim. In the past these various methods have been used for different purposes, the decisive element in their choice being the availability and not the potential of each method. The effective and efficient use of a method will be influenced by the contents which in turn will depend on the aims of the intervention. One can use, for example, mass media to transmit information or to influence social norms. Whereas, in the former case there are also other more efficient methods of transmitting information, in the latter case they are practically the only way to achieve that aim.

5. *Resources*:   one should consider different kinds of resources a.e. personnel, technology and finances. One has to recognise the present difficulties in recruiting appropriate personnel for a health education intervention which are due to the way this activity has been developing. The health education specialists are usually masters of intervention methods but are not qualified in the contents. This is not so much a problem in situations where the content specialists a.e. medical professions are easily available and can be mobilised to participate in an action. It becomes of crucial importance in situations where they have to work on their own, and where their knowledge in medical matters

is not sufficient, or even if they have the knowledge, they lack the professional status which is necessary for the protection of their clients. Attempts are being made to compensate for their lack of knowledge and many courses for health educators or in health education for other professions do include a considerable programme in basic medical knowledge under the assumption that anybody engaged in health educating others should have at least the same amount of medical knowledge and skills as it is expected from the target population. The question of professional responsibility, however, has not as yet been resolved and will require continuous efforts to find an acceptable solution.

Some of the problems and methods require a strong support of audiovisual aids, which depend on the state of *technological development* in a country and on access by the target population. In the past it was assumed that countries with high technological development, which includes also mass means of communication, can depend on using them for health education purposes. People may use different technologies for specific purposes which may not include information about health as is the case with TV programmes where millions are watching entertainment, and only a minority the educational programmes.

Whatever the approach and the method chosen, it always involves *financial expenditure*. Planners are usually under great pressure to ensure appropriate financial support for any planned activity. The agencies or institutions responsible for providing finances have their own language and code of practice which the planners of health education should master before setting of to find financial support.

The grant givers may be more willing to give money for equipment than for courses and personal expenses, trips and meetings. It is usually difficult to get money for a training course or for getting higher qualifications, whereas requests for certain types of hardware are acceptable (although transport is definitely out). For planners it is important to know the difference between recurrent and one-off or nonrecurrent expenses and the possible maintenance costs involved in acquisition of certain hardware. It is, therefore, very important for any planner to get all the information about financial policies of agencies and institutions before approaching them for financial support. Planners should also be aware that receiving support places them under obligation to the supporter, and this aspect should be thoroughly investigated before any commitment is made.

Finally one should mention that very often the problem is not to get finance, but how to spend it once it has been received. An emotional cause such as cancer can generate great financial support, but practically none of the programmes that have been financed from this money have as yet produced the final solutions to certain preventable forms of this disease. A review of research literature in this field shows the diversity of approaches and scientific rigour applied and at the same time indicates that distribution policies may favour the established names with little chance of new blood entering into the field. Another problem in acquiring financial support is related to the demand for accounting for the expenditure. Some institutions will demand practically in advance the results before they are willing to part with the money, others will appreciate the risk involved and will wait for results.

The situation with attracting money for health education is becoming increasingly complicated with the role distribution between health promotion and health education. Whereas health education can make a more obvious case for spending money in connection with health improvement, health promotion may need to spend money on activities which are only indirectly related to health, and yet are of vital importance for changes in life-styles or for solution of some social problems affecting the social wellbeing (according to the WHO definition of health). The new emphasis on self-reliance and self-help has brought into the arena new contenders for limited resources, such as community workers or leaders of self-help groups. It is becoming increasingly obvious that very often financial support will depend on political and emotional as well as purely health arguments.

6. *Execution*: theoretically it is easier to distinguish between the separate parts of a health education intervention, than it is in practice, where there seems to be an overlap between the parts and stages of a programme. While planning the details of the intervention, one is already engaged in sounding out the potential sources of financial support, and while choosing the agents one is already designing instruments and deciding on the methods. One has, therefore, to consider the process of planning within the formal health education system, as an ongoing process, where the consultations with the target

population are a part of a continuous process, and planning certain in-terventions is a part of it, if and when the need and the opportunities arise. A sign of good planning is that the aims are clearly defined, the roles allocated and the indicators and criteria chosen. In that case the development and pretesting of instruments and methods becomes an initial part of the execution of a health education intervention.

Often, however, there is a need to synchronise the onset of an interven-tion with the progression of health promotional activities which should support and reinforce the health education intervention. In practice, the health promotion activities should precede the health education activity, because the effects of health promotion can require some time and usually represent an ongoing process. Ideally one would expect that health promotion is an ongoing process in a community; that the members of that community express their needs for health improve-ment and show willingness to participate in the planning process; and that the formal health education system launches its intervention in such favourable conditions. Launched in such a way, health education interventions become a part of regular activities of health education in-stitutions, in the same way as health promotion activities should be a part of regular activities of all the other relevant professional groups and institutions. To follow the planned stages and phases is then a part normal daily activities, which should also include monitoring and evaluation.

An important aspect of any intervention is the public awareness that the intervention is in progress, public information about its progress and the publication of outcomes. In this way the community is not only actively involved in planning, but is also active in the execution, and can assess the progression towards the defined aims. Very often, in case of difficulties, it will be the community leaders and members that will have to help in overcoming barriers and checking for negative side-effects. During the execution, it will be necessary to keep accurate records about the expenditure as well as about the activities. The accounting is often demanded by grant-giving bodies, or is a regular part of any bud-geting exercise. This requires that the person in charge of a programme is a master of management skills, which include accounting and bud-geting as well as dealing with colleagues and the clients. This manage-ment aspect is very often lacking from training programmes in the field of health promotion and education.

Health promotion

Health promotion deals with external factors from the physical and social environment and plans interventions to improve the living conditions of the general population as well as of certain high risk groups.

It is based on the understanding of the medical, social and political aspects of the problem and its solution.

Definition of specific aims

Taking into account the definition of the given health problems in medical terms, with special reference to the intervention required on a societal and a personal level, the definition of specific aims of a health promotion aspect of the intervention will be in the following areas:

  1. *physical and social environment*

The physical environment may need improvement to provide the people with a possibility to stay healthy. In the same way the social environment may need modification in social norms and individual perception of the same to enhance people's chances of survival and improvements in health. Depending on the existing situation the aims of a health promotion intervention will, therefore, be:

  a. *physical environment* - the aim could be to remove any health hazards and improve living and working conditions in an area;

  b. *social norms* - the aim could be to modify or reinforce existing norms or create new ones according to whether they are conducive or not to health;

  c. *perception of norms* - the aim could be to change or reinforce individual perception of norms, since individuals may perceive that there are norms when no norms exist or they may wrongly perceive the sanction associated with norms.

2. *community services and lay support systems*

The aim of health promotion intervention can be concerned with improvement of existing services and provision of support from self-help groups. Specific aims can, therefore, be:

a. *community services* - the aim could be to improve or reinforce existing or to create new services which can include health as well as social services according to whether they are conducive to health and satisfy the needs of the community;

b. *lay support systems* - the aim could be to support existing or help in developing new lay support systems in the form of self-help groups according to the character of the health problem and the needs of the community.

Definition of objectives

The way the chosen aim or aims will be realised can be expressed in terms of objectives of the intervention. These could include:

1. *physical environment*

The definition of the problem and the choice of the solutions with regard to physical environment should be included in the objectives of the planned intervention;

2. *social environment (norms)*

Depending on the chosen aim the objectives could include creation of new norms or reinforcement and improvement of existing norms, as well as adjustment of individual perception of norms:

a. *social norms* - the objectives could be concerned with creation of new norms and reinforcing or changing existing norms. In addition to changing norms, the objectives could also be differentiated according to whether the norms in question are general or specific. The objectives of the intervention could also be specified according to which of the following aspects of a norm needs to be modified: legitimation, coercive power and/or social support;

b. *perception of norms* - the norms can only be as effective as the people perceive them and conform to them. The objectives could, therefore, also include the changing or reinforcing of individual perception of a norm and its specific characteristics.

3. *services*

Depending on the aims their achievement will require a different set of specific objectives:

a. *community services* - the objectives may include reinforcement and improvement of existing services or creation of new community services according to the needs of the population. They may also include the improvements in accessibility and attractiveness of the services to improve the utilisation and compliance within the community.

b. *lay support systems* - the objectives may include specific measures for financial and/or expert support for the existing lay support systems, or they may initiate the creation of new lay support groups in the form of self-help groups.

Methods

The achievement of objectives will require the choice of a combination of appropriate methods. These will be mainly concerned with the manipulation of the external factors and the individual adjustment to the same. One should not forget that any change will depend on a combination of health promotion and health education approaches, and that here we are mainly concerned with the former. The most commonly used methods include:

1. *advocacy*

This concept defines the role of the health promotion agents (bearing in mind the multisectoral approach) as advocates for the rights and need-satisfaction of a population or group. They can fulfil this role within the system (for example "advocates-planners") or by placing themselves outside the system (as for example some community workers).

In either case, advocacy is an important part of a health promotion intervention;

2. *mass media*

The mass media approach is most effective in changing social norms or expectations and will also be effective in changing people's perception of these norms. It is also very effective in transmitting information about certain health threats or diseases and the availability of relevant services, including the creation of new formal or lay services if and when necessary. When using mass media one should consider the following:

a. *the source* - will influence the credibility of the message;

b. *the message* - will be most successful if it is composed in a clear way, with the right appeal, using the appropriate language, showing relevance to the reader and providing the reader with an acceptable solution (who, what, when, where, how);

c. *the medium* - should be easily accessible to people and form a part of their usual way of acquiring information on a variety of subjects;

d. *the legitimising agent* - should participate in any mass media campaign and reinforce the message either publicly or on a person-to-person level;

3. *community organisation*

Community organisation as a means of ensuring community participation in the prevention, management and treatment of disease will be useful in creation, improvement and management of services in a community. Communities could be faced with three kinds of problems, each of which will require specific approaches:

a. *problems they themselves can solve* - and which will require mobilisation of community resources and active participation of community members;

b. *problems which they can solve only with outside help* - which means that community resources are not sufficient and outside help in expertise or resources will be required;

c. *problems that require outside help* - and where the community members need to have the knowledge and skills for mobilising this help, and which will usually include a multisectoral coordination of efforts and resources.

Indicators

Any evaluation of the achievement of the aims and objectives of a health promotion intervention will require a definition of appropriate indicators:

1. *changes in the physical environment*

Diagnosing the problem within a physical environment will provide the basis for the selection of appropriate indicators such as reduction of unemployment, of air pollution, improvement in transport and communications, establishment of services etc.

2. *changes in norms and their perception*

Any change concerning norms is a social process and will require social indicators, whereas the changes in personal perception of norms should be measured by surveying the individuals in a population. Both types of measurement will have to use indicators which are sensitive enough to measure the changes in the following aspects of norms and their perception:

a. *content* of a norm in relation to a health threat or disease and the expectations concerning people's behaviour and action;

b. *specificity* of the expectations which will be needed to assess people's behaviour in terms of conformity, variance and deviance;

c. *prevalence* or the awareness of the existence of a norm in a population or a specific population group;

d. *coercive power* of a norm in terms of sanctions related to the deviant behaviour;

e. *legitimation* of the expectations by the professions and important others;

f. *social support* which can be expected for conformist behaviour from the immediate and wider social environment.

3. *utilisation of services and self-help*

There is a whole range of indicators which have been developed for the measurement of utilisation of services which could be useful in evaluating a health promotion intervention, although new indicators will be required to measure the effectiveness of community participation in planning and management of existing and the creation of new services. New indicators will also be required in measuring the level of self-reliance in a community and the changes following a health promotion intervention. .

a. *services* - In addition to standardised indicators for the measurement of utilisation of services, new indicators will have to be developed for the establishment of existing or newly created social mechanisms enabling or preventing community participation in the planning and management of services according to the objectively established social needs;

b. *self-help* - Since there is no standardised way of measuring the development of self-help movements in a community, which is a social process, new indicators will have to be developed, which will include the measurement of the existing levels of self-reliance and self-help in a community in general and specifically for the problem relevant to the health promotion intervention in question; the community need for social support in general and specifically in relation to the problem in question; the changes achieved by the health promotion intervention.

Criteria

Criteria represent the units that will be used in the measurement of the contribution of a certain objective to the achievement of a specified aim. They also include a value judgment about a measured level of achievement. On a population level, the planner may, for example, be faced with making the following decisions:

1. how to measure the different *aspects* of "awareness" to be able to establish which ones are contributing most to an activity, or lack of which is associated with non-activity;

2. how to measure the different *levels* of different aspects of "awareness" to be able to establish the "optimal", compared to the "absolute" or "maximal" level, which can then be used as a measure of success or failure;

3. how to choose the *target population* for such measurements in terms of relevance, accessibility and representativeness for the study population;

4) how to measure the *prevalence* of the expected action, accepting the limitations of "reported" as compared to "observed" behaviour, and the problems of validity and reliability of the collected information.

The Instruments

Once the indicators have been chosen and criteria for their measurement and assessment have been agreed upon, the planner will have to translate them into instruments which will then be used for the collection of desired information.

There is a whole set of different forms that such instruments can take, from structured questionnaires and "aide memoire" to diaries and scaling methods.

The value judgment about the expected levels of change as compared to those observed will be important for the analysis and for justifiable inferences.The instruments should be tested for validity and reliability.

Resources

The resources necessary for a health promotion intervention will vary in kind and origin. Since any health promotion intervention is by definition dependent on a multisectoral coordination and cooperation the resources will originate from different institutions and government bodies. The kinds of resources required are:

1. *financial*

Any improvements in the physical environment will be dependent on the available financial support. This has to be taken into account when planning an intervention and will be ensured by community participation in the planning process. Health promotion also depends on the use of mass media which are in most cases commercially run and are very expensive. It will be, therefore, necessary to make provisions for covering the expenses of production and publication of messages in mass media; since these and other similar activities require professional expertise they will also require financial support; evaluation which includes population surveys will also require financial support;

2. *material*

The preparation and publication of material to be distributed in different forms will have to be done by experts, since people are exposed to high quality of advertising and public relation products in their everyday life. In addition to technical experts, it will be necessary to plan for communication experts to be involved in the choice and formulation of the messages;

3. *personnel*

Although a health promotional intervention requires a multi-sectoral involvement, it will be necessary to have a group of experts who will act as coordinators and initiators of the activities and who will supervise the monitoring and evaluation of the intervention.

Monitoring and Evaluation

Evaluation of any social intervention can be only as good as is the precision of defining the aims and objectives, although, one must accept that since one deals with social processes, it will be impossible to measure all the side effects of such a social intervention. The indicators used should ensure that social changes are measured by social indicators and changes on a personal level by using personal indicators, and that a number of measurements are included aimed at recording any negative side-effects. Monitoring and evaluation should include:

1. *base-line data*

The base-line data define the situation before a health promotion intervention has taken place. They should include the information about the following:

a. *the problem* which is the part of the aims; its distribution in the population, the available solutions and the available services to deal with the problem;

b. *the mechanisms* which are necessary to achieve a change and improvement by means of health promotion; their utilisation in community participation; their support for building up of community self reliance;

2. *outcome*

The post-intervention data collection should enable a comparison with the situation before the intervention and the achievements of the intervention. It should be utilised by means of a feed-back mechanism to inform the planners about the achievements and eventual problems.

3. *inferences*

Pre- and post-surveys and measurements will indicate any changes that have been recorded. The inferences can include according to the indicators used, the following:

a. *what occurred* in terms of changes recorded and how does this match to the expectations defined in the aims;

b. *why it occurred* in terms of causality and the direct links between measures of intervention and the changes recorded, which should provide the theoretical basis for the practical actions;

c. *any negative consequences* in terms of unplanned changes or consequences which could be due to the lack of a defined cause-effect relationship between interventions and outcomes.

Health education

Health education in its reduced scope since the introduction of health promotion, deals mainly with personal and small group factors. It should, however, be recognised as the necessary and complementary aspect to health promotion, for any intervention aimed at improving health of a population.

Definition of specific aims

Once the problem has been defined in medical terms which means that one knows what are the required specific actions which will protect or improve health and prevent or help in the management of a disease, it will be possible to carry out an educational diagnosis and define the aims of a health education intervention. These may include:

1. *knowledge*

The aims can be to increase, correct or improve the existing knowledge or lack of it, concerning a health threat or disease and the available solutions in terms of prevention, management or treatment of that specific health problem;

2. *attitudes*

It still seems to be accepted that in general attitudes can enhance or inhibit a health action or behaviour modification. It has been, however, doubtful that changes in attitudes will always result in changes of behaviour. The aims could, therefore, include the acquisition of positive attitudes or a positive way of resolving cognitive dissonance if attitudes cannot be changed;

3. *skills*

Behaviour modification usually depends on skills to manage the transitional period and to establish new behavioral patterns. Skills are also required in coping with new situations (childbirth, bereavement, unemployment, divorce etc.) and form an important part of a health education intervention. The aims of health education must take these required skills into consideration when trying to achieve self-reliance and competence in improvement of one's own and family health.

Definition of objectives

The achievement of aims will depend on the setting of appropriate objectives. Concerning knowledge, attitudes and skills, these can be differentiated in terms of the following processes:

1. *acquisition*

It will be necessary to define in a specific way which objectives will be most promising for the achievement of knowledge, desirable attitudes and necessary skills required for improvements in health. Each of the three aims mentioned will require different objectives concerning the processes involved and methods used;

2. *modification*

The set of objectives to achieve modification of existing knowledge, attitudes or skills will have to take into account the approaches and methods which have been shown to be effective in achieving such a change..

Methods

Depending on the aims and objectives health education interventions have a set of different methods at their disposal:

1. *information*

Transmission and acquisition of information is associated with knowledge necessary for the awareness of a threat and the availability of ways to prevent it. The methods used include mass media, public lectures, group work and individual advice. The theories which explain the relevance of an approach include learning and communication theories, advertising and market research;

2. *counselling*

To enable individuals to cope with a health problem in terms of behaviour modification, adjustment of their subjective reality, the desired role performance and a general increase in their personal competence, they may require an intensive support in the form of counselling. This can take a variety of forms which have to be adjusted to the individual's needs and capacities;

3. *group work*

Changes in attitudes as well as coping with certain emotional problems may require a supportive environment which can either be found in a family or in a group of a specific kind. It has been found that group dynamics can be conducive to changes in attitudes and resolution of cognitive dissonance, changes in self esteem, a help in improving self assertion and readjusting the perceived locus of control. Groups are also helpful in accepting commitments through negotiation and group pressure.

Indicators, criteria, instruments

The aims and objectives will have to be defined in such a way that they can be measured in terms of the initial situation and the subsequent changes:

1. *specific indicators*

It is recognised that when the aim is an improvement in health by means of changing a life-style, it may be difficult to select specific indicators which could monitor and record such a change. It will be necessary to define a life-style as a system, decide on the relevant factors within that system and plan an evaluation of changes within these factors or in their interrelationship.

2. *criteria for optimal change*

Most of the behaviour associated with an increased risk from a disease or a health threat is a necessary part of the everyday life and survival (eating, exercise, sex, etc.), and only a few are irrelevant and represent acquired habits (alcohol, smoking, etc.). Any evaluation of a health education intervention will have to define the criteria in terms of the "minimal" and "optimal" degree of change required for the prevention, management and treatment of a disease.

3. *instruments*

Any population study will require questionnaires for the collection of information which can then be translated into quantitative data. It is, however, appreciated that qualitative data can provide a better insight into more subtle changes which follow a health education intervention, in addition to more crude changes in overt behaviour. The instruments developed for the exploration of indicators and criteria can, therefore, range from postal questionnaires to in depth case studies.

Resources

The new concept of health education as an intensive and personal intervention, requires greater resources in terms of money, time and personnel:

1. *financial*

The financial support will be required for the establishment and maintenance of supportive services required by individuals, for the cost of educational programmes and for monitoring and evaluation of the interventions;

2. *material*

The material resources will include provision of special premises and means of transport, educational material for schools and inservice training programmes, for special educational programmes concerning new health threats and for new educational and information technology;

3. *personnel*

Individual work is labour intensive and will require a much greater number of educators than previously envisaged, additional inservice training for the acquisition of a professional status, and expertise in monitoring and evaluating planned interventions.

Monitoring and evaluation

It is not possible to envisage an intensive personal intervention of a professional standard without monitoring and evaluating the processes and outcomes. The criteria will be the level of benefit for the clients and professional responsibility will be expressed in avoiding any unforeseen negative side-effects. To achieve this, monitoring and evaluation will include:

1. *base-line data*

Collection of base-line data is necessary for any assessment of change in terms of benefiting the clients. The aims and objectives of the intervention will decide on the kind of base-line data required and the population to be included in the monitoring and evaluation programme;

2. *processes*

It will not be sufficient to establish the outcome of an intervention which takes place during a time interval. It has been shown that the processes that go on during an intervention are as important as the final outcome. Monitoring the processes may indicate the reasons why an intervention did or did not succeed;

3. *feed-back*

Any evaluation programme should include a feed-back mechanism which will allow for timely corrections in the process of an intervention without waiting for the final outcome;

4. *inferences*

The final assessment of an intervention will be carried out on the basis of the indicators and criteria developed in accordance with the aims and objectives set out in advance.

EXAMPLES

Example: The British Social Attitudes Survey

(Jowell R, Airey C.Ed. "British Social Attitudes", Gower Publishing Co.Brookfield, Vermont, USA)

An example of the existing social attitudes in a country is the yearly publication of the report "The British Social Attitudes" produced by Social and Community Planning Research. There are 5 national reports and one international report, dealing with the following topics:

1984 Report:

- political attitudes
- economic policy and expectations
- social policy and the welfare state
- educational issues and priorities
- social and moral values

1985 Report

- shades of opinions
- prices, incomes and consumer issues
- sex roles and gender issues
- attitudes to defence and international issues
- right and wrong in public and private life
- local government and the environment
- measuring individual attitude change

1986 Report:

- do people have consistent attitudes?
- work and the work ethics
- political partisanship
- a green and pleasant land?
- British and American attitudes
- interim report: education
- interim report: public spending and the welfare state
- interim report: housing
- interim report: social and moral issues

1987 Report:

- citizenship and welfare
- business and industry
- political culture
- nuclear reactions
- food values: health and diet
- family matters
- interim report: the countryside
- interim report: party politics

1988/89 Report:

- the price of honesty
- education matters
- trends in permissiveness
- working-class conservatives and middle-class social-ists
- the public's response to AIDS
- an ailing state of national health trust in the estab-lishment

- one nation?
- interim report: rural prospects
- interim report: woman's work

1989 Special International Report:
- measuring national differences
- international patterns of work
- the role of the state
- inequality and welfare
- kinship and friendship
- understanding of science in Britain and USA
- pride in one's country: Britain and West Germany
- interim report: the changing family

The wide variety of topics serve as a very useful background to any interventions based on health issues related to the topics mentioned. There are some, such as the family, attitudes to the health services, to food, work, housing, etc. all of which are associated with health issues.

Example: Operational research in problem definition

(Baric, L. "Operational Research", Int. Journal for Health Education, vol xi, 2, Geneva, 1968.)

There are a number of different approaches which can be used in health services research. All of them emphasise the complexity of research methods concerned with organisations, their problems and activities. Since a number of causes of medical problems can be due to certain operational aspects of health care organisations, it is necessary to bear in mind the complexity of any research in this field.

Operational research is one of many approaches which could be useful in studying the health care system. The main characteristic of operational research is its applied aspect. It has been defined in many ways and for our purposes it can be described as "the application of scientific, methods, techniques and tools to problems involving the operations of a system so as to provide those in control of the system with optimum solutions to the problems". It is important to emphasise the systems approach of operational research which is very important in the study of the provision of health care which is a system in its own right.

In setting up an operational research project it will be necessary to follow certain steps of procedure. The first step will be *defining the system* since it will be necessary to limit the area of investigation when dealing with such a complex system as the provision of health care. An important aspect in defining the system under study will be to set up the boundaries of that system. One can well imagine that one could not study the whole health care system and a study of hospitals or general practices could be an example of choosing a specific system within the overall system under consideration. One has to be aware that the optimal solution arrived at in such a study will apply only to the specific system and not necessarily to the general system as a whole.

The second step will be to set up a *model of the system*. A model is a simplified representation designed to incorporate or reproduce the relevant features of the system which are considered to be significant for the research. It takes pieces of information about parts of the general system and assembles them into a representation of the specific system under study. For the study of some aspect of the health care system an "operating model" will be appropriate since it represents a dynamic system and reproduces the processes in action. In this way one can study the relationships and the changes over a period of time. It is, however, important to bear in mind that models are simplified representations of a system and will include only those factors which the researcher deems relevant to the problem; they are neither true nor false and may represent the reality well or not so well and are only a conceptual framework designed by the researcher to represent the system under study. One of the advantages of using models is that they allow us a simulation approach which means that one can change the relationship between different parts of the model and find out the consequences without actually interfering in the real life situation.

The third step will be choosing the appropriate methods and techniques for *data collection and analysis*. In most cases operational research will use standard methods of data collection which include participant observation, analysis of records, surveys, interviews etc. These methods will be used within specific approaches according to the nature of the problem under study. Some of the approaches are briefly described here:

1. *Linear programming*: uses linear equations to describe the relationships between two or more variables to find the optimal solution. This kind of analysis is widely applied in the study of production processes where, for example, output and cost are functionally related;

2. *Game theory*: is a branch of mathematics which deals with situations of conflict, involving decisions where the outcome will be affected by two or more decision makers. It deals with games of strategy, as opposed to probability theory which deals with games of chance. An important aspect of this theory is that the players must know and apply the rules of the game. This approach can be useful in studying interactions between professionals and their clients to find out the reasons for possible conflicts arising from such an interaction. A simple reason for a breakdown in communications could be, as in the case of doctor-patient interaction, that each of the players applies a different set of rules of the game.

3. *Queuing theory*: as a mathematical theory serves to calculate for any given situation what kind of a queue will result, how long people will have to wait before service and how to work out the optimal solution taking into account all the restrictive elements within the system. It can be used, for example, in the study of the usage of hospital beds, reduction of waiting time in clinics, etc. This approach makes full use of the advantages of modelling since it can try out different kinds of solutions without actually disturbing the operational system.

4. *Simulation method*: uses models to try out different solutions and their consequences. It is, however, more important for predicting trends and future developments as consequences of certain interventions. It allows for cost benefit analysis of each approach, their effects on resources and for experimentation with new methods and technologies.

5. *Statistical analysis*: is the most widely used technique for describing and interpreting collected data and information. Out of the enormous number of techniques available, for operational research, the most commonly used are tests which enable us to make a distinction between real and chance occurrences; calculation of the probability with which certain events will occur in particular situations; measurement of correlation between different attributes; estimating errors which may occur in measurement and inferences.

Example: Measuring intelligence (IQ Test)

(Based on: Babbie, E. 1989 ,"The Practice of Social Research", Wadsworth, Inc. Belmont,California)

Scientist are still trying to find a definitive definition of intelligence. In common use are three explanations of intelligence:

a) the capacity of organisms to learn by experience and make adaptive responses to new situations as contrasted with instinctive or reflex responses;

b) the faculty of understanding, intellect; that is the cognitive aspect of mental functioning and in particular the higher thought processes and conceptual activities, and the grasping of relationships;

c) a measurement of the common element or factor underlying successful performance at varied mental tasks such as those included in intelligence tests or intelligence quotients (IQ).

These definitions represent three different approaches (biological, psychological and statistical). Piaget has tried to bring them together by explaining the development of associative mechanisms in the brain in terms of the product of genetic potentialities for the formation of schemata (neuron assemblies in the association areas of the brain), and of experience or stimulation by the environment. From the point of view of the mental tester, intelligence is a fluid collection of overlapping abilities, rather than any single identifiable faculty.

The construct 'intelligence' has a widespread use in scientific circles as well as in common language. There is no wonder that it attracted a great number of scientists engaged in developing and refining test to measure this construct. There are a great number of tests which have been developed for the measurement of intelligence. Although different in a number of ways, most of them produce results which are reasonably correlated with each other.

Whichever test one uses, the IQ score has been found to be correlated with a great many abilities, aptitudes and various other achievements, such as scholastic, associated with learning and problem solving, occupational performance, income, etc. In recent years the notion of "creativity" has become popular. The implication is that there is an inverse correlation between creativity and intelligence, i.e. people with low intelligence can be highly creative. This notion is questionable since there is no acceptable definition of "creativity" as such.

Attempts have also been made to link IQ with nonintellectual activities such as personality adjustment, social responsibility, delinquency, crime, etc. These have not been greatly successful in establishing a causal relationship between IQ and such traits, although statistical associations may be found.

There has been some evidence that IQ is associated with physical correlates such as brain size. The established correlation, adjusted for body size and weight, is statistically acceptable. It is explained in evolutionary terms as an explanation of the rapid increase in human brain size as an adaptive advantage in human evolution. Other similar associations have been attempted between IQ and the pattern of brain waves, stature, basal metabolic rate and obesity, and myopia.

Example: Measuring competence in looking after children

(From: Baric, L. "Measuring Family Competence" WHO, Geneva,1982)

Children are born into families which can have different structures and organisational forms (single parent family, extended family etc.). In most of them there is a mother that looks after the new born baby and children during their first few years of life. This period is very important for the immediate and future state of health of a child and will require a high level of competence of a mother and other members in the family in protecting the child's health. It can be assumed that the health of the child will, in addition to mother's competence, also depend on mother's health during pregnancy and delivery. It is because of this that the measurement of family competence in this specific area of activity covers the whole period from conception, through delivery to at least the end of the first year of a child.

The concept of family competence is a theoretical construct which can only be measured by means of indicators which are used to translate abstract or unmeasurable social concepts into operational terms and thus allow consideration and analysis of such a concept. Since indicators are measures they must be quantifiable, e.g. expressed in numerical terms. One cannot, however, consider family competence in a social vacuum, which implies that it is necessary to establish the environmental conditions under which the assessment of family competence will take place.

Designing indicators requires that the concept be clearly defined in terms of its constituent parts, which should then be translated into indicators, enabling the collection and the analysis of appropriate data. When a concept, such as family competence, is complex, it is not possible to rely on one indicator, so that an indicator system or set is necessary. This indicators set will contain a number of relevant domains of investigation, each of which will include criteria used for measurement and the instruments designed for the collection of data.

The domains of an indicator set concerned with measuring family competence in looking after their own health include a) health of the respondent, b) health of the children and c) health of other adult members of the family.

The criteria used for each domain include i) recognition of symptoms, ii) management of possible crises or chronic cases and prevention of same, and iii) mobilisation of help and support in such situations.

Brought together, the domains and criteria include:

DOMAIN 1 : HEALTH OF THE RESPONDENT

Criterion 1.1 :Recognition of symptoms and possible health threats.
- Recall of most common diseases in that area;
- Previous experiences with illnesses;
- Knowledge about causes, processes and outcomes.

Criterion 1.2 : Management of possible crises or chronic cases and prevention of same:
- Knowledge and skills in preventing most common diseases;
- Knowledge and skills in managing and treating most common diseases;
- Personal experiences in prevention and management of diseases;

Criterion 1.3: Mobilisation of help and support:
- From family, friends and community;
- From alternative health care system;
- From medical and paramedical professional system;

DOMAIN 2: HEALTH OF THE CHILDREN

Criterion 2.1 : Recognition of symptoms and possible threats:
- Recall of most common childhood diseases in the area;

- Previous experiences with childhood diseases;
- Knowledge about causes, processes and outcomes;

Criterion 2.2 : Management of possible crises or chronic cases and prevention of same:

- Knowledge and skills in preventing most common childhood diseases;
- Knowledge and skills in managing and treating common childhood diseases;
- Personal experiences in prevention and management of childhood diseases;

Criterion 2.3 : Mobilisation of help and support:
- From family, friends and community;
- From alternative health care system;
- From medical and paramedical professional system;

DOMAIN 3: HEALTH OF OTHER ADULT MEMBERS OF THE FAMILY

Criterion 3.1: Recognition of symptoms and possible health threats:
- Recall of most common adult diseases in the area;
- Previous experiences with adult family members' diseases;
- Knowledge about causes, processes and outcomes;

Criterion 3.2: Management of possible crises or chronic cases and prevention of same:

- Knowledge and skills in preventing common diseases of adults;
- Knowledge and skills in managing and treating common adult diseases;
- Personal experiences in prevention and management

of adult diseases;

Criterion 3.3: Mobilisation of help and support:
- From family, friends and community;
- From alternative health care system;
- From medical and paramedical professional system.

Each of the three domains mentioned is subdivided into criteria which are used to define family competence in preventing most common diseases or managing them if they occur. To establish family competence in each of these three domains, the respondents will be asked questions about their knowledge and experiences, which will be analysed and grouped into categories denoting any possible problems which can be translated into health promotion and health education actions during the intervention study using the community participation approach.

The assessment of competence of each family is based on the respondents answers to the questions which are of a general nature and allow the interviewer to explore each question area and make the assessment of competence by marking the answers in terms of existing knowledge and the actions taken by the respondents. For this purpose the interviewers need to have a professional background and should be trained in the assessment procedure. The group approach of training interviewers will enable them during the discussion to establish common standards of assessment and ensure comparable findings for each respondent.

The actual assessment is based on the concepts of "adequate" knowledge or action at the one end of the spectrum and "ignorance" or "wrong" action on the other end. This assessment of knowledge and actions will be relative, since it is carried out within the existing experiences and opportunities of the individual respondent. For example, if a person did not have experience with a disease such as pelagra, then the lack of knowledge or action concerning pelagra becomes irrelevant for the assessment of "competence". In other words, competence is being assessed within the framework of individual experiences and on the basis of knowledge and actions relevant to these experiences.

The intervention is based on the respondent's needs for increased knowledge and skills, as well as on improving the opportunities for necessary actions and will be followed by a repeat survey to measure the changes that may have occurred.

Example: Measuring competence in first aid

(From: First Aid Manual, 1982, St John Ambulance Association, London)

The main competence in looking after one's own or other people's health is to master the skills of first aid. This topic has been sadly neglected by people engaged in health promotion and education and is still considered to be the domain of certain institutions associated with first aid, such as The Red Cross, St.John Ambulance, or some others.

There are many first aid courses and manuals which can be bought which deal with this topic. They cover in general the same ground which includes the following topics:

The principles and practice of first aid

The definition of first aid is given as: "the skilled application of accepted principles of treatment on the occurrence of any injury or sudden illness, using facilities or materials available at the time. It is the approved method of treating a casualty until placed in care of a doctor or removed to hospital".

Although many people in different situations can be called upon to help someone, the term First Aider has a semi-professional connotation, since it defines a person who has received an authorised certificate qualifying him/her to render first aid.

The responsibility of a First Aider is to:

- assess the situation;

- identify the disease or condition from which the casualty is suffering;

- give immediate, appropriate and adequate treatment, bearing in mind that the casualty   may have more than one injury and may require a more urgent attention than others;

- arrange without delay, for the disposal of a casualty to a doctor, hospital or home, according to the seriousness of the condition.

Major first aid techniques

structure and functions of a human body. The course and the manual for first aid gives the necessary facts in association with the parts of the body affected by certain most common injuries. Based on this general knowledge, the First Aider can use certain methods and techniques to help the casualty.

The most common techniques include what is known as ABC or taking care of person's vital needs which are:

- an open AIRWAY

- adequate BREATHING

- sufficient CIRCULATION

For life to continue a person must be able to take oxygen into the lungs, from where it will be distributed by blood throughout the body. It is important to bear in mind that some organs cannot survive for long without fresh blood supply (brain cells die after 3 minutes without blood supply). The three emergency situations are: lack of breathing and/or heartbeat; severe bleeding; state of unconsciousness which can disrupt any of the vital functions. For each of these situations the First Aider must be able to diagnose the situation, to provide help and to mobilise professional help.

It is also important to make sure that the injured person is in a position which will enable the normal functioning of the body and help in recovery. This is known as the 'recovery position' which places the unconscious casualty who is breathing and whose heart is beating, to lie on the belly with one leg slightly bent, the arms on the side of the body and the head to one side. In this way the air passage is free, and in case of vomiting the mouth can drain freely.

The First Aider must also know the techniques of using bandages, im-mobilisation and transport of the injured.

The course and the manual of First Aid deals with the major problems and situations which include:

The respiratory system and asphyxia

Asphyxia is a condition in which there is commonly lack of oxygen in blood. The cause of this condition may be the lack of oxygen in the air that the person is breathing or the lungs and heart have ceased to func-tion effectively.

The causes for this condition are most commonly the blocking of air passage (food went the wrong way), drowning, bronchitis, asthma, smoke, irritant gases, hiccups), obstruction (the tongue falling to the back of the throat in an unconscious casualty, a foreign body in the air passage, swelling of tissues of the throat), suffocation (by pillows, plas-tic bags), compression of the neck (strangulation, hanging, throttling), compression of the chest (compression by earth,a fallen object etc., crushing against a wall, pressure in a crowd, damaged chest), condi-tion affecting the nerves which control respiration (electrical injury, poisoning by drugs, gases liquids, muscle contraction as in tetanus, par-alysis as in apoplexy or in injury to spinal cord), conditions preventing the use of oxygen by the body (carbon monoxide poisoning, cyanide poisoning, air containing insufficient oxygen as in smoke filled rooms, change in atmospheric pressure as in high altitudes or deep sea diving) and continuous fits preventing adequate breathing.

If a casualty is not breathing the first step will be resuscitation or an at-tempt to restore breathing. The First Aider must know the techniques of checking breathing, opening and clearing the airways, and taking over the function of breathing for the casualty. This can be done by mouth-to-mouth ventilation or by the Holger-Nielsen method which requires the injured to lie on the stomach and by raising the arms, the chest becomes extended and allows for air to flow into the lungs.

Different causes of asphyxia will require different treatments. For example, in case of drowning the first step will be to clear the air pas-sage by emptying the water from the body. In the same way, in case of strangulation due to hanging special measures will have to be taken to lower the body before rendering first aid. This is also true in case of electric shock, where the cause of the shock must be dealt with to protect the injured as well as the First Aider, before rendering resuscitation.

If the casualty's heart is not beating, the First Aider will have to assist in establishing blood circulation. This includes external chest compression, or a combination of ventilation and chest compression.

The circulatory system, bleeding and shock

The First Aider must understand the circulatory system of the body, must differentiate between external and internal bleeding, the difference between bleeding from arteries or veins and how to deal with shock, which is usually the consequence of blood loss.

The First Aider will try to stop bleeding, protect the wound to prevent infection and deal with shock. It will be necessary to know the application of bandages, pressure points to stop severe bleeding, and how to deal with foreign bodies which may be lodged in the wound.

Special parts of the body will need specific treatment of bleeding such as the head, nose, mouth, ear, chest, belly, arms and legs, fingers, etc..

The bleeding can be caused by different wounds such as incised or clean cut, lacerated or torn, contused or bruised, punctured or stab and gunshot wounds.Each type of wound requires special techniques to stop bleeding which the First Aider must master.

Shock is a condition resulting from the lessening of the activities of the vital functions of the body from a lack of blood supply. The severity of shock will depend on the nature and extent of injury and may vary from a feeling of faintness, loss of consciousness to death. It may be caused by severe bleeding from an artery or ruptured varicose vein; loss of plasma from the circulation due to burns or crush injuries; heart failure; acute abdominal emergencies (ruptured appendix, perforation of the stomach); loss of body fluid (recurrent vomiting due to sea-sickness or severe diarrhoea, dysentery, etc.); nerve stimulation (nerve shock).

The signs and symptoms of shock are paleness and clammy skin with profuse sweating, feeling of faintness, sickness, blurring of vision, anxiety, loss of consciousness, increased pulse rate, shallow and rapid breathing.

The treatment requires immediate hospitalisation and possible blood transfusion. In the meantime the injured should be kept warm and comfortable; attention should be paid to possible vomiting and loss of consciousness. The injured should not be overheated (hot water bottles) or be given anything to drink, and not be moved unnecessarily.

Injuries to bones

A fracture is a cracked or broken bone. It can be closed (where skin surface is not broken) or open (where there is a wound leading to the fracture, or a fractured bone is protruding through the skin), or even 'complicated' if in addition to a fracture there are other organs affected by the fracture (brain, lungs, liver, etc.).

If a fracture has caused severe bleeding, this must be seen to in the first place. The treatment of fractures is mainly concerned with immobilisation of the fractured limb or other parts of the body by temporary fixation and before attempting to move the injured. Immobilisation can be by means of body bandages and/or splints.

There are special treatments of fractures of certain parts of the body, such as head, jaw, arms and legs, spine, chest, etc. The First Aider must know how to handle each one without causing further damage or unnecessary pain to the injured. All fractures or suspected fractures must be dealt with in hospitals.

The nervous system and unconsciousness

The nervous system consists of two parts - the cerebro-spinal system and the autonomous system. These together control the movements and functions of the body and the level of consciousness. The cerebro-spinal system includes the brain, the spinal cord and nerves which can be sensory nerves (loss of sensation) and motor nerves (loss of movement). The autonomous system consists of nerves which regulate involuntary muscles and regulate vital functions of the body (breathing, heartbeat, digestion, etc.).

Unconsciousness can be the result of a number of injuries to the nervous system and will require special treatment according to the severity of the condition, which can range from slight drowsiness to coma.

The treatment will consist of insuring appropriate breathing, seeing to injuries and control bleeding, making the injured comfortable and ensuring a speedy removal to hospital. Any person who has been unconscious even for a brief moment should be seen by a doctor.

It is useful to check whether the unconscious injured person has any identification or treatment card or bracelet, which may be helpful in choosing the best treatment.

Burns and scalds

One can differentiate between superficial and deep burns. They can be caused by dry or moist heat, electricity, corrosive chemicals, or radiation.

The symptoms are pain, redness, or shock.

The aim of the First Aider is to reduce the local effects of heat; to relieve pain; to prevent infection; to replace fluid loss and lessen shock; remove the injured to hospital.

The treatment consists of reducing heat by cold water, covering the injured part with a clean cloth, transport to hospital in severe cases. No ointment or pricking of blisters is allowed. In case of chemicals, the burn must be washed out to prevent further damage. Any clothing soaked in chemicals or boiling water must be promptly removed.

A special case is sunburn which is very common and can range from mild redness to severe blistering. In the latter case medical help should be sought.

Poisoning

A poison can be any substance (liquid, gas or solid) which if taken into the body may affect health or even life. A poison may be taken accidentally or intentionally through lungs, by mouth, by injection or by absorption through the skin.

Through the lungs a poison may enter the body by breathing poisonous fumes, smoke; by the mouth it may enter the body by swallowing some poisonous substance which may cause reaction directly on the food passage (from poisonous berries, infested food, etc.) or on the nervous system (from alcohol, drugs, etc); by injection under the skin (from bites of poisonous reptiles, some animals, some insects, by hypodermic syringe as in drug taking, etc.); by absorption through skin (by pesticides, etc.).

The treatment consists of finding out what happened if the injured is conscious, and preserving any signs of the poison such as tablets, chemicals, etc. If there are burns in the mouth the injured should be given a lot of water, milk or any other mild liquid to dilute the poison; clothing soaked in chemicals should be removed. If the injured is unconscious, he/she should be placed in the recovery position to help in breathing or given artificial respiration. In any case immediate transport to hospital is vital for survival and reducing of further damage.

Emergency childbirth

In an emergency childbirth, the first steps should include sending for a doctor or a midwife. One should not panic, pull the baby, the cord or the afterbirth out, cut the cord until it stops pulsating. One should keep calm, let the nature take its course, protect the baby from falling on the ground, and when delivered, keeping it warm and handing it over to the mother to hold it.

The First Aider should know the stages of delivery, how to protect the mother and the baby from infection, and how to assist during the birth if necessary by reassuring the mother, checking where the cord is and releasing it if it is around baby's neck, and removing the membrane if it is over the baby's face.

When the baby is born, it should be held upside-down to let any fluid drain out from the mouth and nose, and allow the baby to take the first breath. If that does not occur within two minutes, it will be necessary to start resuscitation, by ventilating baby's lungs by blowing very gently.

Shortly after the birth of the baby the afterbirth will be expelled and it should be kept for examination by a doctor or a midwife to see that it is complete. The cord of the baby should be tied in two places and cut in between the ties.

Example :   Definition of the Coronary Heart Disease problem

(From: Baric L. "Formal Health Education and the Prevention of Coronary Heart Disease", Report on the Salford (1973) study, University of Manchester.)

Description of the problem

In general terms, the problem we are dealing with can be described as disease of the heart and its blood vessels. Here the first clarification should be made: there are blood vessels that supply the heart with blood which is then pumped through it to other parts of the body, and there are blood vessels which supply the heart muscle with blood. The latter are known as coronary blood vessels because they form a 'corona' or a crown encircling the heart.

Usually we use different terminology, such as cardiovascular disease, ischaemic heart disease, coronary heart disease, arteriosclerotic heart disease. This is bound to confuse workers with non-medical background. However, even those in the medical profession may be uncertain because of different terminologies usages, as is shown by different ways causes of death have been registered in different countries.

According to the International Classification of Disease (ICD 1965 Revision), heart diseases come under the general category of diseases of the circulatory system.   It is sub-divided into the following sub-categories: (numbers given in brackets are ICD numbers).

(390-392)	Active Rheumatic Fever
(393-398)	Chronic Rheumatic Heart Disease
(400-404)	Hypertensive Disease
(410-414)	Ischaemic Heart Disease
(420-429)	Other Forms of Heart Disease
(430-438)	Cerebrovascular Disease
(440-448)	Diseases of Arteries, Arterioles and Capillaries
(450-458)	Disease of Veins and Lymphatics, and other diseases of the Circulatory System.

In this example, since we are concerned only with the sub-category of Ischaemic Heart Disease, it will be useful to see its further sub-divisions:

(410)   Acute Myocardial Infarction
        Cardiac infarction
        Coronary (artery) embolism
                  "   occlusion
                  "   rupture
                  "   thrombosis
        Infarction of heart, myocardium or ventricle
        Rupture of heart
           "   myocardium
        Any condition in 412 specified as acute or with
        a stated duration of 8 weeks or less.

(411)   Other Acute or subacute forms of Ischaemic Heart Disease
        Angina decubitus
        Coronary failure
          "   insufficiency
        Intermediate coronary syndrome
        Micro-infarct of heart
        Pre-infarction syndrome
        Sub-endocardial infarction

(412)   Chronic Ischaemic Heart Disease
        Aneurysm of heart
        Arteriosclerotic heart (disease)
        Cardiovascular arteriosclerosis
                 "   degeneration
                 "   disease
                 "   sclerosis
        Coronary (artery) arteriosclerosis
                 "   atheroma
                 "   disease
                 "   sclerosis
                 "   stricture
        Healed myocardial infarct
        Ischaemic degeneration of heart
          "   of myocardium
        Ischaemic heart disease
        Post-myocardial infarct syndrome
        Any condition in 410 specified as chronic or
        with a stated duration of over 8 weeks

(413)   Angina Pectoris
          Angina NOS (no other signs)
               "   pectoris
          Angina syndrome
          Cardiac angina
          Stenocardia

(414)   Asymptomatic Ischaemic Heart Disease
          Ischaemic heart disease diagnosed on ECG
          but presenting no symptoms.

In diseases of the coronary arteries or ischaemic heart disease (ischaemia means bloodlessness of a part of the body), the blood supply to the heart muscle is affected and this in turn affects its function. This can be due to contraction, spasm, constriction or blocking of the blood vessels.

The function of the heart muscle can be affected either by inadequate blood supply or by complete blockage of a blood vessel supplying the heart muscle.   Inadequate blood supply, such as in arteriosclerosis, occurs when the blood vessels become narrow in places and slow down the blood supply to the heart muscle. Complete blockage of a blood vessel can occur due to embolism or thrombosis. (Embolism refers to the blocking of a small blood vessel by material which has been carried through the larger vessels by the blood stream; thrombosis refers to the formation of a blood clot within the vessels of the heart). When a complete blockage of a coronary artery occurs it results in a cardiac infarction. (Infarction refers to changes which take place in an organ when an artery is suddenly blocked, leading to the formation of a dense, wedge-shaped mass in the part of the organ supplied by the artery).

An obstruction in the blood supply to a part of the heart muscle will affect the functioning of the heart. The result may be sudden death, or angina pectoris which manifests itself in violent paroxysms of painful sensation in the chest, typically when physical activity leads to extra demands on the heart.

Arteriosclerotic changes in coronary artery disease can be due to either atherosclerosis or to atheroma. Arteriosclerosis is a condition of thickening and rigidity involving predominantly the middle coat of medium sized arteries and can happen in any part of the body. When it is caused by fatty degeneration of the middle coat of the arterial wall then it is called atherosclerosis; atheroma is a degenerative change of the inner coat, but involving the middle coat in time, and manifests itself as small nodes or swellings here and there on arteries (Thomson, 1967).

Nearly all of the factors discussed in the previous section have been found to be directly or indirectly associated with the incidence of coronary heart disease. For purposes of preventing the disease through health education certain requirements are necessary: we must know how to identify the people who are at higher risk from developing the disease or suffering from its consequences, and we must know what changes in their living conditions and behaviour patterns to promote.

Morris with his colleagues (1966) examined the natural history of ischaemic heart disease in stages and divided it into *'causes'* (inheritance, experience and mode of life), *'precursor'* pathology (as causes begin to show effects in disturbed function and structure, without as yet any evidence of the disease), and *'early incidence'* (as disease, possibly reversible, appears).

Among causes, it was found that all of the factors included (age, family history, stature, obesity, occupation and cigarette smoking) contributed to the individual risk from the disease. Occupation was the most powerful contributor, whereas stature and obesity contributed very little.

Systolic blood pressure and plasma cholesterol were found to have a very good predictive value for higher risk from ischaemic heart disease. Men with higher level of each of these precursors have a greater risk of developing the disease.

Signs of early disease, such as non-ischaemic ECG abnormality, contributed very little to the prediction of risk, when added to 'causes' and *'precursors'*.

Morris draws the following conclusion: ".....it seems that these causes (occupation, obesity, and the rest), operate largely through these precursors......it seems that much of the predictive power of these precursors is due to these causes". And he continues: "....There is a new optimism that the modern epidemic of ischaemic heart disease of middle age can be controlled. In the first place, investigators are adjusting themselves to the idea of "multiple causes" - their existence, identity, how they connect, and that conceivably there is no essential cause except perhaps for some threshold of nutrition which must be reached. Public health campaigns relating to these causes - e.g. education on the dangers of cigarette smoking or on the need for sedentary workers to take regular exercise - could be effective. But the dominant hope today is that action at the stage of precursor pathology (hypertension and hypercholesterolaemia in particular) may still achieve true primary prevention. Individuals shown to be susceptible will be identified and prophylactic measures directed at them. Prevention will be translated into the clinical field....."

Let us now try to summarise what we know about the problem and what can be done to reduce it. In the first place there is no doubt that ischaemic heart disease is the main cause of death in most European countries, that the overall mortality rates are rising and that they represent the major health problem for preventive medicine. This implies that a study of effectiveness of health education in this field should have priority and full support in most of the European countries.

The second thing to examine is whom does it mostly affect. Males between 45-65 years of age have twice as high a death rate as the females of the same age group. Younger people (20-35 years) are also more affected than before, and the death rate from coronary deaths has increased nearly sevenfold between 1930 and 1960 with ischaemic heart disease now accounting for nearly a third of all heart disease deaths at that age. In spite of such an increase, because of the overall reduction of death rates for this age group, the total number of deaths for this age group in 1963 was relatively low (193) as compared with other causes of death (2,300 from road accidents). The argument for preventive measures should, therefore, be based on the increase of deaths in the middle age (45-65), i.e. well below the age of retirement.

Although the disease is more or less evenly spread throughout all the social classes, because of the existing differences in diagnosis and the pattern of attendance at checkups, it is still probable that the men in higher social classes are more likely to be diagnosed as having angina pectoris or coronary disease. This implies that the chances are greater for those people to be in the high risk group and, therefore, in the target population of an educational programme.

The health problem as such causes a number of problems which must be taken into consideration when planning a health education programme. Dawber and Kannel (1963) try to answer the question whether coronary heart disease is a disease entity which can be studied by epidemiological methods. They conclude that macroscopic epidemiological approach (looking at prevalence and incidence of disease and associating this with other gross observations such as mortality from arteriosclerotic heart disease as defined by the International List - 120 before its 1965 revision) in the case of coronary heart disease is not warranted. The microscopic epidemiological approach (carrying out detailed studies of a population and determining prevalence or incidence of a disease and relating this in turn to population characteristics) is more promising but poses also certain problems concerning the definition of the disease. Definition of coronary heart disease in terms of atherosclerosis is of no value in the living population, since it can be used only in post-mortem examinations. It is, however, possible to define the disease in terms of clinical syndromes: angina pectoris, myocardial infarction and sudden death. The first of these, angina pectoris, can be defined only on the basis of subjective sensations of the person afflicted and is not very reliable for comparative purposes. Myocardial infarction can be defined by methods of objective examination (ECG) and can be used for epidemiological studies. So can the third clinical syndrome, sudden death, since the major cause of unexplained sudden death occurring in an apparently healthy adult is mostly due to impaired coronary blood flow.

The doubts voiced by Dawber and Kannel are of importance for this study, since they can be reflected in the attitudes of the medical profession in general, concerning the causal relationship between the disease and some of the risk factors examined in a great number of limited and isolated surveys.

It is a long step between establishing some statistical association between a risk factor and a disease on the one hand, and undertaking certain large scale actions on the other hand, affecting large numbers of people and involving considerable expenses. For example, the association found between the areas with soft water supply and increased mortality from coronary heart disease, should, theoretically, prompt local authorities to increase the hardness of the water which is now technically possible. However, we do not as yet know of any large scale measures of this kind.

On the basis of the existing literature and the conclusions drawn by experts attending two meetings organised by WHO Regional Office for Europe (Bucharest, 1965: Copenhagen, 1965), it can be stated that "there is a lack of scientific evidence on the effectiveness of the measures usually recommended for the prevention of ischaemic heart disease in general and myocardial infarction in particular."

Nevertheless, a number of clinical and epidemiological studies have shown that apparently healthy individuals with certain characteristics or habits have a greater incidence of ischaemic heart disease than expected. These risk factors are listed below as they are described in the WHO documents mentioned, and divided into two groups: the first group, where something may be done through health education, and the second group where health education cannot contribute directly.

Group I :

a) *Cigarette smoking*: epidemiological studies have presented evidence that cigarette smoking is associated with a high incidence of acute myocardial infarction (Doll & Hill, 1964). With regard to angina of effort, there is no significant correlation between cigarette consumption and this symptom of ischaemic heart disease.

b) *Weight gain in adults*: this was presented as a risk factor in the development of hyperlipidaemia and of arterial hypertension. Weight gain per se is not regarded as a risk factor in the pathogenesis of ischaemic heart disease.

c) *Physical inactivity*: this can be a risk factor in the pathogenesis of ischaemic heart disease, although the scientific evidence on this point is equivocal. It is, however, generally accepted that regular exercise is a useful preventive measure against the development of ischaemic heart disease, although strict scientific proof is lacking.

d) *Nervous tension*: this may play a role in precipitating acute myocardial infarction, but there is serious doubt regarding its significance as a predisposing factor in angina of effort, although it probably plays a large role in the pathogenesis of arterial hypertension.

Group II :

a) *Hyperlipidaemic states*: marked hyperlipidaemia - genetically determined - is the only risk factor strong enough to produce ischaemic heart disease in the younger age groups, i.e. under 40 years (Oliver and Boyd, 1953). Long-term studies of attempts to lower serum-lipid levels in hyperlipidaemic subjects through diet or pharmacological remedies have not yet provided unequivocal evidence of a beneficial effect in preventing or delaying the course of ischaemic heart disease (Oliver and Boyd, 1961 : Rose, 1965). However, owing to recent progress in dietetics and pharmaceutics, it is now possible to shift the serum-lipid levels of most hyperlipidaemic subjects into the normal range.

b) *Arterial hypertension*: this is an established risk factor in the pathogenesis of ischaemic heart disease. However, therapeutic control of severe arterial hypertension has not yet demonstrated a protective influence against ischaemic heart disease.

c) *Diabetes mellitus and hyperuricaemia*: both of these diseases are a risk factor in the development of ischaemic heart disease.

d) *Genetic factors*: several risk factors, such as arterial hypertension, hyperlipidaemia and diabetes mellitus, may be found in greater proportion in the relatives of the diseased. Examination of the relatives provides an opportunity for the early detection of asymptomatic risk factors and for the early institution of control measures. In this sense, genetic factors are important in the pathogenesis of ischaemic heart disease.

The three main risk factors of importance for health education activities are: cigarette smoking, over-eating and lack of physical activity. The aim of health education in this field should be to try to influence human behaviour and to achieve the desirable changes. For purposes of a health education programme, these three factors should be treated as a behavioral syndrome and the effectiveness of the programme should be assessed by changes in all three and not in each separately, possible at the expense of the others (as in substituting over-eating for smoking).

It appears that there are certain differences in opinions concerning risk factors mentioned, as between cardiologists and general practitioners. Before launching on a large scale evaluative study of a health educational programme, the limits of this possible difference should be established, its reasons analysed, and conclusions drawn, since it may well be that the success of an educational programme will for the greater part depend upon the support and reinforcement given to it by general practitioners, or the medical profession in general.

Example: Doctor-patient interaction

(From: Baric,L. "Formal Health Education and the Prevention of Coronary Heart Disease", Report on the Salford (1973) study, University of Manchester)

This is an aspect of a *dyadic* or two-person interaction. Each person comes to the encounter as a result of *motivations* which can be satisfied by the happenings in the encounter. Each interactor emits verbal and non-verbal signals and the interactors perceive the behaviour of the other, and meet in a situation defined by the culture with defined rules and role-relationships. A simple way to look at the interaction is to use the S-R (stimulus-response) model, whereas a more complex way would be to look at the whole system including the patterns of behaviour of both actors.

The latter could include the assessment of social skills of the actors and the cognitive processes which may be involved, such as taking the role of the partner in the interaction. The social skills model postulates that the interaction is a part of the social skills of the two actors and as such can be learned and improved. It includes in the first place the attainment of certain *goals* for which purpose the actors will use some specific form of interaction conducive to the achievement of such a goal. This may include *reward/punishment* as a means of stimulating the desired responses from the partner in the interaction. It includes the *selective perception of clues* to which the actors are sensitive, to which they will respond and which may be a part of verbal or non-verbal communication. The *central 'translation' process* will help in translating the incoming stimuli into a plan of action. This action may be expressed in a series of *motor responses* including facial expressions or body postures which will help the interaction. The response in the form of a *feedback* mechanism will help in mid-course adjustments of the interaction to be made.

The interaction can be examined using the **exchange** theory approach which postulates that each actor aims at maximising the gain and minimising the loss, regardless of what happens to the partner. To be able to work, this approach has to take into consideration certain rewards for the partner to avoid breakdown of communications.

Another way of looking at such an interaction is to treat dyads as a **social system**. This means that the interaction is examined from the aspect of both actors. One way of achieving this is to use *game theory* models which not only examine the cost-benefit relationship, but also include the concept of payoffs as a means of strategy controlling the interaction. The interaction can be seen as a set of interpersonal strategies with one move depending on the next move by the partner, etc. There are other theories which examine such an interaction in terms of the *affective* quality of relationships (friendship, love, etc.).

The general approach

Bloom (1965) proposed a systems model for the examination of the doctor-patient interaction which includes the following:

- the doctor as a person, as a professional, as a member of the immediate and the wider social environment;

- the patient as a person, having an occupation, as a member of his immediate and wider social environment;

- the professional normative system defining the role performance of each partner;

- the socio-cultural system within which the interaction takes place;

- the medical problem which initiates the interaction.

The field of doctor-patient interaction is, however, one of the main concerns of medical sociology as well as sociology of medicine, and different authors have been using specific models for their analysis. They range from linguistic differences between doctors and patients on the one hand to the problem of dependency and medicalisation of human behaviour on the other. They include the concept of "sick role" and the consequences of "labelling", the patient "career", the problems of institutionalised patients, and the changing role of the patient as a "consumer" with increasing understanding of the processes and consequences of illness, with the choice of doctors and the treatment on offer, and the ability to evaluate a doctor's performance.

The new tendency of promoting community participation in defining the health policy, enables the individual (patient or potential patient) to have a say in the allocation of limited resources and the running of the health care delivery system.

The relatively recent phenomenon of self-help and consumer groups, enables individuals to have his complaints heard and acted upon. This is of importance in the case of iatrogenic (medically induced) diseases and accidents which have in the past been disregarded as accidents not meriting any compensation. The same applies to illness caused by environmental factors, which are becoming increasingly recognised and have resulted in numerous litigations.

An important part of doctor-patient relationship is based on the communication process. This communication process is not always effective due to certain barriers: consequently barriers are considered to be negative and need to be removed.

Instead of accepting this premise and proceeding to list all the possible established or imagined barriers that do or could exist in a doctor-patient relationship, this paper aims to cover only the following aspect of this general problem:

     1. Barriers examined in terms of expectations;

     2. The definition of barriers linked to the conceptual model used;

     3. A detailed examination of a few of the large number of possible barriers; and

     4. The role of health education in removing and/or perpetuating some of the existing barriers.

The field of doctor-patient communication has been a favourite area of investigation for a great number of social scientists, recorded in books and articles which could comprise a whole library on its own. Because of this, in this paper only an example of references in each problem area will be mentioned, in the hope that other references could, if so desired, be readily found in any library index. Thus, this presentation should be viewed as a glimpse into this problem area, but still in some ways an unorthodox glimpse instead of a literature review, in the hope that it will generate some new ideas concerning an old problem.

Doctor-patient interaction, based predominantly on the process of communication between the two actors, is purposeful and formalised. Both actors have a specific purpose in mind, the achievement of which is formalised, which means that there are certain rules of procedure. These rules can be formal as contained in the code of ethics of the medical profession or informal as in the case of social expectations concerning the patients behaviour in this interaction situation.

What we are in fact dealing with is an interaction governed by a whole set of formal and informal norms as in any other professional interaction. Norms are generally described as sets of expectations of a number of possible varieties. Thus, any study of barriers to communication must start with an examination of expectations involved.

It is accepted that whenever an interaction takes place between tow or more individuals, the expectations of each individual partner need not be fully satisfied. The reason for this failure can be described as a "barrier to complete fulfilment of these expectations". There are different kinds of expectations. When the two partners occupy *formally recognised statuses* with accompanying roles as in the case of the "the doctor" and "the patient" then we are faced with at least two kinds of expectations: the ones defined by the structure and the functions of the formal system within which this interaction takes place and the others due to the *personal interpretations* of these by the individual actors. The diagram illustrates the two types of expectations for each of the two actors with areas of overlap.

The doctor as one actor in this dyadic interaction process carries with him a whole set of his professional expectations concerning the patient. The patient as the other actor, by changing from an individual to a patient, also brings with him into the situation a whole set of formally rec-

ognised expectations. Since neither of them can detach their individual personalities from their formal status within such a situation they
both will be influenced by their individual personal expectations.

In addition to the characteristics of the actors, their expectations will
depend on the reasons for which such an interaction is taking place.
The reasons can be simple or complex and can be classified according
to the desired outcome.

Let us examine various possible reasons for a doctor-patient interaction from the point of view of each of the two actors. From the patient's
point of view an interaction will take place because the patient has a
"problem" which causes him distress or prevents him from fulfilling his
social obligations. It can be a simple physical incapacity (a boil on the
neck) or a more complex physical incapacity linked with a state of mental anxiety (blood in sputum).

From the doctor's point of view the problem presented to him by the
patient may require an action on his part alone (diagnosis and prescription or intervention), or referral to a specialist as well (surgeon-
operation). If the patient's problem is complicated by an
accompanying state of anxiety then in addition to an intervention the
doctor will be required to talk the problem over with the patient to relieve the accompanying feelings of anxiety as well. In this way the reason for an interaction will be defined by who initiates it and by the
expected outcome. At this point the first diagram can be extended to
illustrate the complexity of the influences on the expectations of each
of the two partners in such an interaction .

Both actors, the doctor and the patient, belong to specific cultural entities from which they derive their value system. They can come from
two different cultures or from the same cultural background. How
great the overlap between their value systems is will depend on a number of factors, such as closeness in education, social class, sex, age, etc.
By definition their value systems can never completely overlap nor be
completely detached. The reason for the former is that each individual internalises the value of his or her culture in a subjective and specific way, whereas in the latter case all cultural systems share certain
basic values characteristic of the human species.

A certain part of the value system is either explicitly or implicitly contained in norms which represent the expectations concerning human behaviour. An example of explicit norms is the legal system of a country with all its laws and regulations. The explicit norms usually provide for a certain range of freedom in their interpretation and this range is usually define by implicit norms which establish the latitude of acceptance in the variation of their interpretation as well as possible exceptions. Other implicit norms cover areas of social life that have not been regulated by formal or explicit norms.

Conceptual models

It should be clear by now that the analysis of barriers to a satisfactory communication process between two actors in a specific situation will depend on the way we choose to look at this interaction process.

Stating it more precisely, the analysis of barriers will depend on the conceptual model we apply and the theories that describe the relationships between the parts of that model.

A word should be said about models and theories. Especially in the field of communications there are several models in current use and we will be forced to choose between them before we proceed to examine the possible barriers.

There are many definitions and descriptions of the meaning of the term "model"; in this context a model is considered to be a representation of a system, defining its structure and the different parts that constitute it.

In the case of the doctor-patient interaction system a simple or a complex type of model can be used. In the simple model the system is represented by locating the two actors and describing by arrows the two way interaction, a part of which is in terms of the communications, that are taking place. The complex model shows the same situation but the system is much more complex in terms of the number of actors and the number of relationships that bear on the interaction process.

Models - whether simple or complex - are however, only of limited use without the accompanying theories. Theories, which define the relationships between the parts of the system, are generalisations based on a number of observations, and represent formalised and ultimately testable explanations concerning specific characteristics of such a relationship.

To return to doctor-patient interaction, whether we use simple or complex models, the understanding of the relationship between their different parts will require an examination of the underlying theories in the general field of communication.

The problem of communication is closely related to the problem of doctor-patient interaction as well as health education in general. Different researchers have applied different models and used different approaches, consequently generating different theories concerning a specific aspect of this problem. Although we have a great number of models available, there are few theories developed which explain the relationships between their parts.

Some of the barriers explored

As we stated earlier, the problem of doctor-patient interaction has been at the centre of research carried out by a number of researchers from various fields; doctors, patient-associations, sociologists, economists, psychologists etc. The number of works published and the number of barriers established is so great that it could fill a complete small library. As an example of some better known works quoted by Cox and Mead (1975), I will mention here those carried out by Cartwright, Mechanic, Zola, Freidson, Bloom, Stimson and Webb, and Robinson, although this is by no means a comprehensive or fair selection. The more obvious barriers explored, not necessarily by those mentioned include noise accompanying a message, differences between the sender and receiver, the discriminatory process of selection by the receiver, language barriers, direction of communication and the discrepancy in the social position of the two actors, lack of feedback, literacy of the receiver, different cultural values and expectations, as well as many others.

Because of the limited time and space I will concentrate on only a few barriers in the hope that this may throw new light on the health education methods used and their anticipated effectiveness.

The first has been mentioned by Freidson, (1975) and deals with the different orientation of doctors and their patients with respect to the symptoms and the interpretation of the outcome of an interaction between the two. Whereas the patient has simple explanation for the commonly used categories of complaints such as sneezing, noises in the head, a running nose and fatigue, the doctor will probably diagnose it as an upper respiratory infection. He will also bear in mind that these symptoms could be due to something else such as an allergy or even approaching deafness. He will not mention them, but he will bear the possibility in mind although it may not be highly probable. The doctor making such a diagnosis is taking into account the statistical possibility of being sometimes wrong.

There is a difference between the perception of such problems among patients and doctors. The patient knows what he feels and what he hears. He feels terrible and the doctor tells him that there is nothing to worry about. A friend, however, tells him that he knew someone with exactly the same symptoms who dropped dead after being declared healthy by the doctor. This places the patient in a dilemma, when to insist on special attention due to his feelings and when to accept the doctor reassurance that there is nothing seriously wrong. When can the patient decide that the doctor may be wrong? There is no "right" answer to this question since we all know of situations when the doctor was wrong, but also know of many more situations when the patient was wrong.

To sum up, the doctor draws on his general knowledge about a disease and its probable outcome when dealing with a specific problem, whereas the patient draws on his experiences, feelings and observations, and forms his opinion about the disease in general. The doctor considers the seriousness of the possible outcome whereas the patient considers the seriousness of his symptoms or feelings at the time. Both run the dangers of committing one of the basic fallacies related to the theory of probability, i.e. to apply a general probability of an event occurring, computed from a population, to a particular case.

Another barrier in doctor-patient communication is described by Bloor and Horobin (1975) and is known as the so called "double bind" in which the patient finds himself because of the doctor's expectations about him. The doctor expects the patient to be a rational well-informed person, able to recognise the importance of a whole set of early signs which could be symptoms of a disease, carry out self-diagnosis, overcome any inhibitions and come to see him without any delay. Once he enters the surgery a complete metamorphosis should take place. The patient should forget anything he knew, heard or felt about his symptoms and manifest complete trust in doctors opinions, actions and recommendations.

This implies that the doctor expects his prospective patient to be a "well informed" citizen as far as self-diagnosis and seeking medical help are concerned. This is also the aim of health education which endeavours to increase patients' knowledge of health matters so that they can seek appropriate and timely medical help.

The problem lies in the transition from the role of a healthy person to that of a patient. At that moment the patient is expected to forget everything he knows about his condition and accept without question the opinion of the doctor. This is a "double bind" situation where the patient is expected to carry out a reasonable diagnosis of his condition to determine whether and when to seek medical treatment which includes diagnositic and prognostic abilities, which have to be forgottten when one sees the doctor and becomes a patient. In this way a person who does not feel well is first encouraged to participate in the decision-making process only to be expected later to become completely dependent on the doctor's opinions. This implies a possibility of a conflict which is more likely the more educated the patient is. The best example of this is the study of doctors as patients and the problems they have compared to working class patients.

The doctor's expectations concerning the patient's behaviour are the main source of potential conflict in doctor-patient relationship. The less informed patient may present the doctor with a whole lot of trivial information and miss out some important symptom, whereas the better informed patient may feed the doctor with the right kind of symptoms associated with a certain condition and thus unwittingly influence the doctor's diagnosis, or be more critical of doctor's decisions.

The third barrier is the difference in the opinions about the amount of optimal communications for a successful doctor-patient interaction. A number of studies examined the average time spent by a general practitioner with an "average" patient in an "average" consultation and found that the average time of consultation was between 3-10 minutes per patient. This is often cited by the critics as an obvious barrier in the doctor-patient communication. This common-sense interpretation can be questioned if one takes into consideration everything that has already been said about the social distance, language differences, orientation to scientific facts etc., which differentiates a doctor form his patient.

It seems that the problem lies in the different expectations of each actor, where the patient wishes to get information, advice, intervention and respect as an individual, and the doctor wishes to streamline the interaction within the boundaries of optimal efficiency.

There are two different hypotheses: one says that the more time the doctor spends with his patient (implying that the time is spent in communication) the better the chances of patient's recovery; the other suggests that there is an optimal amount of time (implying an optimal amount of communication) in doctor-patient interaction for a successful outcome of the patient's illness, and that an increase in the time, i.e. communication, need not always benefit the outcome of the disease. Illustrations of this point can be found in the findings of a great number of studies into the question the patient's recall of what the doctor told him.

The dilemma of health education

The fact that most of the general practitioners see most of their patients during a year implies that the general practitioner must be an important factor in the health education of the patient.

The few problems concerning doctor-patient communication, that have been illustrated in this paper, raise the question of the role that health education can and should play in increasing the effectiveness of this interaction.

One of the questions that requires an answer is, how far should a doctor comply with his patients needs and vice versa.

Freidson (1975) describes this problem in the following way.

He asks how a doctor can adjust himself to a patient's lay and sometimes bizarre expectations without endangering his own standards of practising modern medicine. There is a difference between a rigid adherence to professional doctrine and sacrificing one's professional standards. In the latter case, the doctor will manifest a certain degree of flexibility which will include the understanding of the patient's point of view without sacrificing the professional standards. This kind of doctor would be considered to be a "better doctor", one who will remain within his professional limits and not act irresponsibly. The conflict in the doctor-patient relationship can be reduced by the manifestation of understanding by the doctor for the patient's views, although the doctor must be trained to recognise how far he can accommodate the patient and where to draw a line and still remain a professional. The implies that the final decision is in the hands of the doctor, but also means that there will be patients whose expectations cannot be met by the doctor.

The ideal situation would occur if one could define the point at which the doctor has to stop adjusting to the patient and the patient must begin adjusting to the doctor. Since it is not possible to define this threshold of adjustment, health education has endeavoured to increase the patient's knowledge and understanding of modern diseases and available treatments so that he or she can approach the problem in the same way as the doctor, although without knowing all the details.

If one takes such potential conflicts into consideration, one could question the justification of any health education at all. On the other hand, a patient without any health education would present the doctor with a situation which is commonly associated with veterinary surgeons, where the patient can only by crudest means indicate what is wrong. It is because of the way medical science has developed, depending on a feed-back from the patient in making a diagnosis, it will be necessary to improve the patient's knowledge through health education.

The question could also be raised about the virtues of working with patients who have no health education. The most obvious one is the total dependence of the patient and the total control of the doctor in such an interaction. In the case of the veterinary surgeon it allows him to physically restrain the patient who does not want to cooperate.

This is, however, not acceptable for medical practitioners even in the case of uncooperative patients.

One could, therefore, agree that there are certain advantages in working with a patient who has a certain level of health education. It could be expected that such a patient would have sufficient knowledge to recognise symptoms and seek help in time and cooperate in the treatment.

It could be assumed the more health education the better. This is not always the case as the studies of doctors as patients have shown. It has been found that a person cannot objectively assess his own condition and that an expert could be over-optimistic in assessing the existing dangers. An illustration of this is the existence of doctors who are drug addicts and alcoholics. They know the symptoms but may wrongly believe that they are still in control when they have already lost control and become addicted. A doctor who has the highest possible level of health education may be more likely to be critical of his colleague's work, or may even inhibit the normal reactions of his colleague in his diagnosis and prescription of treatment.

It is difficult to say whether health education promotes or inhibits conflicts in the doctor patient relationship. It will probably depend on the situation and the "optimal" leval of health education of the patient. the level of health education of a patient should be treated as a continuum, where at the one end will be the patient without any health education and at the other end the patient with "complete" health education. The optimal level would lie somewhere between those two extremes and will shift according to the situation and the problem in question.

Within the limits of time and space a number of points have been raised which could throw new light on the problem of doctor-patient interaction as a potential health education situation.

The interaction is fraught with potential obstacles and barriers, some of which are due to the system, some to the kind of interaction, and some to the expectations of the two actors.

It is postulated that the outcome of any study of this problem area will depend on the conceptual model used, and that there are already several different models in coexistence. It is further postulated that in spite of a great number of different models, there is still very little theoretical knowledge to explain the relationship between the parts of a model.

For example, a model of doctor-patient communication can include time as one of the relevant factors. This seems to be a very reasonable way of looking at the problem. Very little empirically validated knowledge, however, exists to provide a theoretical generalisation about the kind and direction of the relationship between the time spent and the effectiveness of such an interaction. Commonsense assumptions, such as "the more the better" seem to be refuted by existing experience.

Another similar example is the problem of how far can a doctor accommodate a patient's expectations and still retain his professional integrity without which the patient's interest may be endangered. If we measure this by the level of patient's satisfaction we will get one extreme value, and if by doctor's effectiveness, another. The answer lies somewhere in the middle denoting the 'optimal' point of mutual accommodation.

Once again there is no theory to define what is this 'optimal' point to be used as a basis for the evaluation of doctor-patient communication.

Summary

In conclusion, it can be said that the awareness of existing barriers is not an answer to the problem of doctor-patient communication, but only a necessary precondition for the building of models, which again are of no great use on their own. What we need is more research aimed at developing theories which will allow for the generalisation of findings and provide a possible standard for evaluation of that problem area.

One should also mention the changing situation following the reform of the UK National Health Service and the new role of general practitioners in health promotion and health education (Baric & Murphy, 1991). The new contract provides for payment which can be claimed by the GPs when they run Health Promotion Clinics. This will lead to a rapid increase of such activities within general practice which will bring about a whole set of new problems requiring new solutions.

Examples: Behaviour modification clinics

(Based on Bandura A., "Principles of Behaviour Modification",Holt, Reinhart and Winston, New York, 1969)

Antismoking clinics

Most of research in this area has been concerned with the working of anti-smoking clinics. An overview of this work as reported by Bandura (1969), shows the type of clinics and the methods used with the outcomes which illustrates the enormous variety of approaches and the limitations of the outcomes.

The smoking withdrawal clinic has become increasingly popular in the last decade. The first of these was started in Sweden in 1955 by Ejrup (Ejrup, 1964). Since then the idea has spread mainly to the United Kingdom and the United State and recently over other European countries especially Germany, Holland, France. Thus, recently the smoking cessation clinic has become a popular means through which smoking withdrawal is attempted.

Specific treatment techniques, number and length of meetings, and other factors vary considerably across clinics, but most of them involve groups of self-selected smokers who come to receive help in quitting from experts who usually provide some combination of health information, encouragement, group therapy, moral support, social pressure and suggestions for resisting the temptation to smoke (Schwartz and Dubitsky, 1967; Ketzer, 1968; Bernstein, 1969).

Basically the clinics are divided into two categories: clinics employing medication and clinics not employing medication. In Ejrup's original clinics and in many of those that followed, various kinds of medication were employed as an aid to quitting. On the other hand, the famous 'five-day-plan' medication was not used.

It is not intended to review comprehensively all the clinics reported in literature, such reviews were made by several writers (e.g. Schwartz and Dubitzky, 1967; Bernstein, 1969; and recently Bernstein and McAllister, 1976; Raw, 1977). However, a brief sketch of the existing literature will provide an idea about the extent of the movement and about the variety of approaches. Most clinics have not followed up their clients but those that have done so for 12-18 months report high success rates of the original participants who have stopped smoking. Nevertheless, the success rate at one year follow-up shows a remarkably similar long-term success rate of 15% to 25%.

The reason for these similarities may be deduced from findings of Hunt et.al (1970, 1973) who have measured recidivism over time. They found that two-thirds resumed smoking three months subsequent to clinic attendance and three-quarters resumed within six months. However, a quarter remained abstinent at one year follow-up.

As mentioned before, one of the earliest and best known clinics is that of Ejrup (1963), although his therapy changed over the years from 1956 to 1960. As a rule the would-be quitter received information and education regarding his smoking behaviour, explanation of treatment techniques and one or more drugs, (mainly Lobeline). The percentage of smokers who ceased to smoke increased over time and the figure reached 88% in 1960. The cessation rate for all 2,271 smokers is 60% (Ejrup, 1964). However, 70% of the patients who had been successfully treated had relapsed after a year. Similar methods are reported by Edwards (1964) and Hoffsteadt (1964).

Backman (1964, 1966) has reported results of 8-week anti-smoking 'courses' run in groups (using Lobeline). At the end of treatment 62% had stopped smoking completely. Follow-up data was not clearly presented, but the general impression is that after periods ranging from two months to one year 77% of 44 clients were still not smoking.

Lawton (1962) used a 'group therapeutic' approach with 19 smokers. At the end of the meetings twelve were not smoking (63%). At the 12-week follow-up only eight (42%) were still abstinent, and this figure dropped to three (15.7% after eighteen months).

The Philadelphia Project (1966) compared smoking rates of the actively treated parents with a group of parents who attended an introductory meeting but none of the group meetings. 50% of the participants quit smoking at the end of the clinic. This figure shrank to 38% after six months. At the 18-month follow-up date, 18% of the control group, contrasted with 26% of the experiment group, were not smoking.

Mausner (1966) provided seven sessions of non-directive group ther-apy with college girls and found little difference in final smoking levels between the therapy group and a non-treated group. In a later study, Lawton (1967) compared four group methods of smoking withdrawal. The overall success rate (total abstinence) of subjects who completed the entire treatment programme, was 26% at 1-week after treatment, 18% at seven months and 8% at fifteen months. There was no demon-strable superiority of one treatment method over another.

Schwartz and Dubitzky (1967) compared drugs, individual counselling and group counselling in an 8-week treatment programme: 22% of those assigned to the drug treatment were successful, compared with 42% who had counselling and 37% who attended group meetings.

Percentages of success at the 4-month follow-up decreased respective-ly to 18%, 24% and 20%. None of these was statistically better than a control group which took the original test but received no treatment.

Ross (1967) summarises the results of 24 clinics at the Roswell Park Memorial Institute in Buffalo, New York, with an average of 50 - 95 volunteers attending each clinic. The treatment programme featured drugs, films, lectures and group discussion, with group meetings once a week for four weeks. The immediate abstinence rate was 34%, fall-ing to about 20% one year after treatment.

Five years later about 18% were not smoking (West et.al, 1977). How-ever, it was found that variations in clinic protocol in terms of drugs and education methods had no relation to long-term smoking withdra-wal.

The clinics of the 'five-day-plan' use a combination of medical, relig-ious, educational and fear arousing communications, will-power, the buddy system and a guide book of living instructions for the five days. The results reported a success rate ranging between 70% and 85%. However, follow-up surveys at three months and at a year after treat-ment indicate that only about 34% and 15% to 20% respectively of these are still non-smokers (McFarland, 1964, 1965; Falkenberg, 1964; Thomson and Wilson, 1966; Fritz, 1974).

In the clinics of the Central Middlesex Hospital (Mair, 1970), 63% stopped smoking by the end of treatment. Nevertheless, after three months only 10% of this group remained abstinent and in the first and second year follow-up the figure was 19%.

Nemzer (1973), reported that 70% of the participants in his clinic in New York gave up smoking, but after twelve months only 20% remained non-smokers.

The Canadian study (Delarue, 1973) reported that the rate of abstinence after one year for all participants in the clinic study was 28.6%. Recent studies (Grodon, 1976; Russell, 1977; Raw, 1977) showed similar success rates for most smoking cessation programmes.

To sum up, it can be concluded that although the immediate success rates of most of the clinics are fairly high (up to 80%), there seems to be a clear pattern of relapse, so that 20% to 30% remain abstinent at one year follow-up. Thus, smoking withdrawal in the clinics tends to be temporary and/or not clearly different from that accomplished through subjects unaided efforts.

In the light of the above evidence, smoking withdrawal clinics have been a source of controversy. Whilst some writers (e.g. Burton, 1977) suggest that clinics and group methods are superior over individual counselling, hypnosis and other similar methods, others state that "most clinics represent a great deal of wasted time and effort" (Bernstein, 1969, p.431; 1976, p.91).

Weight reduction clinics

In terms of popularity these clinics attract the greatest number of members. One of the largest Weight Watchers operates on an international level and it is estimated that over half a million people pass through their doors every week. Others, like TOPS (Take off pounds sensibly) has 300,000 members in 12,000 chapters in 29 countries (Gartner & Riessman,1977). A high proportion of members (over 90%) are women.

The problem of weight can be physical, medical, emotional or related to fashion. Most of the clinics treat it as an emotional problem due to defective emotional control. The clinics or groups as they prefer to be called, are run by non-professionals who have training in running such groups. The methods are in accordance with the definition of the problem as emotional, , and include opening singing or recital of the pledge, and public announcement of each members gains or losses in the past week. There is a strong support in terms of cheering and public praise for those who lost weight and booing and public criticism for those who gained weight. The method of reducing weight differs in terms of limitation of calories, which is accompanied with different rituals (like preparing special recepies at specific times of day).

In general about half the members give up after few months and the rest continue for several years in some cases. In this way the clinics deal mostly with self-selected persons who have decided to loose weight and are willing to stay on the programme. The results are comparable with some medical programmes, although with a much greater variation between groups.

'Alcoholics Anonymous'

Although it is not recognised as a 'clinic' the groups have a well defined structure, strict rules and uniform method of dealing with the problem of alcoholism. They are a good example of a variety of 'anonymous' groups which deal with addictions to drugs, gambling, overeating, etc. The AA (as it is universally known) is one of the largest organisations of this kind and most researched with an enormous bibliography of written works and reports. The success is remarkable and widely recognised, among others by the World Health Organisation.

The main characteristics of AA are high level of authoritarianism, blame the victim approach, acceptance of social stigmatisation, recognition that it is a chronic problem with specific symptoms related to behaviour. There is a recognition of the important role of ex-members (former alcoholics) and dependence on group support. It is accepted that alcoholism can newer be cured but only controlled, and that former alcoholics are always in danger of relapse.

The members (75% men) are all volunteers who stay anonymous, there are no records and no external controls or influences. The behaviour (life style) is strictly regulated starting with total abstinence. AA has "Twelve Suggested Steps of AA" and "The Twelve Traditions of AA", which encompass the AA philosophy and the rules of behaviour of the members. These are recited at the start of a meeting, commented on, after which each member is called upon to give a "weather report" which is a form of public confession. It usually includes an admittance that the person has hit bottom, statements of self-degradation, recognition that AA is the only help, and the affirmation of the dependence on the group. This is followed by approval from the chairman and old members (ex-alcoholics) who continue to participate in the meetings, since one of the 'traditions" is to continue to help other alcoholics.

Example: A Community Intervention

(Baric,L. "A New Approach to Community Participation", J. Institute of Health Education, Vol28 No2, 1990)

The new ideas are best illustrated by an example of an intervention study which could be aimed at developing and testing a new approach to "community participation" within an ecological approach using the methods of health promotion and health education. The exercise will provide an opportunity for empirically testing the method and at the same time provide an outlet for practical experiences in community health education. This exercise is being carried out (1990) in Sudan in collaboration with the University of Gezira The intervention study is envisaged in two parts:

Creating a movement

The importance of external factors in promoting healthy life-styles and the self-reliance and self-determination of communities is recognised in terms of the following planned activities:

1. A mass media campaign will be designed with the aim of popularising the idea of "healthy communities" and explain the commitment and involvement of communities in creating a healthy environment with healthy people living there;

2. It is important to obtain support and cooperation of representatives of national, provincial and local authorities, who should be identified with this movement; to achieve this a set of meetings and consultations with these leaders will be organised;

3. The health education team, including the members of the University of Gezira, will produce supporting literature, reports and explanatory texts to back-up this activity;

4. Meetings with representatives of local press and mass media will be organised to work out a campaign programme to popularise the movement;

5. A background document will be prepared explaining the general principles as well as details of procedures related to community commitments;

Community participation

1. It is expected that the outcome of a mass media campaign will be the interest of certain communities to participate in the movement and take on commitments associated with declaring a village or town a "healthy community";

2. A meeting with the interested leaders will be held to explain the commitments and work out a detailed plan of action;

3. University of Gezira will organise a workshop for community leaders with the aims of enabling them to carry out the commitments and to raise their competence and provide them with skills necessary to achieve improvements in their communities;

4. To achieve these aims the Workshop will include the following objectives::

- knowledge about the administrative processes involved in attracting support for local programmes;

- knowledge about the local power structure an decision making processes involved in taking on and fulfilling commitments concerning the participation in the "healthy community movement;

- knowledge about collecting and interpreting information about local problems as well as about available solutions;

- information about proposed intervention, the methods used and the indicators which will form the basis for evaluation;

- management skills in running a programme of this kind.

5. At the end of the Workshop the participants should be able to undertake definite commitments and be able to carry them out.

6. Following the commitments a second thrust of publicity should include information about the communities participating and the leaders involved in it. It should indicate that a systematic monitoring has been introduced and that the public will regularly be informed about the progress as well as problems encountered and the ways of solving them.

The intervention programme

1. After completion of the Workshop and return to the community, the leaders should organise a meeting with local people some of whom will have an active role in carrying out the programme. The aim of this meeting is to ensure a multisectoral participation and involvement in the programme;

2. The outcome should be the creation of a team with the following tasks:

- to establish the local problems and rank them according to priority of tackling them using the criteria of seriousness, distribution and potential for successful solutions;

- the guiding principle in selecting the problems should be the achievement of an "optimal" instead of a "maximal" improvement. The optimal improvement is defined as the improvement within the constraints of the problem and the available resources;

- to assess the necessary as well as locally available resources; to devise methods and procedures in attracting outside support if necessary; d. to discuss the methods of approach, adjust them to local needs and possibilities, and to make a role distribution among the community members;

- to carry out the programme;

- to ensure a continuous monitoring, evaluation and feed-back mechanisms for the duration of the programme;

- to design and pretest indicators, criteria and instruments for evaluation;

- to ensure continuous flow of information to the mass media about the progress of the programme, the problems encountered and the ways they were solved.

3. At the end of the two year trial period a more general assessment of a number of such community programmes will be made and lessons will be drawn from the shared experiences;

4. The communities participating in this programme can be used as outlets for field training programmes within their various teaching programmes.

5. The final assessment of the intervention programme will be made according to the improvements achieved, the usefulness for field training of students, and the outlook for a more permanent endeavour of these communities to deal with their problemsand satisfy their felt needs within the principles of self-reliance and self-determination.

6. The interim as well as the final reports will serve as documentation of empirically tested methods within the framework of the new interpretation of the meaning of "community participation".

Resources needed

The resources required for such an exercise will include the cost of training the local leaders and the community members, the preparation of necessary materials and the cost of evaluation.

Example: A Workshop for Leaders

The proposed Workshop is a part of a pilot study aimed at testing a new approach to community participation in health improvement through self-care and self-determination. The approach to be tested involves in the first phase popularization of a movement concerned with declaring certain communities (villages, cities) as "healthy", and the actions of communities in achieving such improvements.

The second phase includes the raising of competence of community leaders and/or representatives in four major areas: **initiating, organising, managing** and **evaluating** the community activities.

This example deals with a blueprint for the organisation of a Workshop aimed at raising the competence of community leaders and representatives, intended to be organised at the Medical School of the University of Gezira.

The participants of the Workshop will be leaders and/or representatives of communities which have shown interest in participating in this movement. They are expected, after attending the Workshop and learning about the requirements for this involvement, to take on the commitment for participating in the movement.

This movement is based on a similar concept of "healthy cities" developed in some European countries, Canada and the USA, and already spreading with a number of cities declaring themselves as "healthy cities". In June 1987 the first European Congress on Healthy Cities is taking place in Dusseldorf, W. Germany. Attempts are now being made to translate this concept into "healthy cities and communities" and to adjust it for the needs of EMR. This Workshop is a part of such an attempt planned to be carried out in Sudan.

The background qualifications of the participants will be different, from highly educated religious leaders to maybe illiterate community members.

The teaching programme of the Workshop is divided into four modules: initiating, organising, managing and evaluating a community programme.

WORKSHOP MODULE 1: Initiating a programme

The **aims** of this module are to enable the participants to become familiar with and competent in "selling" the idea of declaring their community as a "healthy community" to the people living in that community, by emphasising the advantages and presenting the realistic contributions expected from each community member.

At the end of the "initiation period" the community should have established a "working team", examined the existing problem and selected the priorities in preparation for the development of the "organisation programme." The stages of the "initiating" process include:

1. The "Softening" Process

Initiating a community activity requires the support of community members expresses in their active commitment to certain activities. To achieve the general acceptance of the idea of declaring a community "healthy" the first step should be discussion of the concept and the idea with individual members of the community. This will create awareness about the possibilities as well as responsibilities associated with such a commitment.   The individuals will be chosen for their influence, possible opposition, control of resources, etc. At the end of this process the idea should be known in the community and people should have had the opportunity to sound out the "significant others" whose opinions they value and respect.

The part of the Module 1 covering this stage in the process should enable the participants to acquire skills in "directive interviewing", i.e. individual conversations with the aim of acquainting the partner with the idea and sounding out their opinions and possible objections.

The content should include information about raising issues, listening to opinions, providing arguments, answering questions, as well as about the way of conducting an interview (introduction, questions and answers, conclusion).

The method of acquiring this knowledge as well as skills related to interviewing should include simple explanation of the major points supported by numerous illustrations and followed by practice in the form of role play.

The assessment will include the expression of confidence by the participants, the opinions of their partners and the external observers, as well as the assessment of the supervisor.

2. Mass Meeting

Following the general preparation, the initiating process will include the organisation of a mass meeting. This can be a special meeting or a part of an existing mass meeting. The organisation includes the following stages:

a. The advertising of the meeting, including the title, the time, the place, the agenda and the speakers.

b. The agenda should include the clarification of the concept, the outline of advantages and possible disadvantages and the role distribution of potential participants.

c. The "questions and answers" period should be allowed sufficient time for clarification of any issues and constructive treatment of any objections.

d. The outcome of the meeting should be the acceptance of the community as a whole to undertake the commitment and enter into the exploratory process of finding out in reality what this commitment implies.

e. The follow-up should sound out individuals according to the role definition presented as part of the agenda, and organise a meeting with the members who agreed to actively participate in the attempts to improve the "life" of the community, which could also include health issues. The part of the Module 1 covering the organisation of a mass meeting should enable the participants to acquire skills in planning, advertising, organising, leading and participating in such meetings.The contents should include information about attracting the attention and using mass media; the considerations to be taken into account when planning a meeting (place, size of the auditorium, seating arrangements, acoustics, lighting, chairing and running a meeting, presentation of speeches, leading a discussion, answering questions, dealing with troublemakers, and getting a commitment or opinion by sounding out the participants. The method of acquiring this knowledge and skills should include some general advice, a task and role play. The assessment will include the subjective feelings of the participants and subsequent evaluation of the meetings organised by the participants.

3. Forming a Working Team

The individuals concerned with the issue and willing to actively support the movement who come to the smaller meeting following the mass meeting, should be concerned with these topics:

a. Forming a "working team" from among all the people interested; and

b. Distributing the tasks among the members in relation to the organisational programme;

c. Taking on the task of studying and defining the problems in the community;   The part of the Module 1 dealing with forming a working team should enable the participants to individually approach different members at the mass meeting, recruit them for a working team and distribute tasks among them. The contents should include the understanding of the rationale for such a team, familiarity with the general problems in the community, the skills in collecting and storing information, ability to assess the potential contributions of each member, gaining their commitment and setting the task of objectively establishing the problems in the community.The method will include some simple explanations about team leadership; practical skills in collecting and storing data, data analysis, and presenting the findings in an interesting and relevant way; these skills will be acquired during the work on tasks and practical examples.The assessment will be based on the preparations for the next mass meeting and peoples reactions to the presentations; it will also be based on the choice of priorities and the level of commitment of the population.

4. Second Mass Meeting

Once the work of the team has been completed, it should call a mass meeting to discuss the findings and inform the people about the progress made towards organising certain activities. The outcome of this meeting should be a general agreement of the community about the priority of problems according to their seriousness and feasibility.

The part of the Module 1 dealing with organising the second mass meeting should enable the participants to learn from the experiences gained during the organisation of the first mass meeting and avoid most of the mistakes made.

The contents should include ways of critically analysing the outcomes and possible improvements.

The method should include the simulation process in the form of tasks, where the participants get information about an imaginary meeting and carry out the exercise of improving on it.

The assessment will be based on the outcome of the exercises as well as by the level of confidence expressed by the participants. A long term assessment will include the evaluation of the second mass meeting.

5. Programme Planning and Organisation

These preparation should produce a programme and Module 2 deals with its planning and organisation.

WORKSHOP MODULE 2: Programme planning and organisation

Once the general idea of commitment has been understood and the people have expressed their readiness to participate in this "movement", the AIMS of this module are to enable the participants to become competent and confident in drafting a programme for action, testing it with the people in the community and producing a final organisational and operational programme for action.

The first step in planning and organising a programme for action will be to make a diagnosis by examining the causes and prescribing relevant solutions. The "medical" diagnosis will be available from the medical profession and it will include medical "causes and solutions". For a health promotion/education intervention it will be necessary to carry out a different diagnosis with the emphasis on "health promotional/educational solutions".

If one accepts that health threats and risky behaviour are a function of external factors and community members' actions and behaviour, then the programme should include both of these aspects in the chosen solutions. The success of such a simultaneous set of activities in two interacting areas will require a mechanism for coordination, evaluation and feedback. The main steps can be envisaged as follows:

1. Commitment

The implementation of the chosen solution will require the agreement and commitment of both institutions and members of the community concerning certain required actions. This commitment can include resources, working time, expertise, services etc. It will be defined by the nature and the character of the solution prescribed.

2. Tasks

Once the general commitment of the institutions and community members has been acquired, the next step will be to specify the solution in terms of activities. These activities should then be distributed in the form of task distribution for institutions and role definition for individual members of the community.

3. Actions

Setting the whole programme into motion will require actions on the institutions and community members according to the task distribution and role definition. These actions will have to be synchronised to achieve maximum effectiveness.

4. *Coordination of activities*

Synchronisation of activities will require a mechanism for coordination as well as close cooperation of all the actors involved.

The task of such a mechanism for coordination of a programme will depend on the management skills of the team, and this is the aim of Module 3.

WORKSHOP MODULE 3: Management of the programme

The **aims** of this module are to enable the participants to acquire knowledge about issues involved in management of a programme as well as skills in carrying it out.

The main objective of management is to *coordinate* the various planned activities involving a number of institutions and a great number of individual community members. This coordination is vital for *simultaneous actions* to take place.

Some of the solutions will depend for their success on *synchronicity* of actions as for example changing norms, values and opinions of communities.

The management of the programme should include synchronising the commitments of both the institutions and the members of the community, their acceptance of specific tasks and roles, as well as the adjustments of their actions with the aim of supporting and reinforcing each other. The success will have to be evaluated and this is dealt with in Module 4.

WORKSHOP MODULE 4: Evaluation and feedback

The **aims** of this Module are to provide the participants with an understanding of the need for and the skills necessary for evaluating a programme, as well as making use of the feedback mechanism for the adjustments and corrections of the programme.

Evaluation should be included in the planning stages of a programme. To achieve a successful evaluation, the following preconditions should be met:

1. the programme should have aims and objectives defined in a measurable way; the measurement will require a set of indicators defined by criteria for assessment and translated into instruments which can be used to carry out the measurements;

2. the programme should be divided into steps or phases and each one will require a specific evaluation of the achievement of each sub-aim or sub-objective;

3. the programme should include a mechanism for utilising the feedback information and adjusting the programme accordingly;

In terms of a community action, the phases involved are:

1. commitment: it will be necessary to critically assess the commitments undertaken by institutions as well as by individual community members; these should be synchronised and should be supportive as well as specific; they should also be relevant to the aims of the programme; any problems noted at this stage should be fed back into the system and corrected before one proceeds with the next phase;

2. tasks and roles: it will be important to distinguish between the general and specific aspects of commitments, the specific commitments will enable the task distribution and the role definition; any problems due to the mismatch between the institutional tasks and individual role performance should be fed back into the system and adjustments should be made;

3. actions: evaluation will have to link the commitments undertaken with the distribution of tasks and roles and the actions carried out; it will also have to link the actions monitored with the actual achievements in terms of programme aims; since a number of actions and activities will be carried out within the framework of the pro-

gramme aims, each one will have to be assessed separately; the feedback mechanism will enable corrections and adjustments at certain points in time since any community action represents an ongoing programme and a continuous activity as a part of the changing community life style.

Summary

The Workshop is intended for participants with various educational background who should be able to understand the basic ideas behind such a movement as the creation of "healthy cities/communities".

The Modules developed in this paper are sufficiently precise to help the organisers of such Workshops in choosing the relevant aspects of knowledge and skills needed for the performance of different roles within such a programme.

The participants should know which "questions" to ask and whom to ask them: this is the basis for the external support provided for any community activity.

The problems identified and chosen as priority will attract solutions according to the resources the community has at its disposal and can mobilise from outside. Because of this, the criteria for evaluation will not be comparable since the achievements will be community-specific and should be individually assessed.

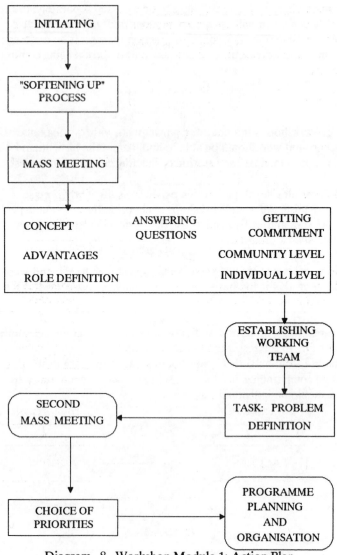

Diagram 8 Workshop Module 1: Action Plan

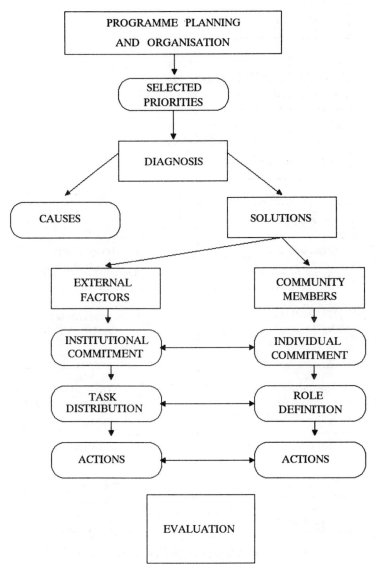

Diagram 9 Workshop Module 2: Action Plan

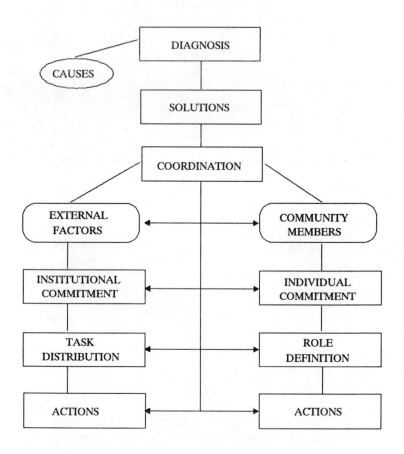

Diagram 10   Workshop Module 3: Action Plan

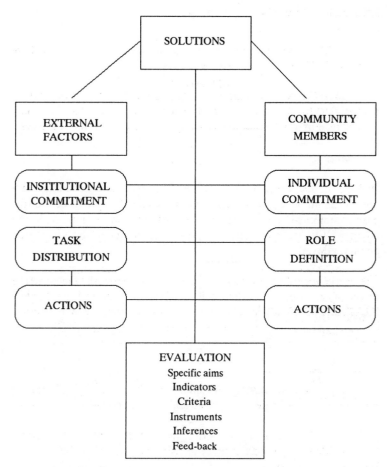

Diagram 11 Workshop Module 4: Action Plan

Example: The AIDS campaign

(DHSS: AIDS Monitoring response to the public education campaign Feb.1986-Feb1987, HMSO,1987)

An interesting example of the use of advertising as a part of a larger campaign is the AIDS programme which has been evaluated and can give an insight into the campaign programme as well as its outcomes.

The campaign

In 1986 the Department of Health and Social Security (DHSS) embarked on an advertising campaign to prevent the spread of the disease commonly known as AIDS. The campaign was organised by the Central Office of Information (COI) and developed by the advertising agency TBWA.

The aim of the campaign was to educate people about the facts and the myths of the disease, to offer advice and reassurance and to influence the climate of opinion in relation to the disease, with the objectives of:

- increasing awareness and knowledge, both among the general public and those at risk;

- changing attitudes, again both among the general public and those at risk;

- and thereby modify behaviour among those at risk.

The Central Office of Information commissioned the British Market Research Bureau Ltd (BMRB) to undertake a series of surveys among both the general public and certain "at risk" groups in order to evaluate the effectiveness of the campaign.

The campaign used initially the national press media, and subsequently television, posters and leaflets for every household throughout the U.K. in addition to other methods such as telephone help lines. Throughout the campaign there was extensive editorial coverage in the major press and television media.

Because of the use of mass media aimed at the whole population it was impossible to design evaluation by using an experimental and a controlled group. It was, therefore, impossible to isolate specific advertising effects. It was, however, possible to measure general changes in the population before and after the campaign and to check on advertising recall in the population.

The aim of the research programme was, therefore, to examine changes in awareness, attitudes and behaviour during the first year of the advertising campaign, and if possible to relate these changes to the advertising input. The feed-back of the findings during the first year served as an important element in strategic planning of the government's ongoing publicity and educational programme.

Evaluation

The report published by the DHSS gives an overview of the evaluation carried out. In the period between February 1986 and February 1987 four waves of interviewing were conducted covering over three thousand adults (18-64 years of age) and nearly eight hundred young people (aged 13-17). Those people were interviewed in their homes and additional nearly one thousand homosexual men were interviewed in gay clubs and pubs around the country. The interview lasted forty to fifty minutes. The overview states:

"There is considerable evidence from these surveys that major progress has been made over the year in terms of the objectives of the government's publicity campaign to increase awareness and knowledge, to change attitudes and thereby to modify behaviour.

There were major increases in knowledge of the ways in which AIDS can be transmitted, and increasing awareness of ways of avoiding or reducing risk. The majority of people became aware of the main ways in which AIDS can be caught and many of the myths were dispelled.

Many substantial changes have occurred in public attitudes, in the direction intended, and in some cases the time pattern of change indicated that the government's advertising campaign had played a significant part in this.

There appear to have been major changes in the claimed sexual behaviour of homosexuals using the evidence obtained from gay pubs and clubs, but it is felt to be likely that the campaign played only a very minor role in bringing these about. Changes in heterosexual behaviour of any significant scale were not detectable.

Awareness of the government advertising was extremely high and believed to be greater than for any other social persuasion advertising campaign in the country. The leaflet that was the subject of a universal household drop had acclaimed readership of four out of every five people aged under 65.

Although the specific effects of the official campaign cannot be disentangled from those of the many other influences brought to bear, it seems fair to conclude that the campaign made a significant contribution to the progress made since February 1986."

Discussion

From the statement of the aims and objectives of the advertising campaign it is obvious that the campaign used the conceptual framework of the KAP (knowledge attitude practices) model and that the outcomes were examined within this conceptualisation. This raises two questions, i.e. whether this model is effective and whether the effectiveness of the model was evaluated appropriately.

There is sufficient evidence from the literature to justify the assumption that a KAP approach need not be effective, nor efficient, in changing people's behaviour. This assumption has been supported by the findings from the evaluation study which record the changes in awareness and attitudes but not in behaviour. There has been some "reported" change in behaviour among the "at risk" or gay population which is not encouraging in terms of the composition of the sample (3,000 adults, 800 young people and 1,000 homosexuals) or the general population at which the campaign was targeted.

The evaluation was concerned with changes on a personal level (awareness, attitudes, behaviour) and did not examine possible social changes, which should have been taken into account since it was a social intervention on a population scale.

The positive aspect of the campaign was the increased knowledge related to the nature of the disease, ways of transmission and means of prevention. The campaign publicly recommended the use of condoms and the awareness of the sample population confirmed that the message got through. It seems that the campaign was successful in reducing the myth about different ways of transmitting AIDS such as being bitten, kissing, being spat on, drinking from the same glass, coughs and sneezes, toilet seats and touching, with the exception of "being bitten" which stayed relatively high. There was an increase in knowledge about who is at risk and people believing that promiscuous people and those who have casual sex were a high risk group. The report states that these changes have occurred at an even pace over the year and cannot unequivocally be attributed to the advertising campaign.

The changes in attitudes have been most noticeable in connection with the preventive aspects of using condoms and cutting down the number of sexual partners. There were positive attitudes towards the government programme for young people and towards the need for the government to spend more on the research and prevention of AIDS. There have been no changes in attitudes to homosexuality and, therefore, no evidence has been found of a backlash against homosexuals as a result of the increased awareness and knowledge acquired about AIDS.

It should be kept in mind that the behavioral aspect of the surveys relied on "reported behaviour" and that there were no ways of checking the accuracy of the statements made. There was no evidence that people changed the number of partners during the year due to the advertising campaign. Very few (one in five) reported using a condom on the last occasion they had sex, although the number is higher for the sixteen to seventeen year old group (46%).

The main reported changes have been in behaviour among homosexuals with the halving of the number of partners during the year of the campaign. There was also an increase in the use of condoms among this group. It is interesting to note that in answering the questionnaire, as compared to the interview, only 4-5 out of 10 claimed to be completely homosexual on a 10 point scale and about 3 in 10 reported a heterosexual relationship in the last twelve months. These proportions did not change during the year of the campaign.

REFERENCES

**** (1989) *Competing for Health*, Nuffield Institute for Health Services Studies, Leeds.

**** (1972) *First Aid Manual*, St. John Ambulance Association, St. Andrew's Ambulance Association, The British Red Cross Society, London.

Allport, G.W., (1969) *Pattern and Growth in Personality*, Holt, Rinehart and Winston, New York.

Argyle, M. (Ed.) (1981) *Social Skills and Health*, Methuen, London.

Atkinson, J., (1967) *A Handbook for Interviewers*, HMSO, London.

Babbie, E., (1989) *The Practice of Social Research*, Wadsworth Publishing Co. Belmont, California.

Bandura, A., Walters, R.H., (1969) *Social Learning and Personality Development,* Holt, Rinehart and Winston, London.

Bandura, A., (1969) *Principles of Behaviour Modification*, Holt, Rinehart and Winston, New York.

Baric, L., (1968) "Operational Research" in *International Journal of Health Education*, Volume 11, No.2.

Baric, L., (1973) "Formal Health Education and the Prevention of Coronary Heart Disease" Report on the Salford Study, University of Manchester.

Baric, L., (1976) "Preparation of Manpower for Health Education - A Comparative View", *Health Education Monographs*, Volume 4, No.3.

Baric, L., (1978) "Levels of Uncertainty in Health Action" in Bell, C. (Ed.) *Uncertain Outcomes*, MTP Press, Lancaster.

Baric L., (1980a): "Evaluation - Obstacles and Potentials", *Int.Journal for Health Education*, Vol23, No.3.

Baric L., (1980b) "Evaluation of the 10th International Conference on Health Education, in the Report on 10th International Conference on Health Education, International Union for Health Education, Geneva.

Baric, L., (1982) *Measuring Family Competence in the Health Maintenance and Health Education of Children*, WHO, Geneva.

Baric, L., (1985) "The Meaning of Words: Health Promotion", *Journal of the Institute of Health Education*, Volume 23, No.1.

Baric, L., (1990) "A New Approach to Community Participation", *Journal of the Institute of Health Education*, Volume 28, No.2.

Baric L.& H.M.Curtis (1986): Report on Evaluation of Teaching Methods of the MSc in Health Education, University of Manchester, Health Education Authority Library,London.

Baric L. & B.Duncan (1987): Report on the Evaluation of the Contents of the MSc in Health Education, University of Manchester, Health Education Authority Library, London.

Baric, L., Harrison, A. (1977) "Social Pressure and Health Education" Paper presented at the Joint Meeting of the Society for Community Medicine and the Rennes School of Public Health, Manchester.

Baric, L., McArthur, C., Sherwood, M., (1976) "Smoking in Pregnancy", *International Journal of Health Education*, Volume 19, No.2.

Baric, L., McArthur, C., Fisher, C., (1976) "Norms, Attitudes, Knowledge and Behaviour Related to Smoking Among Students" in *Health Education Journal*, Volume 35, No.1, London.

Baric, L., McArthur, C., (1977) "Health Norms in Pregnancy" in *British Journal of Preventive and Social Medicine*, Volume 31, No.1.

Baric,L., Murphy,G. (1991) "The New Contract for General Practitioners - an Opportunity for Health Promotion." in *Journal of the Institute of Health Education,* Vol.29, No.2.

Becker, M.H., (Ed.) (1974) "The Health Belief Model and Personal Health Behaviour" in *Health Education Monographs,* Volume 2, No.4.

Bell, C.R., (Ed.) (1979) *Uncertain Outcomes,* MTP Press, Lancaster.
Berger, P.L., Luckmann, T. (1967) *The Social Construction of Reality,* The Penguin Press, London.

Bloom, S.W., (1965) *The Doctor and His Patient,* Free Press, New York.

Bloor, M.J., Horbin, G.W., (1975) "Conflict Resolution in Doctor-Patient Interaction" in Cox, C. and Mead, A. (Eds.) *A Sociology of Medical Practice,* Collier, MacMillan, London.

Broom, L., Selznick, P. (1973) *Sociology,* Harper & Row, U.S.A.

Carter, C.O., Peel, J., (Ed.) (1976) *Equalities and Inequalities in Health,* Academic Press, London.

Cartwright, D., Zander, A., (1953) *Group Dynamics,* Row, Peterson & Co., New York.

Catalano, R., (1979) *Health, Behavior and the Community,* Pergamon Press, New York.

Cherry, C., (1963) *On Human Communication,* John Wiley & Sons, New York.

Chester, R., Peel, J., (Eds.) (1977) *Equalities and Inequalities in Family Life,* Academic Press, London.

Cohen, J. (1964) *Behaviour in Uncertainty,* George Allen and Unwin, London.

Cohen, J. (1972) *Psychological Probability,* George Allen and Unwin, London.

Cook T. and C.L.Gruder (1978) *Metaevaluation Research, Evaluation Quarterly*, 2:5-15.

Cook, J.A. (1973) "Language and Socialization: a critical review" in Bernstein, B. (1973), *Class, Codes and Control*, Routledge & Kegan Paul, London.

Dager, E.Z., (Ed.) (1971) *Socialization*, Markham Publishing Co. Chicago.

Danziger, K. (Ed.) (1970) *Readings in Child Socialization*, Pergamon Press, London.

Dawber, T.D., Kannel, W.B. (1963) "Coronary Heart Disease as an Epidemiology Entity", in *American Journal of Public Health*, Volume 49, No.10.

Dean, J.P., Rosen, A.,(1955) *A Manual of Intergroup Relations*, The University of Chicago Press, Chicago.

Dember, W. N., (1969) *The Psychology of Perception*, Holt, Rinehart & Winston, London.

Denzin, N.K., (1977) *Childhood Socialization*, Jossey-Bass Publishers, San Francisco.

DHSS (1987) AIDS - *Monitoring Response to the Public Education Campaign*, HMSO, London.

DHSS (1989a), *Promoting Better Health*, HMSO, London.

DHSS (1989b), *Working for Patients*, HMSO, London.

DHSS (1989c), *General Practice in the NHS*, DHSS, London.

Dittmar, N. (1976) *Sociolinguistics*, Edward Arnold, London.

Doll, R., Hill, A.B. (1950) "Smoking and the Carcinoma of the Lung" in *British Medical Journal*, Volume 2, p.739.

Douglas, M., (1986) *Risk Acceptability According to the Social Sciences*, Routledge & Kegan Paul, London.

Douglas, T., (1976) *Group Work Practice*, Tavistock Publications Ltd, London.

Douglas, T., (1970) *A Decade of Small Group Theory (1960-1970)*, Bookstall Publications, London.

Dubos, R., (1965) *Man Adapting*, Yale University Press, London.

Dubos, R., (1960) *Mirage of Health*, Harper, New York.

Duhl, L., Hancock, T., (1988) *A Guide to Assessing Healthy Cities*, WHO Healthy Cities Papers No. 3, WHO, Copenhagen.

Egan, G., (1986) *The Skilled Helper*, Brooks/Cole Publishing Co., Pacific Grove, California.

Engel, J.F., Blackwell, R.D., (1982) *Consumer Behaviour*, The Dryden Press, New York.

Fagence, M., (1977) *Citizen Participation in Planning*, Pergamon Press, Oxford.

Fellner, C.H., Marshall, J.R., (1970) "Kidney Donors" in J. Macauley and L. Berkowitz (Eds.), *Altruistic and Helping Behaviour*, Academic Press, London.

Freidson, E., (1975) "Dilemmas in the Doctor Patient Relationship" in Cox, C. and Mead, A. (Eds.) *A Sociology of Medical Practice*, Collier, MacMillan, London.

Gartner, A., Riessman, F. (1977) *.Self-Help in the Human Services*, Jossey-Bass Publishers, London.

Goslin, D.A. (Ed.) (1971) *Handbook of Socialization Theory and Research*, Rand McNally & Co. Chicago.

Gould, J., Kolb, W.L. (Ed.) (1964) *A Dictionary of the Social Sciences*, Tavistock Publications, London.

Green, L.W. (1990) *Community Health*, Times Mirror/Mosby College Publishing, Boston.

Hancock, T., Duhl, L., (1988) *Promoting Health in the Urban Context*, WHO Healthy Cities Papers No.1, WHO, Copenhagen.

Harlow, H.F., Harlow, M.K. (1965) "The Affectional System" in A.M. Schrier, H.F. Harlow and F. Stollnitz (Eds.), *Behaviour of Non-human Primates*, Academic Press, New York.

Hatch, S., Kickbusch, I., (1983) *Self-help and Health in Europe*, WHO EURO, Copenhagen.

Henderson, P., Thomas, D.N., (Eds.) (1981) *Readings in Community Work*, George Allen & Unwin, London.

Henerson, M.E., Morris, L.L., Fitz-Gibbon, C.T., (1987) *How to Measure Attitudes*, Sage Publications, London.

Himmelfarb, S., Eagly, A. H., (1974) *Readings in Attitude Change*, John Wiley & Sons, New York.

Hovland, C.I., Janis, I.L., Kelley, H.H., (1963) *Communication and Persuasion*, Yale University Press, Yale.

Hudson J. & McRoberts H.A. (1984): "Auditing Evaluation Activities" in Rutman (1984) *Evaluation Research Methods*, Sage Publications, London (pp.219-236).

Illich, I., (1974) *Tools for Conviviality*, Calder & Boyars, London.

Jehu, D., (1967) *Learning Theory and Social Work*, Routledge and Kegan Paul, London.

Jowell, R., Airey, C. (Eds.) (yearly) *British Social Attitudes*, Gower Publishing Co. Vermont, U.S.A.

Kanfer, F.H., Goldstein, A.P., (Ed.) (1981) *Helping People Change*, Pergamon Press, New York. Katz, E., Lazarsfeld, P.F., (1964) *Personal Influence*, The Free Press, New York.

Kickbusch, I., (1989) "Health Promotion: A New Approach at the Workplace" in Kaplun, A. and Wenzel, E., (Eds.) (1989) *Health Promotion in the Working World*, Springer-Verlag, Berlin.

Klein, J., (1963) *Working With Groups*, Hutchinson & Co., London.

Krumboltz, J.D., Thoresen, C.E., (1976) *Counselling Methods*, Holt, Rinehart and Winston, New York.

Kuhn, T.S., (1970) *The Structure of Scientific Revolutions*, University of Chicago Press, Chicago.

Laver, J., Hutcheson, S., (Ed.) (1972) *Communication in Face to Face Interaction*, Penguin Books Ltd, Harmondsworth, Middlesex.

Leathar, D.S., Hastings, G.B., Davies, J.K., (1981) *Health Education and the Media*, Pergamon Press, London.

LeVine, R.A. (1973) *Culture, Behaviour and Personality*, Hutchinson, London.

Lieberman, D.A., (Ed.) (1974) *Learning and the Control of Behavior*, Holt, Rinehart & Winston, New York.

McGrew, A.G., Wilson, M.J. (Ed.) (1982) *Decision Making*, Manchester University Press, Manchester.

McKeown, T., Lowe, C.R., (1977) *An Introduction to Social Medicine*, Blackwell Scientific Publications, Oxford.

McQuail, D., (1975) *Communication*, Longman, London.

McQuail, D., Windahl, S., (1981) *Communication Models*, Longman, London.

Minar, D.W., Greer, S., (1969)   *The Concept of Community*, Aldine Publishing Co., Chicago.

Moore, C.M., (1987) *Group Techniques for Idea Building*, Sage Publications, London.

Morris, J.N., Kagan, A., Pattison, D.C., Gardner, M.J., (1966) "Incidence and Prediction of Ischaemic Heart Disease in London Busmen", *Lancet*, II, No. 7463.

Navarro, V., (1978) *Class Struggle, The State and Medicine*, Martin Robertson & Co. Ltd, London.

Oates, J. (Ed.) (1979) *Early Cognitive Development*, Open University Press, Croom Helm Ltd, London.

Ogilvy, D., (1983) *Ogilvy on Advertising*, Pan Books, London.

Oliver, M.F., Boyd, G.S., (1953) " Ischaemic Heart Disease" in *British Heart Journal*, 15, 387.

Oliver, M.F., Boyd, G.S., (1961) "Preventing Ischaemic Heart Disease" in *Lancet*, 2, 489.

Pfeiffer, J.W., Jones, J.E., (Yearly) *The Annual Handbook for Group Facilitators*, University Associates Inc., San Diego.

Piaget, J., (1959) *The Language and Thought of the Child*, Routledge & Kegan Paul Ltd, London.

Popper, K.R., (1959) *The Logic of Scientific Discovery*, Hutchinson & Co., London.

Porterfield, J.D. (Ed.) (1966)*Community Health*, Basic Books, New York.

Pride, J.B., Holmes, J. (Ed.) (1972) *Sociolinguistics*, Penguin Books, Harmondsworth, Middlesex.

Rapoport, R.N., (1960) *Community as Doctor*, Tavistock Publications, London.

Robb-Smith, A.H.T., (1967) *The Enigma of Coronary Heart Disease*, Lloyd-Luke (Medical Books) Ltd, London.

Rose, G.A. et.al (1965) "Reducing Risk from Ischaemic Heart Disease" in *British Medical Journal*, 1, 1531.

Rosenstock, I. (1974) " The Health Belief Model and Preventive Health Behaviour," in Becker (Ed.) *The Health Belief Model and Personal Behaviour*, Health Education Monographs Volume 2, No.4.

Royal College of Physicians (1989), *Medical Audit*, Report of the Royal College of Physicians, London.

Rutman L. (1984), *Evaluation Research Methods*, Sage Publications, London, Second Edition.

Scherer, J., (1972) *Contemporary Community*, Tavistock Publications, London.

Schramm, W., (Ed.) (1960) *Mass Communications*, University of Illinois Press, U.S.A.

Sieghart P., (1989)*AIDS and Human Rights*, British Medical Association, Foundation for AIDS, London.

Smith, A.G., (1966) *Communication and Culture*, Holt, Rinehard & Winston, New York.

Smith, A., (1968) *The Science of Social Medicine*, Staples, London.

Sola Pool, I. de, Schramm, W., (Eds.) (1973) *Handbook of Communication*, Rand McNally, Chicago.

Strauss, B. & F., (1957)*New Ways to Better Meetings*, The Viking Press, New York.

Suchman, E.A., (1963) *Sociology and the Field of Public Health*, Russell Sage Foundation, New York.

Suchman, E.A., (1965) "Social Patterns of Illness and Medical Care" in *Journal of Health and Human Behaviour*, Volume 6, p.2-15.

Tallman, I., Marotz-Baden, R., Pindas, P., (1983) *Adolescent Socialization in Cross-Culltural Perspective*, Academic Press, New York.

Teevan, R.C., Birney, R.C., (1964) *Theories of Motivation in Learning*, D. Van Nostrand Co., Princeton, New Jersey.

Thelen, H.A., (1954) *Dynamics of Groups at Work*, The University of Chicago Press, Chicago.

Thomson, W.A.R., (1967) *Black's Medical Dictionary*, Twenty-seventh Edition, A. & C. Black, London.

Tones, K., Tilford, S., Robinson, Y. (1990) *Health Education Effectiveness and Efficiency*, Chapman and Hall, London.

Townsend, P., Davidson, N., (Eds.) (1980) *The Black Report : Inequalities in Health*, Penguin Books, London.

Waterson, N. Snow, C. (Ed.) (1978) *The Development of Communication*, John Wiley & Sons, New York.

Weber, M. (1966) *The Theory of Social and Economic Organisation*, Free Press, New York.

Weiner, B., (1972) *Theories of Motivation*, Rand McNally, Chicago.

Whitaker, G., (Ed.) (1965) *T-Group Training: Group dynamics in management education*, Basil Blackwell, Oxford.

WHO EURO (1984)*Concepts and Principles of Health Promotion*, Copenhagen.

WHO EURO (1984) *Health Promotion Concept and Principles : a discussion document*, WHO, Copenhagen.

WHO EURO (1988a) *Promoting Health in the Urban Context*, WHO Healthy Cities Papers No.1., Copenhagen.

WHO EURO (1988b) *Five-Year Planning Framework*, WHO Healthy Cities Papers No.2., Copenhagen.

WHO EURO (1988c) *A Guide to Assessing Healthy Cities*, WHO Healthy Cities Papers No.3, Copenhagen. WHO (1989), *Ethics in Health Promotion*, WHO EURO, Copenhagen, (EUR/ICP/HSR 634, 5119v).